D1738484

WITHDRAWN
UTSA Libraries

Republicanism and Anticlerical Nationalism in Spain

Republicanism and Anticlerical Nationalism in Spain

Enrique A. Sanabria

REPUBLICANISM AND ANTICLERICAL NATIONALISM IN SPAIN

Copyright © Enrique A. Sanabria, 2009.

All rights reserved.

First published in 2009 by
PALGRAVE MACMILLAN®
in the United States—a division of St. Martin's Press LLC,
175 Fifth Avenue, New York, NY 10010.

Where this book is distributed in the UK, Europe and the rest of the world,
this is by Palgrave Macmillan, a division of Macmillan Publishers Limited,
registered in England, company number 785998, of Houndmills,
Basingstoke, Hampshire RG21 6XS.

Palgrave Macmillan is the global academic imprint of the above companies
and has companies and representatives throughout the world.

Palgrave® and Macmillan® are registered trademarks in the United States,
the United Kingdom, Europe and other countries.

ISBN-13: 978–0–230–61331–7
ISBN-10: 0–230–61331–4

Library of Congress Cataloging-in-Publication Data

Sanabria, Enrique A.
    Republicanism and anticlerical nationalism in Spain / Enrique A.
Sanabria.
        p. cm.
    Includes bibliographical references and index.
    ISBN 0–230–61331–4
        1. Spain—Politics and government—1886–1931. 2. Republicanism—
Spain—History—20th century. 3. Anti-clericalism—Spain—History—
20th century. 4. Nakens, José, 1841–1926. I. Title.

DP233.S26 2009
946'.074—dc22   2008039103

A catalogue record of the book is available from the British Library.

Design by Newgen Imaging Systems (P) Ltd., Chennai, India.

First edition: April 2009

10 9 8 7 6 5 4 3 2 1

Printed in the United States of America.

Library
University of Texas
at San Antonio

For the Angela I once knew
and
for Delia Margarita Sanabria De la Cruz,
in Memoriam.

Contents

Figures and Table

Figures

Table

Acknowledgments

This book would not have been possible without the enormous support of Pamela Beth Radcliff who selflessly went beyond the call of duty as my graduate mentor at the University of California, San Diego, by being my role model for the past fifteen years. Those of us who are lucky enough to call ourselves her students refer to her as "St. Pamela," and I fear I will never be able to thank her enough for all that she is and what she has done for me. While at UCSD I was also blessed to be exposed to the erudite minds and generous spirits of David R. Ringrose, Kathryn Ringrose, Christine Hunefeldt, Susan Kirkpatrick, Carlos Waisman, Bob Edelman, John Marino, Cynthia Truant, and the warm friendships of Michael Bernstein, Steve Cox, David Gutiérrez, David Luft, Paul Pickowicz, Eric Van Young, and Alexander Vergara. I also wish to recognize and thank Stanley G. Payne of the University of Wisconsin and Peter Pierson of Santa Clara University, who are most directly responsible for fanning the flames of my interest in Spain, its history, and the profession and craft of the historian.

I am proud to call myself a member of the Society for Spanish and Portuguese Historical Studies, which has exposed me and my work to excellent Hispanists from both Europe and the United States. I want to thank the Best Dissertation for the Years 1999, 2000, and 2001 Committee for believing in my thesis. The Society's conferences have given me the opportunity to present my work, receive valuable feedback, and enjoy important conversations with José Alvarez Junco, Carolyn Boyd, William Christian, Dan Crews, Jesús Cruz, Victoria Enders, George Esenwein, Sandie Holguín, Geoff Jensen, Judith Keene, Jack Owens, Allyson Poska, Adrian Shubert, and John Tone.

It is thrilling to have forged lasting friendships with graduate school colleagues both at Wisconsin and UCSD who are currently flourishing in the academy and in their personal lives, and who graciously gave part of themselves by commenting on my work, studying alongside me, sharing their insights, cheering me on, or socializing with me during that frustrating transition we call grad school. To Charles Bodie, Brian D. Bunk, Daniel Berenberg, Krista Camenzind, Jordi Getman-Eraso, Barnet Hartston, Maggie Hirthe, Kevin Ingram, John Hoon Lee, Eric Maiershofer, Sarah Malena, Wendy Maxon, Douglas McGetchin, Elizabeth Munson, David Ortiz, Jr., Sean Perrone, Rachel D. Shaw, Theresa Smith, Gabriella Soto-Laveaga, Hamilton Stapell, Daniel Stuber, Ana Varela Lago, Don Wallace, Mark Wild, Clinton Young, Jackie Zucconi, and especially Will Kropp and Phoebe S. Kropp, who, among other things, have given me the frustrating opportunity to mismanage a fantasy baseball team year after year: thank you from the bottom of my heart for giving me your gift of collegial friendship. Indispensable administrative support at UCSD came from Mary Allen, Ivonne Avila, and Bonnie Heather Merrick.

During various trips to Spain I was lucky to befriend Terry Berkowitz, Jodi Campbell, Morgan Hall, and Dan Kowalsky who were fellow Fulbright scholars, as well as Paloma Aguilar Fernández, Rafael Cruz, Julio de la Cueva, Juan Hernández Andreu, Manuel Pérez Ledesma, Juan Carlos Sola, and Nigel Townsend. I especially want to thank Patricia Zanisher for helping me with archival and bibliographical access in Madrid in 1996 and 2002.

I now call Albuquerque and the University of New Mexico home, and I feel privileged to have been welcomed into an intellectual family here replete with exceptional scholars who have not only taken the time to read and comment on my work, but also challenged me to become a better historian and teacher. I am deeply grateful for the mentorship of Melissa Bokovoy and Jane Slaugther, and also the comments, advice, and friendships of Durwood Ball, Cathleen Cahill, Eliza Ferguson, Tim Graham, Linda Hall, Elizabeth Hutchison, Cynthia Radding, Barbara Reyes, Patricia Risso, Richard Robbins, Jay Rubenstein, Virginia Scharff, Andrew Sandoval-Strausz, Jason Scott Smith, Sam Truett, and, of course, the late Tim Moy. Administrative support selflessly came from Yolanda Martínez, Helen Ferguson, Dana Ellison, and Barbara Wafer.

Funding for the research and writing of this book and the dissertation from which it emerged was made possible by a Fulbright Fellowship, a Presidential Writing Fellowship from the University of California Office of the President, a Faculty Research Allocation Grant from the University of New Mexico, and grants from the Center for German and European Studies at the University of California,

Berkeley, and the Center for Iberian and Latin American Studies at UCSD. I wish also to thank the helpful library and archival staffs at the *Archivo Histórico Nacional* (Madrid), the *Archivo Histórico Nacional de la Guerra Civil* (Salamanca), Spain's National Library, the *Hemeroteca Municipal* (Madrid), the *Archivo de la Villa de Madrid*, and the Mandeville Special Collections of UCSD's Geisel Library, especially Lynda Claassen. The Interlibrary Loan Office Staffs at both UCSD and the Zimmerman Library at University of New Mexico were extremely reliable, industrious, and helpful with my plentiful requests.

Christopher Chappell and Rachel Tekula, my editor and production manager, respectively, helped make my experience with Palgrave Macmillan go smoothly, and Chris Schmidt-Nowara and my two anonymous readers improved my manuscript immensely. Any errors or omissions remain my own failings, of course.

Sadly, my mother Delia M. Sanabria De La Cruz did not live long enough to see this book in print and on her bookshelves, but I pray she is pleased and at peace today. To her and to my invaluable writing partner Angela Allen, I dedicate this book. I also thank my father Enrique E. Sanabria, my brothers Eduardo and Eric Sanabria, my aunt Alma Goss, Susie Ughe Bodine, Melinda Barlass-Ackerman, Ann McGinley and the rest of my family and friends for their interest and enthusiasm for this book.

Finally, I thank my two closest friends, Cecily Kuehl Shank and Jessica Messier, for practically living through the rollercoaster ride that was getting this book in print and filling my days with such joy and tenderness. Thank you both for the gifts of love, serendipity, and infinite possibility.

Introduction

On May 27, 1936, Marcelino Domingo Sanjuán, Minister of Education during the Second Spanish Republic, received a letter from Don Victoriano Ciller Medrano (editor-in-chief of a small Barcelona-based anticlerical newsletter produced by members of the "José Nakens" Masonic Lodge) soliciting support for his petition for a commemorative José Nakens postage stamp. A rabble-rousing republican during the Restoration of 1875–1923, Nakens made a name for himself throughout Spain as editor of the rabidly anticlerical-republican weekly *El Motín* (The Riot or The Mutiny), published between 1881 and 1926. According to Ciller Medrano, his newsletter titled *El Ateo* (the Atheist) had been dedicated to "educating the masses that jaunt themselves into burning down churches, exciting religious fanaticism, [which] leads to street fights" since the Berenguer Dictatorship of 1930.[1] He argued that since other great republican leaders such as former presidents of the First Republic, Francisco Pi y Margall, Emilio Castelar, and Nicolás Salmerón, and the novelist turned *fin-de-siècle* political activist, Vicente Blasco Ibáñez, had received such an honor, it was only fitting for the Republic to give Nakens his due. Furthermore, Ciller Medrano saw himself and *El Ateo* as inheritors of Nakens and *El Motín*'s cause, and asked Domingo to transfer all or some of the government pension Nakens's daughter had been awarded by the Republic to *El Ateo* in order to offset the costs of production.[2] Domingo diplomatically responded that he believed tributes to Nakens were scarce, but passed the buck suggesting Ciller Medrano contact other republican officials.[3]

This book offers a general history of Spanish anticlericalism during the Restoration, specifically between its inception in 1875 and the assassination of Prime Minister José Canalejas in late 1912. Anticlericalism shall be presented as one part of a bazaar of nationalist discourses put forward, in this case by republican journalists and politicians, at a time when other nations of the world were fixing national identities and engaging in nation-building projects and a time when Spain's national identity was in flux or in doubt. Of these competing articulations of the Spanish nation, anticlericalism, not in and of itself always related to nationalism, was one of the most successful discourses because of its ability to transcend material issues that divided the middle and working classes. Anticlericalism was therefore a fundamental weapon in the discursive arsenal of liberal progressive Spain, which had locked horns with Catholic-traditionalist Spain at the start of the nineteenth century.

The absence of a state-backed nationalist project in Spain, like those evident in the French Third Republic or Victorian England, did not preclude the presence of dynamic nation-building projects.[4] What is particularly distinctive about Spain during the nineteenth century is that there were a plethora of groups wrestling each other in an attempt to assert their version of what the Spanish nation ought to have been. Because I focus on Restoration anticlericalism specifically, this book will use José Nakens Pérez—the best known Restoration anticlerical ideologue obsessed with the complete de-Christianization of Spain who is largely neglected by historians—and his contributions to a Restoration "anticlerical industry" to show how republicans looked to and adopted models of nation-building from other European nations in the hopes of nationalizing, democratizing, and modernizing Spain.[5] The fact that anticlerical nationalism struck a chord among socialists, anarchists, and other members of the working class speaks to the resentment for the Church and clergy and the role it played in quotidian life during the Restoration.

This is the first book-length English-language study of Spanish anticlericalism since Joan Connelly Ullman's 1968 classic *The Tragic Week*,[6] and I incorporate new perspectives on nationalism, gender, and the politics of religion in order to update our understanding of an anticlerical tradition that existed before the Second Republic (1931–1936) and civil war (1936–1939), both of which ushered in remarkable anticlerical mob violence in Spain's streets and countryside. Heretofore, that mob violence had been an aspect of anticlericalism that drew Hispanists' attention.[7] However, by focusing on the discourse and ideology of anticlericalism, I join a growing group of Spanish scholars who have looked critically at anticlericalism during the Restoration and established it as a fundamental phenomenon of political, cultural, and social life.[8]

In exploring anticlericalism, and the brand of anticlericalism purveyed by José Nakens, I build upon the extensive investigation into republican culture by the Spanish historian, José Alvarez Junco, who shed light on how Spanish republicans borrowed heavily from Christian morality to shape their emotional appeals. Alvarez Junco also pioneered the link between modern forms of anticlericalism and nationalism,[9] but has shoved the pivotal Nakens to the proverbial sidelines and also presented republican nationalism as an extremely serious and solemn affair.

Solemn, serious, and moralistic though many of the late-nineteenth-century republican leaders may have been when it came to nationalism, it would be foolhardy to overlook the importance of humor in the nation-building efforts of some republicans such as Nakens and Alejandro Lerroux. Anthropological inquiry into "humorology," spearheaded by Mahadev Apte, has emphasized the social nature of humor and joking relationships, which signal individuals recognizing a special kinship or other types of social bonds between them.[10] Humor and joking relationships mark group identities, signal the inclusion or exclusion of others or new individuals, and manifest a consciousness of group identity or solidarity.[11] Though uncouth in his anticlericalism, Nakens was the leader and model for Restoration radical republicans who appreciated the importance of bridging the gap between cultured elites and the general public to build community and generate a mass political following for their movement. For this reason, Nakens' words and the images in *El Motín* and other similar republican and Masonic journals inform this study of the confluence of republicanism, anticlericalism, nationalism and, at times, humor.

As peculiar as it may seem that Nakens be lumped into the same category as Pi y Margall or Salmerón, he was indeed an important figure in republican circles during the Restoration. Only recently have scholars begun to rediscover the man who was

> Exalted by many as a model of honesty and coherence; fought by many others for his anticlerical sectarianism; excommunicated by those who had the power to do so; criticized with great frequency by his own coreligionists; detained, imprisoned, tried or fined on many occasions….[12]

Though known primarily for his anticlerical *raison d'être* Nakens also energetically tried to unify the fractured republican movement in 1903 with the Republican Assembly. At that meeting, Salmerón, given complete control of the movement, invited Nakens to serve on the resultant party's directorial commission. Though Nakens was never the principal spokesman of the Restoration republican movement, he represented an intermediary actor between the old-fashioned conspiratorial ideas of men such as Manuel Ruiz Zorrilla and the mass mobilization of a younger generation of republican demagogues such as Lerroux and Blasco Ibáñez.

Furthermore, seemingly oblivious to the power of his vitriolic anticlericalism, Nakens's republican circles intersected with revolutionary leftist circles. He interacted with the two most infamous anarcho-terrorists of the Restoration: Michele Angiolillo, before he assassinated the Prime Minister of Spain in 1897, and Mateo Morral, after he attempted to assassinate the King and Queen on their May 1906 wedding day. Indeed a testament to Nakens' legacy and importance was how he was not forgotten by subsequent generations of republican journalists and politicians despite his run-ins with the revolutionary left and the law. At the dawn of the Second Republic, as the Parliament (*Cortes*) entered days of passionate debate about the place of the church and clergy in Republican Spain, numerous speakers alluded to the anticlerical vision of the old republican, José Nakens, who had passed away nearly five years before he could have seen the fall of the Monarchy and the (temporary) triumph of liberal democracy.[13]

The life and work of José Nakens are important because they offer a window to myriad political currents that functioned dynamically—as well as convulsive episodes that exploded—beneath the apparent stability of the Restoration oligarchy's control. For this reason his newspaper *El Motín* as well as his contributions to the "anticlericalism industry" inform this exploration into how republican journalists and politicians in Spain conflated their anticlericalism with their nationalism, and in doing so associated anticlericalism with forging a modern nation.[14] While not professing to be a biography of José Nakens, this book uses his life and work to shed light on the attempts by radical republicans, particularly in Restoration Madrid, to construct an anticlerical-nationalist vision of Spain during the crucial transition to a mass politics of nation-building.

El Motín and the Masonic weekly *Las Dominicales de Libre Pensamiento* are Spanish examples of a Europe-wide genre of satirical newspapers that very quickly drew large readerships primarily among the middle class in the late nineteenth century. For instance, Italy's *L'Asino*, which dates to 1892, responded to the challenge of Catholic worker syndicates and clerical opposition to a state-backed divorce bill in 1902 by launching an often fierce and crude campaign against the Vatican and the Italian clergy that included Gabriele

Galantara's caricatures of venal, avaricious, gluttonous, rapacious, and lascivious priests and monks.[15] Nakens and *El Motín* employed similar tropes and images in an effort to define the nation as liberal, secular, and republican. I approach *El Motín* as Michael B. Gross has approached a similar paper in Germany, called *Gartenlaube*, which he argues serves as an "antimonastic map of German Liberalism."[16] Though certainly more widely circulated and highbrow than *El Motín*, *Gartenlaube* championed middle-class liberal values while obsessively poking fun at the Vatican, the German Catholic Church and clergy, and German Catholics.[17] The very same discourses that ridiculed Catholic superstitions and fanaticisms and stereotyped Catholics as antipathetic to science and individualism are present in both *El Motín* and *Gartenlaube*.

Because Nakens' anticlerical campaign was nationalist and rooted in demonstrating to as many Spaniards possible that the Spanish nation was decayed and dishonored by the Catholic Church and clergy, I argue that he is particularly important to understanding how anticlericalism, itself not necessarily a political discourse but a traditional language of opposition to a private institution, served as an articulation of an alternate national identity to that put forward by the Catholic-traditionalist Right. But this type of anticlerical nationalism truly went beyond language and symbols for the sake of language and symbols; Nakens's anticlericalism and his nationalism were rooted in a fundamental belief in progress and liberal modernity that was anti-Catholic because he desired complete de-Christianization and understood Catholicism and the clergy as obstacles to Spanish greatness. In addition, Nakens's anticlericalism offered an alternative nationalism at a time when the Restoration state was unable, or unwilling, to establish the symbols of the nation and avoided the controversy of nation-building altogether.[18]

On Nationalism and Spanish Nationalism

The amount of recent scholarship on European nationalism has been dizzying. While some important theorists of nationalism insist the essence of a nation lies in the kinship offered by sharing the same ethnicity, which coalesced long ago around shared religion, language, vernacular literature, or collective memory,[19] other influential scholars point to modern forces and moments such as the French Revolution, industrialization, print capitalism, and secularism that helped form the "imagined community" that Benedict Anderson defines as the nation.[20] Despite disagreements regarding the origins of nations, most scholars stress the "constructedness" of nationalism in the nineteenth century because, as Geoff Eley and Ronald Grigor Suny argue:

> creative political action is required to transform a segmented and dis-united population into a coherent nationality, and though potential communities of this kind may clearly precede such interventions (...) the interventions remain responsible for combining the materials into a larger collectivity.[21]

Nationalism is the manipulation or creation of symbols of the nation (flags, anthems, state and civic ceremonies) as well as establishing dictionaries, academic curriculum, musical style, art, theater, and popular festivals, and this process dates to the nineteenth century. Nationalists attempted to adapt artifacts of the past, including but not limited to historical memory, to further their modern political and national goals such as creating new or dividing old political groupings, democratizing governments, protecting wealth and social structures, advancing modernization, and/or building empires and generating popular support for empire.

In the last two decades, studies on Spanish nationalism have also exploded onto the scene, though most of them focused attention on the rise and the strength of peripheral nationalisms centered in indus-trialized Catalonia or the Basque Country.[22] There used to be a dearth of studies that looked at Spanish nationalism (as opposed to Iberian micro-nationalism), but with the publication of recent major works, particularly Alvarez Junco's *Mater dolorosa*, the historiographical parameters have been established.[23] While specialists on European nationalism have traditionally neglected Spain,[24] Hispanists have very much plugged into the field of nationalist studies and are fur-thering an understanding of the difficulties involved with making a Spanish nationalism or implementing a single fixed understanding of what Spain meant in the nineteenth and twentieth centuries. For instance, Sandie Holguín builds upon the work of Prasenjit Duara to demonstrate that nationalism represents "the site where very different views of the nation contest and negotiate with each other."[25] Holguín argues that because the leaders of Spain's Second Republic did not presume the republican nation existed, they embarked on the political and cultural task of "creating Spaniards" through a variety of ways including literacy campaigns, pedagogical missions, and implanting a republican understanding of the Spanish past.[26]

For the nineteenth century, Alvarez Junco was spurred on by the fact Liah Greenfeld's work neglected Spain—and because a work on Spain comparable to that of Eugen Weber on France, George Mosse on Germany, or Linda Colley on England had yet to be written—to write *Mater Dolorosa*, one of the most significant contributions to the study of Spanish nationalism of our time.[27] In light of the preponderance of research on peripheral nationalism in Spain after the Franco regime that left Spanish nationalism forgotten or nonexistent, Alvarez Junco argues that not only was the construction of Spanish identity underway in the nineteenth century but that Spanish nationalism has been the most successful, certainly the most long-lived, of any of the Iberian nationalisms.[28] He decisively breaks with the primordialists by establishing nations as artificial creations moved by political interests, but distances himself from Marxist modernists such as Eric Hobsbawm who diminish the power of passion people feel for the nation.[29] After tracing the idea of Spain across 500 years of Spanish history, Alvarez Junco argues that efforts to assert what the Spanish nation was began with Spain's War of Independence from Napoleonic France in 1808–1814. Over the course of the nineteenth century, at least two major competing histories and understandings of Spain emerged as partisans of a liberal progressive vision of Spain fighting for liberal progressive reform clashed with a national-Catholic vision of Spain rooted in pursuing unity under a strong monarch, and which cherished the memories of the anti-Islamic *Reconquista* and Spain's Habsburg Golden Age.[30]

The strength of these competing national identities during the Restoration serves as the context for this book. Spain's state was composed of an old traditional monarchy and oligarchy that was troubled by political, economic, and social circumstances, all of which made its effort at nationalization of the masses weak and inefficient.[31] But just as Holguín and Pamela Radcliff have shown that republicans in control of the Second Republic knew they needed to assert the symbols of the Spanish nation and create secular, democratic, and civic-minded Spaniards, I argue that Restoration republicans such as José Nakens were consumed with the task of making Spaniards for an anticlerical modern Spain.

Recently, another body of literature on the relationship between religion, secularism, and nationalism has emerged to explore the Europe-wide fractionalization between liberal, progressive, modernizing forces and their conservative, Catholic, and traditionalist counterparts.[32] Many scholars have noted that though the Europe-wide process of secularization was rooted in separating God and religion from state and society, God never quite went away, as religion gave politicians and nation-builders the rhetoric and symbols necessary to foment nationalist feelings. Secularists and nationalists often learned their skills from the Catholic Church and clergy that were never monolithic in their late-nineteenth-century antipathies to Liberalism, as evidenced by clerical efforts to reconcile faith, liberalism, and the forging of the nation.[33] The fact that liberal priests and clerical forces may have pioneered the attempt to forge the modern nation at the start of the nineteenth century and that some priests and Catholic intellectuals continued to do so during the Restoration was lost on the republicans who both resented and envied the Spanish Catholic Church for its hegemonic grasp over Spaniards. What resulted was a terrible shouting match of competing nationalist discourses during the Restoration in which radical republicans would let ultraconservative or Carlist spokesmen such as Ramón Nocedal speak for all Catholics just as easily as clericals and conservatives could let Nakens, Lerroux, or Blasco Ibáñez speak for the republican movement.

Anticlericalism, Clericalism, and Secularism

Recently, Manuel Suárez Cortina wrote that the "importance of *El Motín* as an instrument of anticlericalism has yet to receive sufficient historiographical attention."[34] I hope to address that need as I assert that Nakens recast anticlericalism as a vehicle for the nation-building projects of the republicans. Heretofore, few scholars of Spain have been attracted to studying modern forms of anticlericalism (broadly defined as opposition to the power of the clergy[35]) because they did not adequately figure into economic and political analyses. Rafael Cruz argues:

> Anticlericalism—much like military intervention in state affairs—was considered marginal to other general topics, perhaps because of the debatable observation that anticlerical behavior constituted an obscurantist, spontaneous, and definitely marginal departure from the continuity of customary politics. In addition, anticlericalism was something of an embarrassment for being consubstantial with a high degree of collective violence: it was considered the reversal of the progress toward modernity and modernization.[36]

This book joins a number of monographs that posit Restoration anticlericalism as wholly modern and a weapon in the discursive arsenal of republican politicians and journalists determined to disrupt the status quo of the oligarchy and the monarchy's grasp on political power.[37] Anticlericalism offered republican purveyors such as Nakens an opportunity to create links between themselves and members of the revolutionary left who had their own grievances with the Church, clergy, and the regime. Thus, anticlericalism served as glue that could bring disparate groups, including among the republicans themselves, together through their antipathies toward the Church and thereby shape one of the two Spains.

Although the word anticlericalism originates in the nineteenth century as a description for lay resistance to the political power of the Catholic Church,[38] Europeans have, of course, lived with some form of anticlericalism for generations. While I am primarily concerned here with anticlericalism in a nation with a strong Catholic Church, even nations such as Great Britain and its historic Catholic minority have witnessed various forms of theoretical, political, and popular denunciations of both the Anglican and Catholic clergies.[39] In Catholic countries, some forms of anticlericalism have come not from lay or nonbelieving opponents of the Church, but from within the clergy or believers, as in the case of mainly conservative medieval anticlericalism, which eventually gave way to the radical Protestant critique of clerical status.[40] But while most forms of medieval and early modern European anticlericalism were anticlericalisms of believers, scholars argue that modern forms of anticlericalism—which sought to truly injure the Catholic clergy or end the centrality of the Church in society—make their appearances in the late eighteenth century, especially with the French Revolution. It is at that time anticlericalism was redefined as a positive affirmation of human liberty and secular society.[41] In this book I am concerned with this new form of anticlericalism because it was an important component in a larger battle for cultural and national identity in nineteenth- and twentieth-century Spain.

Modern anticlericalism grew out of medieval and early modern traditions (be they anti-Papist or rooted in the skepticism of the Enlightenment's *philosophes*), but it was shaped by dominating ideologies such as liberalism, secularism, nationalism, and socialism, which demanded allegiance to institutions or groupings that clashed with traditional ties to the Church and clergy.[42] More directly, modern anticlericalism is a response to an increased presence and intensity of clericalism or the "ascendancy of an institution with a deeply anti-liberal policy that to critics appeared increasingly aggressive in its efforts to force its values on an entire society."[43] Indeed the Western

Europe of the early nineteenth century was rapidly changing and becoming secular, causing great concern among the forces of clericalism. While modern anticlericalism and secularism are not necessarily the same thing, they are very much related, because the latter affected religious forms and practices. Secularism constitutes a context, and impersonal social forces created responses to that context: clericalism and anticlericalism.[44]

As illustrated in figure 1.1, the relationship between the protean forms of secularism and those of both clericalism and anticlericalism suggests that secularization of society increases clerical activity, which in turn spurs modern anticlericalism. In the struggle toward secularism—a noble aspiration seeking to allow the individual to believe or not to believe—anticlericalism can no longer simply be considered a negative ideology but, in the words of Julio de la Cueva, "an often-negative and sometimes violent expression of a broader positive ideology advocating secularity."[45] Modern anticlericalism for radical republicans was a militant attitude that either rightfully or erroneously perceived clericalism as a threat to secularization and progress, and as an even bigger threat to the construction of a new imagined community.

Modern anticlericalism was a feature present not only in nineteenth- and twentieth-century Spain, but also in various European contexts. In 1983, *European Studies Review* published a special issue dedicated

Secularism
Characterized by but not limited to industrialization, urbanization, increased literacy, technological innovation, a differentiation of the secular and the religious, the development of a civil religion or civil loyalties, and emphasis on separating the individual from corporate identities.

▼

Clericalism
Characterized by but not limited to fear of secularization; an increase in forms of religiosity (sacraments and Church attendance); defense of the clergy; and a refusal to accept that any areas of human existence (politics, education, social and economic organization, etc.) lay outside the boundaries of religion.

▼

Anticlericalism
Characterized by but not limited to ideas and actions that develop as a response to clericalism and which seek to curb the influence of the Church and clergy, if not the complete separation of the Church and state. Unlike secularism, anticlericalism often features emotional attacks against the clergy and is more punitive toward the religious.

Figure I.1   The relationship between secularism, clericalism, and anticlericalism

to anticlericalism, and the essays demonstrated that anticlerical-ism had been at the forefront of battles between forces of tradition and political modernity throughout Europe.[46] Nationalists became increasingly intolerant of other collective identities interfering with the identity of the nation they were putting forward. To left-liberals, destroying the power of the Catholic Church was essential to achiev-ing liberty and progress, because not only did the clergy set the moral tone of European societies in general, the clergy's traditional control over schools, hospitals, orphanages, poorhouses, and so on, and its rigid Scholastic doctrines, were incompatible with secularism and Liberalism, which sought to free individuals from premodern insti-tutions and mentalities. When Spanish Restoration anticlericalism is analyzed as part of a Europe-wide struggle between liberals and cleri-cals, it ceases to stand out as peculiar. Nineteenth-century national-ists and statesmen stoked the flames of secularism so that they, rather than the Old Regime institutions of the Throne and Church, could guide and provide for their citizenries.[47]

What did make Spain particular was the relative weakness of the liberal state when juxtaposed with the remarkable strength of both clericalism and anticlericalism. The context of Spanish clerical–anticlerical struggle provided a uniquely important role for the Restoration public sphere because it was within the press, literature, theater, and everyday forms of sociability that the struggle to affirm the meaning of the nation took place.[48] Modern Spanish anticlerical-ism formed a fundamental part of what republicans perceived to be the virtuous attempt to modernize Spain.

The Historical Context of the Restoration

Compared with the tremendously convulsive first three quarters of the nineteenth century in Spain, the Spanish Restoration appeared stable and was, in fact, long-lived. Spain began the nineteenth cen-tury at war with Napoleon, witnessed three civil wars between 1833 and 1876, saw governments come and go as a result of dozens of mil-itary coups, lagged behind much of Western Europe economically, and experimented with non-Spanish monarchs and even a Republic in 1873.[49] With the establishment of a liberal political system that consolidated formal political power for the oligarchy, ratified a lib-eral Constitution in 1876, successfully kept the military, with its his-toric propensity for insurrection, from disrupting the government, and gradually extended basic civil rights such as universal manhood suffrage, it appeared that the Restoration state was a success story of liberal-democratic participatory government.

However, the Restoration's architect, Antonio Cánovas del Castillo, installed a number of illiberal measures to ensure political power remained in the hands of the elites, resulting in a chasm between those elites and mass society. The fundamental feature of the regime was the so-called *turno pacífico*, the peaceful and automatic rotation of the two oligarchical parties. Cánovas strengthened the executive power of the monarchy by enshrining it, rather than the military, as the moderating power between the parties and devised a system that created parliamentary majorities for the ruling party, be it the Conservatives or Liberals.[50] The key word of course is "create," because the Restoration regime depended on an extensive network of local political bosses, called *caciques*, who ensured predetermined outcomes of elections through bribes, falsifications, ballot tampering, coercion, and even violence. Given Restoration Spain's predominately illiterate, rural, and agrarian population, the strength of the rural *caciques* accounted for the regime's longevity, despite growing popular apathy and resentment.

Unlike in other Western European nations where states took an active part in asserting national identity (through the establishment of national symbols, secular holidays, flags, anthems, and rituals), the relatively weak Spanish Restoration state actually avoided such contentious issues as the religious question, nationalism, and educational curriculum.[51] Because the Spanish state was in chronic political crisis from 1808 to 1875 and because exorbitant war debt inherited from the Old Regime plagued the Restoration state, it was completely unable to penetrate the hearts of the Spaniards and generate a unified Spanish identity.[52] The regime was more concerned with maintaining stability and precluding mobilization from either the left or right, which allowed its opposition to emerge as standard-bearers of alternative political cultures.

It is under the regime's apparent stranglehold over formal political power that we see a bourgeoning urban civil society. While the republicans and later the socialists were technically not locked out of seats in the Parliament, they joined the anarchists on the left and the ultraconservative Carlists on the Right as outsiders of the system that Cánovas constructed. Elections were not the only way that nonelites and opponents to the Restoration regime could participate in politics, and as Radcliff observes, "given the restrictions of Restoration liberalism, these groups were most successful when they pursued their political goals outside the national electoral arena."[53] The expansion of the public sphere wherein Spaniards from various classes and backgrounds came together and discussed notions of the common good and forms of good government offered republicans such as Nakens a space to pursue politicization and nation-building.[54]

*   *   *

With these introductory words on anticlericalism and nationalism in mind, I move on to the story of Spanish anticlericalism, the republican José Nakens, and the effort to create an anticlerical national identity in Restoration Spain. Taking anticlericalism's fundamentally liberal and modern qualities as its points of departure, chapter one demonstrates how anticlericalism was at the forefront of battles between the forces of tradition and political modernity not only in Spain but in virtually all other Western European contexts.

Chapter two presents a brief sketch of José Nakens and his political career within Spanish republicanism. Nakens was a transitional figure between the old conspiratorial or militaristic politics of Ruiz Zorrilla and the younger generation of dynamic republican populists such as Lerroux and Blasco Ibáñez. Chapter three specifically deals with Nakens and the "anticlerical industry" of Restoration Spain: the mass-production of anticlerical, pro-republican imagery, and other artifacts or forms of discourse of the anticlerical Spain Nakens envisioned. The anticlerical industry paraphernalia had the goal of making people feel aggrieved about the role of the clergy in their nation so that they would be encouraged to agitate toward a Second Republic that would redress their problems.

Through untangling the attempted regicide of Alfonso XIII and his bride on their wedding day on May 31, 1906, chapter four will show how anticlericalism provided a powerful link across the developing left-wing political culture. Despite the fact that Nakens was antipathetic to anarchism, he and other republicans were instrumental in helping anarchists imagine an anticlerical and antimonarchical community.

Chapter five focuses attention on the gendered language of republican anticlericalism and how republicans represented and understood women. As elsewhere in Europe, republicans envisioned women to be illiberal obstacles to their national vision. A significant component of the anticlerical message of Nakens and other republicans included an effort to convince Spanish men that they must break the bond between their women (i.e., their wives or daughters) and their priests.

Finally, chapter six demonstrates that anticlericalism had been transformed from something republicans had incorporated into their repertoire of protest to a vehicle that even the oligarchic parties could use to appear as spearheads of national regeneration. This was especially true of the Restoration's most "anticlerical decade," 1898–1910, when the *modus vivendi* between the Church and State was most jeopardized, and when the intellectual backlash against the State resulted in a sharpened call for that national regeneration.

There is no denying that modern Hispanists are in some way haunted by the Spanish civil war of 1936–1939. Indeed my own interest in Spanish anticlericalism originally stems from graduate school reading about the violence directed against the clergy during the civil war, which left 6,832 members of the Catholic clergy dead, including 13 bishops, 4,172 diocesan priests and seminarians, 2,364 friars and monks, and 283 nuns.[55] While I certainly do not pin these deaths on José Nakens or other radical republicans who had generated a following by attacking the clergy, they were responsible for contributing to a modern anticlerical tradition implanted in the minds of many Spaniards who believed an effective way to challenge order and authority was through anticlerical violence. However, the marked anticlerical hatred and violence of the civil war perpetrated mainly by members of the working class and peasants point to more than just a shared culture or language of anticlericalism. During the Restoration, Nakens and anticlerical nationalists reflected deep-seated preoccupation with and grievances toward the everyday power and presence of the Church and clergy.

By linking anticlericalism with nationalism, radical republicans put forward a divisive vision of the Spanish nation. Rather than accepting anticlericalism's liberal message or understanding anticlerical nationalism as a path toward modernization, the power to potentially create through destruction was what revolutionary workers took with them into the 1930s. Thus, the anticlerical nationalism of radical republicans helped polarize rather than unify Spanish identity, setting the state for the religious/national antagonism during the Second Republic and Spanish civil war.

Anticlericalism in Modern Spain and Europe: Struggles over Nation-Building

One of the most important legacies of the French Revolution, which was part of a larger secularizing process in France, was the actual application of the theories of the *philosophes* throughout Europe.[1] The period of restoration and conservatism that marked the aftermath of the Napoleonic era did not prevent the subsequent efforts by many liberals, especially left-of-center or pro-democracy liberals, to remove or try to remove the absolutist quality of their governments, champion meritocracy, and question preexisting aristocratic privilege. As a corollary to the victory of nineteenth-century Liberalism, the Catholic Church and clergy were attacked for ideological and practical reasons. A commitment to Liberalism, which mandated that the individual be frcc in his spiritual, economic, ethical, and political life, necessitated significant changes in the relationship between the state and the Church, and between the state and the individual.

Scholars such as Michael Burleigh, however, are quick to remind that many priests and their followers attempted to confront and reconcile themselves and their faith with the moderate forces of liberalism and modernization even before the French Revolution, only to find themselves victims of radical idealists seeking a civic religion in the service of the state.[2] Even those revolutionary traditions pointed to the continued interplay between religion and national identity as Catholicism offered nationalists the linguistic, symbolic, and rhetorical models needed to build a national community.[3] In the case of Spain, Scott Eastman uses Catholic sermons and print culture to argue that religion, ideals of spiritual uniformity, and the Catholic clergy themselves played a crucial role in the forging of the Spanish nation and empire in the immediate aftermath of the French Revolution and Peninsular War.[4] The early nineteenth century touched off contested and convulsive attempts to construct national identity within Spain, a process that would go beyond 1823, and the role the Church and clergy played throughout the century established that competing discourses of national identity continued to be negotiated within the frame of a powerful culture of religious devotion and a liberal tradition that sought to curb clericalism.[5]

Though scholars widely disagree about the origins of modern nationalism, it does seem clear that the experience of the French Revolution and the Napoleonic Wars initiated a discourse of national identity that was linked to the idea of the individual: many who espoused Liberalism conflated the idea of liberating the individual with the idea of liberating the nation from Old Regime institutions such as the monarchy and the Catholic Church, which dominated education and public welfare institutions. In his survey of the rhetoric of nationalism, Craig Calhoun argues that nations were constructed as "super-individuals" whose identities assumed a special priority over other collective identities.[6] The construction of the personal identity of the "super-individual" (the nation) required subordinating all other collective forms of identity, such as membership in the Catholic Church, the family, and so on, in order for the nation-state to be the moral compass and guardian of the individual. Calhoun writes that "membership in a nation is a mediation between the discrete individual and the impersonal forces that affect his or her life while remaining beyond the control of direct, interpersonal relationships."[7]

The nineteenth-century Europe-wide campaign to liberate the individual, and thereby the nation, through a rational secularization of society aggravated clerical groups, especially when radical, revolutionary, or punitive paths to reform were pursued. In these contexts, priests, monks, bishops, and their loyal followers felt threatened by efforts to differentiate the secular and religious spheres, which initiated a vicious cycle. In Spain, for instance, partisans of a radical liberalism and democratic movement would have to wait until 1868 before they could make strides against the intrinsically tied forces of religion and national identity by successfully enshrining the non-confessional state, only to see clerical demonstrations of every stripe rise up to challenge their secular triumph. The emergence of clericalism, both in private pastoral form and public demonstrations, triggered the anticlerical actions and words of liberal statesmen and special interest groups that were not willing to concede any ground to clericalism.

With John N. Schumacher's claim that "the struggle of the Catholic Church against Liberalism in the nineteenth century nowhere, perhaps, took such extreme forms as it did in Spain"[8] as an important point of departure, this chapter explores nineteenth-century anticlericalism in Spain to demonstrate how the battle between anticlericalism and clericalism permeated the political and cultural efforts to create a liberal and national identity. It continues with a comparison of the clerical/anticlerical battles in other European countries during this time of nation-building. I show modern anticlericalism has been a common expression of liberalism, which seeks to erase restraints on individual progress. In Spain, modern anticlericalism is principally rooted in a tension born out of the struggle to establish the parameters of the clergy's function in a society that has become conscious of its own autonomy.[9] Of particular concern here is to understand anticlericalism, especially as put forward by radical republican politicians and journalists, as an expression of Spanish nationalism.

Building the Spanish nation proved to be very difficult for nineteenth-century rulers and elites alike because of the peculiarities of Spanish national identity before the Napoleonic Wars. Alvarez Junco writes that the ethno-patriotic identity of Early Modern Spain was characterized by a fusion between political and religious identity; deep-rooted xenophobia; eurocentrism, or the tendency to evaluate Spain *vis-à-vis* the rest of Western Europe; and a victimized, self-pitying tone.[10] Furthermore, the majority of the population felt more linked to their local rural communities than to any imagined community, given the nation's rudimentary communications and lack of a cohesive economic and cultural marketplace.[11] Within local communities the priest, rather than any representative of the state, controlled the channels of education and communication, which of course hampered efforts to instill liberty and progress among the Spanish. Even during a crisis point such as the French Revolution, the Spanish Church was able to work with the Spanish state to minimize any damage to either's position in society.[12] However, during much of the nineteenth century, the state and Church were often pinned against each other rather than cultivating alliances.

Through this survey of Spain's clerical/anticlerical battles during the nineteenth century, it is important to remember that modern anticlericalism stems from a reaction to clericalism. Modern anticlericalism can only be explained within the context of the politico-religious conflict generated by the processes of secularism and modernization. Demetrio Castro Alfín writes that modern Spanish anticlericalism's "content and expression was decidedly political and the old moral factors were recast and molded to the new cultural framework of competitive party politics."[13] This is a pattern that holds true for many Western European nations during the nineteenth and twentieth centuries because anticlericalism was a wholly liberal response to clerical anxieties. In Spain, clericalism and its multifaceted manifestations (from increased religiosity and missionary activity to the mass-production of clerical literature to Carlism) flared up soon after, and as a response to, the triumphs of Spanish liberalism. This, in turn, led to multifaceted manifestations of anticlericalism designed to curtail clericalism in favor of the continuation of Spain's political, cultural, and economic modernization.

Furthermore, anticlericalism in nineteenth century became more than a form of popular revolt that arose to push back clerical gains. To Spanish radical liberals and democrats in the mid-nineteenth-century, anticlericalism became an intellectual tradition just as it had for triumphant republican politicians and intellectuals in France. For the republicans—late nineteenth-century inheritors of that radical democratic ethos—anticlericalism became a *raison d'être* in and of itself rather than something that merely sprang up whenever clericalism grew strong. Anticlerical's dynamism as both a weapon in the people's repertoire of protest and a weapon in the discursive arsenal of radicals, democrats, and liberals was part of what made anticlericalism such a successful discourse of national identity, because it could transcend the material issues that divided the middle classes and popular masses.

The Convulsive and Vicious Cycle: Anticlerical Responses to Resurgent Clericalism in Nineteenth-Century Spain

The War of Independence, 1808–1814

The close link between religious and political identity became apparent in Spain's so-called "War of Independence" from France (1808–1814). Scholars have pointed to that conflict as a veritable holy war and as the first nationalist expression of the Spanish to assert their Catholic and traditionalist identity.[14] Many who took up arms were priests or monks who fought out of a desire to defend traditional and Catholic Spain from what they perceived as a godless liberal French encroachment. Stanley Payne writes that "there was apparently not a single province in all of Spain that did not produce at least one guerrilla band led by a priest or monk."[15] These priests and monks believed that Spain's Church was not to be a moderate Church, but rather a Church "led by priests who regarded themselves as modern prophets charged with bringing the people of God back to their senses to recreate a theocratic society in which religious and moral values were paramount."[16]

Liberal and moderate Spanish priests have hardly been cited as characteristic of the clergy during the war with Napoleon, though scholars such as Eastman correctly insist upon a more nuanced picture of the clergy and the ways in which they conceived of and imagined national identity.[17] Hispanists have been all too ready to follow the lead of reports and accounts that portrayed the clergy as all-powerful because of their ability to direct the fury of the people against the French. However, just as the altruistic and nationalist motivations of Spanish guerrillas and bandits who plagued Napoleon's armies has come into question, so too has the myth and image of the militant reactionary Spanish clergy.[18] The historiographical problem of neglecting the liberal and moderate clergy is noted, but it is not a major concern of this book, which analyzes an anticlerical-nationalist discourse that was partially predicated upon presenting a clerical enemy that was anathema to alternative political cultures.

Alvarez Junco has argued compellingly that the myth and lore of the War of Independence were more important than the war itself in the construction of Spanish nationalism. Napoleon simply sought to replace the Spanish Bourbons with his brother Joseph, and continue the processes of secularization and rationalization of the state administration already begun during the reign of Charles III; he was out to either threaten or destroy Spanish culture.[19] The "War of Independence" then did not forge a modern Spanish nation, but historians and politicians in the middle of the nineteenth century imagined the conflict as if it had. Whatever the case may be, Spanish liberals after France's ouster were left with a number of militant clergymen and their reactionary followers who had violently resisted the French, and who would resist French-inspired or "Enlightened" attempts to reform the relationship between Church and state. The problem was compounded by the newly restored King, Ferdinand VII, who sought to reward the traditionalist clergy by appointing reactionary bishops in order to solidify his alliance between throne and altar.

The Restoration of Ferdinand VII and the Liberal Triennium (1820–1823): Clerical Renaissance and Anticlerical Response

Spanish clericalism found in Ferdinand VII's antipathy to liberals and the Constitution of 1812 the justification for its mulish resistance to secularism. Ferdinand threw out the Constitution in 1814, reinstituted the Inquisition, and drove out liberal clerics and freemasons, while inviting the Jesuits back into Spain.[20] However, the narrow basis of support that Ferdinand's reactionary government defined for itself was not enough for him to maintain his power. Ferdinand could not control the nation merely with the help of the clergy, especially when Spain was burdened by heavy war debt and suddenly facing a plethora of independence movements in Latin America. His coddling of the clerical movement rankled liberals and set the stage for the emergence of anticlerical disturbances and violence in 1820 when Major Rafael Riego led a military *pronunciamiento* in favor of the 1812 Liberal Constitution.

Reforming the internal organization of the Church was a priority for liberals during the Triennium of 1820–1823. While at no time were the liberal politicians seeking to threaten the Catholic faith, those behind the Constitutional Triennium genuinely sought to address the inequities of the clergy's economic and social existence. They were enthusiastic about removing inherited clerical privileges, creating a fair system of compensation for all priests, and offering the clergy the same rights as all Spanish men, no more and no less.[21] Liberal clergymen came out of retirement or returned from exile and endorsed the need to make the clergy a more efficient body of civil and religious servants. The tenuous accommodation between a largely conservative Church and the liberal state became stressed when the Jesuits were expelled from Spain in August of 1820.[22] The *Ley de Monacales* tried to impose a rational ordering of religious homes and ecclesiastical jurisdictions so that even monasteries big enough to house thirty monks no longer housed two or three "bored" clergymen.[23] Also, the liberal state sold various monasteries, cloisters, and churches, or converted them into hospitals or barracks in an effort to make more efficient use of ecclesiastic resources and address the state's financial despair.

However, scholars sympathetic to the Church and clergy suggest that these reforms are only one part of the story; the reforms also created an anticlerical environment throughout Spain. Although he believes in the need for clerical reform and makes a few apologies for the clergy's reactionary character, Father Manuel Revuelta González,

S. J. is quick to argue that the liberals' "purity of intention" was obfuscated by their self-interest and desire for anticlerical vengeance. In addition, liberals were determined to hurry along the ecclesiastic reform almost overnight, regardless of whether the old clergy was ready for it or not.

Indeed, there is a great deal of truth to characterizing the Triennium as a time of intense anticlerical vindictiveness. Liberals, especially the radical liberals or *exaltados* who controlled the Parliament in 1821, were determined to ensure that the Spanish people be exposed to the Constitution of 1812, and politicians were especially critical of clergymen who resisted the state's program. The regime's decision to institute a limited form of freedom of the press resulted in a remarkable proliferation of newspapers and other forms of media, many of which were unabashedly anticlerical. It should be noted that some of the most widely read anticlerical propaganda came from the liberal clergy who believed that ecclesiastic wealth had come at the expense of Spanish peasantry. For example, Salvador Miñano Bedoya's *Political Laments for a Poor Little Idler Accustomed to Living at the Expense of Others* (1820) articulated an intense frustration with clergymen who did not contribute to society.[24] However, as the tensions between conservative royalists and the liberal state devolved into open conflict, liberal clerics were completely discredited in the eyes of traditionalist Catholics. Still, Miñano's anticlerical works became standard reading for the liberal bourgeoisie, and the anticlerical atmosphere of Madrid permeated not only literature but also the theater and other channels of communication.

The anticlerical sentiment of radical liberals was evident in their belief that the clergy should swallow (*tragar*, or gulp down under duress) the 1812 Constitution, whether they wanted to or not.[25] Many accounts of that period emphasize the atmosphere of tension: it was dangerous for any clergyman to be found in the streets of Madrid and Barcelona. The Absolutist Frenchman Martignac lamented that

> clergymen were ridiculed in the theaters, and were presented to the public as detrimental to the state, as perverse and evil people, and the same applies to the secular clergy. A multitude of offensive songs rapidly spread everywhere, and obscene books were sold without any effort to conceal the deed.[26]

In 1821 Riego himself, along with his aids, joined a boisterous crowd at Madrid's Teatro Principe singing the popular anticlerical chant of

"Swallow it, you dog / you who do not want the Constitution."[27] Callahan argues that this type of popular urban anticlericalism, centered primarily in Madrid and Barcelona, was new. Madrid, as the center of the nation's political life, offered an atmosphere "where the attitudes of liberal politicians could filter down to the streets through pamphlets, broad sheets, and simple word-of-mouth."[28] In the last quarter of the nineteenth century, republicans and their anticlerical industry would thrive in this new urban anticlerical milieu.

Such an anticlerical backlash initiated the sometimes violent omnipresent cycle between clericalism and anticlericalism. The anticlericalism, which had emerged to challenge the resurgence of clericalism between 1814 and 1820, triggered open resistance by some priests to the liberal state beginning in 1821. Priests such as Jerónimo Merino, whose guerrilla exploits against the French had earned him a canonry in Palencia from Ferdinand VII, took to the hills against the liberals.[29] Fr. Merino would later go on to become a Carlist, and eventually he died in exile. However, his enormous fame as a vicious *guerrillero* was furthered by the anarchist novelist Pío Baroja who wrote that Merino "had some of the enigmatic personalities of blood-thirsty men, of assassins and executioners."[30]

By 1822, a civil war broke out in Northern Spain between liberal forces of the state and neo-absolutist (or royalist) councils in the Catalan hinterlands. Once again, reactionary priests and monks took up arms and led unruly troops under the battle cry: "Long live the King and Religion. Death to the Constitution!"[31] Many more priests and monks made every effort to undermine the state and the Constitution through their daily sermons; throughout the nineteenth century, the clergy deftly took advantage of the pulpit to subvert the liberals in Madrid.[32] Clerical involvement in the royalist rebellions of 1822–1823 moved the liberal state and its supporters increasingly toward radical actions. Executions of priests and monks, burnings, and sacking of religious institutions by anticlerical Spaniards became a reality for the first time in Spain's history.[33] In Catalonia, these anticlerical actions were an effort to avenge the execution of liberal prisoners held in Urgell, who were murdered at the hands of ultramontane priests.[34] The die was cast and some form of the clerical/anticlerical struggle would from hereon be a regular feature of nineteenth-century political life.

Clerical Resurgence and the Second Restoration, 1823–1833

Just as in other European nations where attacks on the Church generally increased after periods of clerical rebirth or regrouping, Spanish anticlericalism in the nineteenth century sprang up to combat the clerical revivals. In order to properly understand both the political anticlericalism and the violent popular anticlericalism in the Madrid of the 1830s, we need to realize that reactionary clericalism and absolutism enjoyed one last hurrah between 1823 and 1833. With the permission of the European powers, a French invasion of Spain succeeded virtually without a struggle. The guerrilla priests, who had once taken to the hills to fight the French, now embraced the "100,000 sons of St. Louis" (French King Louis XVIII) in 1823 because the temporary occupation promised the restoration of Ferdinand's absolute power.[35]

During this Second Fernandine Reaction, clericalism gave future anticlericalism its *raison d'être* as the repression of liberals was more severe than the reprisals of 1814. Riego's execution in 1823 gave many traditionalists some degree of satisfaction, but at the same time it created a liberal martyr whose death had to be avenged with the blood of clergymen. On October 1, 1823, all Triennium measures were overturned, initiating an economic comeback for the Church: the full tithe was restored, as were old jurisdictions, and old monasteries were reopened with many properties returned to the Church.[36] Liberal priests were suppressed or exiled, and the reactionary forces within Church demanded that Ferdinand restore the Inquisition to help stamp out Jansenism. The quality of the clergy did not improve significantly over this period of constant flux as eighteenth-century weaknesses such as the poor distribution of resources and dogmatic ignorance persisted throughout the clergy's ranks.[37] Ferdinand himself staffed the Church hierarchy with antiliberal prelates, which placed the Church well behind the intellectual course of European thought in general. Still, as absolutist as he was, Ferdinand did not go far enough and frustrated conservative hopes for a theocratic regime. Many ultraconservative priests and their flock turned their loyalty toward his reactionary brother, Charles.

The First Carlist War (1833–1840): Liberals versus Traditionalists

Spanish liberals' third attempt to displace the vestiges of the traditional monarchy and Church came in the 1830s. Ferdinand dismayed the supporters of Charles in 1830 when he successfully fathered Isabella, his healthy heir to the throne. He repealed the Salic Law, a French Bourbon tradition that prohibited female monarchs since the end of the War of Spanish Succession, and began to drum up support for the infant princess among right-of-center liberals. The hopes and aspirations for a liberal Spain rested firmly in the princess who was to be taught to embrace Spain's liberal tradition from her earliest years. In late 1833, the King died, leaving behind a polarized nation; ultratraditionalist bands took to the hills to fight on behalf of the pretender Charles, while all liberals rallied around the Queen Regent, María Cristina, and infant daughter Isabella.

The First Carlist War of 1833–1840 was the longest and most devastating of the Spanish civil wars in the nineteenth century. Its ferocity can be explained in the way Carlists perceived the conflict. Carlists fought out of a deep sense of patriotism and fierce loyalty toward their faith, and local traditions or *fueros*, which had been in place since the Reconquest.[38] Carlists believed that the implementation of any liberal Constitution jeopardized their faith and their communities' ethos. Thus, religion was one tradition that stood as an obstacle for the liberal state because for Carlists, the old clergy, and their supporters, there was no contradiction between religion and their identity. Religion was not an intermediary loyalty between citizen and nation, it *was* the nation for Carlists. Their desire to go to war for their faith and traditions not only reinforced their local identities over those imposed in Madrid but, more importantly, radicalized the discourse of Spanish nationalism.

It should not be surprising that the overtly hostile clerical responses to the liberals and the Carlist uprisings in 1833–1834 resulted in violent anticlericalism in Madrid. A cholera epidemic had spread from Andalusia to the Ciudad Real Province and into Madrid where the disease claimed over 500 lives each day from July 15, 1834.[39] Anticlerical propagandists spread a rumor that Jesuit priests poisoned the public water supply in order to punish the liberal capital for its impiety.[40] Under the pretext of searching for incriminating evidence an angry mob stormed the city's central plazas, including the Plazuela de Cebada where Riego was executed, and sacked several religious structures and residences. In less than twelve hours the crowd murdered seventy-three priests and friars and left eleven others injured. Some priests were hacked to death with sabers, others were hanged naked in the streets, and many of their corpses were further desecrated. Clerical accounts of the atrocities accuse the police of willfully turning a blind eye to the anticlerical violence under the pretext that they were investigating the veracity of the poisoning rumor.[41] Indeed, there was police and military misconduct during the riot, and Madrid's police superintendent, mayor, and civil governor resigned because of the perception that their units were undisciplined. Of the seventy-nine persons arraigned for the riot, fifty-four were civilians, and twenty-five were either policemen or national guardsmen. Only two men, a cabinet maker and a military musician, were executed for their part in the riot, but both were accused of theft rather than homicide.[42]

Clearly the 1834 Madrid anticlerical riot was more than a spontaneous reaction to an alleged poisoning. The nation was involved in a civil war, the cholera epidemic had created a great deal of anguish over the city's social conditions, the anti-absolutist as well as anticlerical energies had been building throughout the Second Fernandine Reaction, and anticlerical leftist liberals took advantage of this when they made up such a horrible rumor. The Church and the clergy, especially the Jesuits, had become symbols of an absolutist identity that was anathema to men dedicated to the liberal vision of the Spanish nation. Still, atheists and freemasons were not the sole forces behind the riot, and many of the rioters themselves were Catholic. This riot was not so much directed against the Catholic faith but rather a collective unleashing of anger toward symbols of absolute power. For Caro Baroja, the 1834 riot was more than an action based on the polarization between good and bad guys, but rather symptomatic of a society with a fundamental discord between its actors, and also one in which there is no understanding.[43] When the anti-absolutist daily *Eco del Comercio* reported on the anticlerical riot, it transformed the victims into "enemies of the nation (*patria*)," and minimized the violent acts by referring to them as "mishaps (*algunas desgracias*)."[44] Already, the rhetoric of nationalism tied to the liberation of the individual was in place, and it explained anticlerical violence as a way to combat obstacles to the freedoms envisioned by liberals.

The same rhetoric of nationalism took shape around the dichotomy of liberal and antiliberal. The monks and priests were enemies of the Spanish nation because they were symbolic obstacles to Spain's march toward a liberal system. This riot, as well as the civil war within which the riot took place, demonstrated that anything about religion or anything relating to religious reform was a political powder keg; the riots demonstrated the radicalized link between politics on one hand and religion on the other.

One of the results of the popular anticlerical sentiment of the early years of the Carlist War was that the Spanish state now enjoyed the ideal environment in which to force the Church to abandon its Old Regime character. This was accomplished through the disentailment of Church land. The underlying motivations for this new wave of expropriation were to boost the state's finances and create a constituency of bourgeois land owners loyal to the state.[45] Disentailment certainly held pragmatic value for the Spanish State as it tried to centralize and legitimate its authority. While the 540 parcels of Church land entered into the Spanish market for auctions between 1836 and 1844 is impressive, recent research reveals that the 1830s disentailment was a continuation of a longer process begun under Carlos III.[46] Notwithstanding, the Old Regime Church, which had dominated both the spiritual and temporal life of all Spaniards for hundreds of years, could no longer function as it had once the Spanish liberal state asserted itself in 1840.

The Liberal State, 1840–1868: Clericalism Revives

The victory for the new liberal political system was a Pyrrhic one because it came through tearing up the nation; it was the victory of the liberal sector of society over the traditionalist sector. Church leaders had no choice but to acquiesce to the liberal state and abandon their hopes for a theocratic society. However, all was not lost for the Church because the painful transition from the Old Regime to liberalism offered the Church and Catholics political opportunities to use the liberal system to further their interests. The Church and clergy knew they could not go back to the Old Regime alliance with the state, but the Church and clergy could use the legal rights afforded to them by liberalism in order to undermine Liberal Spain. If the liberal ideal of a Church reduced largely to its spiritual and pastoral missions was accomplished after the Carlist revolts were put down and the disentailment of Church property completed, the triumph came at the expense of any possibility that the Church could be put in the service of the liberal state.[47] Thus, if the state were to engage in a political nation-building discourse, it would not find a sympathetic audience among the majority of the clergy and its following.

Aside from a brief but unsuccessful Carlist uprising in Catalonia in 1846 (often called the Martiners' War or the Second Carlist War) and the Liberal Unionist Revolution of 1854–1856, which resulted in a new bout of political anticlericalism primarily stemming from Liberal Unionists' disgust with the 1851 Concordat, the Spanish state and Church were on neutral terms until 1868. Much like the oligarchic Restoration regime that would emerge after 1874, the political and military elite that constituted the government between 1843 and 1868 was primarily concerned with excluding radical democrats (including Spanish earliest republicans) from power and with maintaining social order. There was a noticeable decline in anticlerical violence throughout Spain after 1843.

Anticlericalism was limited to Cathedral break-ins, drunken disruptions of ceremonies, a minority's disrespect for the religion, but it certainly did not constitute a frontal assault on the Church.[48] The sweeping political anticlerical measures of February 1855, which resulted in the confiscation of approximately 143,000 units of property belonging to either the regular or secular clergy, did not prompt any anticlerical violence despite clerical resistance and the corresponding increase in anticlerical agitation by liberal and democratic newspapers.[49] When popular violence did erupt during this period, it was directed at other symbols of power or oppression, such as the Queen Mother's Palace and homes of the notables in 1854, or against commercial enterprises during bread riots in Old Castile in 1856. The Church and clergy, it appeared, were no longer the symbols of the people's oppressors.

This reconciliation between the Church and the Spanish state hampered the prospects for an official nation-building program. The traditional clergy continued to criticize the liberal polity and prevented the faithful from adhering to the liberals' vision of Spain. Borja de Riquer has argued that the 1851 Concordat gave the impression that Catholicism was consubstantial with political conservatism. The Concordat "consolidated the Catholic confessionalism of the state and reinforced the traditional identification of Spain as the 'catholic-nation' *par excellence.*"[50]

The relatively peaceful conditions also allowed the Church and clergy to attempt to re-clericalize Spain. Antonio María Claret, a Catalan prelate who would also become the Queen's confessor, was a key figure in the mid-nineteenth-century religious revival. He used sophisticated marketing methods and a team of missionaries to launch a counterattack on what he considered a depraved secular society. Callahan writes that

> Between 1848 and 1866 the publishing house Claret established printed 2,811,100 books, 1,509,600 pamphlets, and nearly 5,000,000 posters and broadsheets. Claret's adaptation of the mission and his appreciation of the importance of religious propaganda within the new society of liberal Spain provided the Church with an instrument of popular evangelization that to some extent compensated for the near disappearance of the proselytizing religious orders.[51]

These clerical texts maligned rather than supported liberalism and the political system and triggered the expansion of the anticlerical industry during the Restoration.

Clericals also struck a tremendous victory for themselves on November 8, 1857 when the Minister of the Interior, Cándido Nocedal (a moderate liberal who later became an important Carlist leader and founder of the Carlist daily *El Siglo Futuro*), passed a press law that prohibited the publication of any discussion of religious themes without the authorization of the local diocese.[52] These restrictions favored clericals as the state tilted the odds in favor of pro-clerical partisans in their battle against liberalism and socialism. A trigger for anticlericalism, ultramontane elements were also spurred on by Pope Pius IX's *Syllabus of Errors* (1864), a proclamation that condemned liberalism and all other progressive ideologies. In October of 1865, after a long campaign by the Catholic press against Emilio Castelar (a republican journalist and university historian of Early Christianity), the *moderado* government reserved the right to withdraw or withhold academic tenure (*cátedra*) from scholars who were not Catholic, or spoke against the official religion of the state.[53] The political atmosphere that resulted after 1857 was a paradoxical one: though the liberal state depended on the Catholic Church for its base of support and though the Church was more dependent (especially financially) on the state than ever before in the nineteenth century, the state was nonetheless, constantly and legally, maligned by clerical forces. In addition, anticlericalism as an intellectual tradition for those resentful of the proclerical atmosphere grew within liberal professionals, such as Castelar, and democrats seeking to accelerate the secularization of Spain.

The 1868 Revolution and the First Republic: Resurgent Anticlericalism

Of course this new wave of clericalism did not to go unpunished when popular forms of anticlerical revolt again sprang up between 1868 and 1874. The Revolution of 1868 was launched by a coalition of liberal generals and urban radicals resentful of *moderado* dominance since 1856. However, the revolution of these elites was also accompanied by a number of local juntas whose members often included antireligious radicals and republicans. Fernando Garrido, a republican and editor of *La Igualada*, insisted that "The September (1868) Revolution was, more a revolution against religion than a political revolution."[54] In many of Spain's provinces, revolutionary juntas restricted the activities of bishops and priests, looted churches, shot at religious statues, and physically attacked priests.[55]

Popular forms of anticlerical agitation grew when Spain's First Republic was proclaimed in 1873. Anticlerical mischievousness was especially prevalent in Southern Spain where, for example, Seville youths dyed holy water red so that the faithful would emerge with brows tinted the color of the revolution, and in Cádiz, republican bands disrupted solemn benedictions and that city's municipal government changed religious street names to those of the republican litany.[56] A new series of Carlist rebellions in the north of Spain and atrocities against liberal prisoners at the hand of a small minority of priests prompted anticlerical reprisals similar to those during the First Carlist War. The weakened Church of the 1850s, not worth the wrath of the disgruntled mobs, was now once again attacked precisely for its affiliation with the Queen and her conservative state.[57]

As in republican France, Catholic anticlericalism in Spain had begun to give way to a modern form of anticlericalism—that is, an anticlericalism of antireligion. A new generation of radicals that included Garrido and José Nakens—but also Catholic-raised intellectuals such as Clarín (Leopoldo Alas y Ureña), Juan Valera, and Benito Pérez Galdós—viewed religion as a fundamental evil that had to be repressed or even extirpated altogether.[58] For a new generation of Voltairean radicals, the answer to Spain's conflict with the Church was simple: the complete separation of Church and state. However, when their time to rule came in the form of the first Spanish Republic (1873), they lost the opportunities to pursue anticlericalism further because of a number of revolts that necessitated the state's attention.[59]

For various radicals and republicans, anticlericalism became a *raison d'etre* in and of itself rather than something that merely sprang up whenever clericalism grew strong. So long as the forward progress of Spain was hampered by clericals, or at least so long as modern anticlericals perceived that was the case, the modern anticlericals were determined to curb the Church and clergy's presence in society for the good of the nation. Because of the success of anticlericalism throughout nineteenth-century France and especially during the Third Republic, anticlericalism became a lifestyle, a philosophy, and an almost sacred tool in the cosmos of Spanish modern anticlericals. For modern anticlericals, anticlericalism was that which divided liberals from antiliberals, the enlightened from the fanatical, and progressive Spain from absolutist Spain.

The Restoration: Everyday Tensions and Exceptional High Drama

Numerous local studies of the clerical/anticlerical battle in Restoration Spain before 1898 reveal that while acute moments of violence were rare, the drama created by the rhetoric of both sides sustained tension in everyday life.[60] Many of these struggles involved republican agitators, but also agitators from the revolutionary left—anarchists and some socialists—who continued to see the Church as part of the dominant class that both controlled the government and perpetuated an inequitable capitalist system.[61] In the mind of republicans, the Church and the Restoration state were equals; the urban Church's financial wealth was proof that the state favored traditional institutions over the nation's workers and poor.[62] The Spanish clergy's continued dominion over the educational system, particularly primary schooling, was also an important source of conflict during the Restoration.[63]

Anticlericalism and anticlerical violence would spike again in the aftermath of the Spanish-American War, culminating with the Barcelona Tragic Week of the summer of 1909. When anticlerical violence exploded there, three clergymen accidentally died in the violence and dozens of churches and convents were destroyed by angry mobs.[64] While Joan Connelly Ullman makes the provocative suggestion that anticlericalism in Spain did not serve to further any political ideology, and often functioned as radical republicanism's tool to channel a mobilized public's aggression safely away from institutions of political power, Romero Maura's hypothesis of the consubstantiation of anticlericalism and the world view of radical republicans and anarchists is more plausible.[65] Radical republicans and their revolutionary left allies in the early twentieth century sought to destroy the Restoration regime by undermining it through force. When republicans infused their anticlerical dogma into the working classes' hatred of the wealth of the Church, anticlericalism advanced to a revolutionary and violent phase. The conservatism of the Catholic Church and its reliance on the regime made it an impediment to republican rule and, therefore, it had to be removed as well. The Tragic Week was a symptom of a larger polarization between republicans and clericals, a polarization rooted in profound antipathies toward each other. The deep divisions between clerical and anticlerical Spain were severe enough to prevent the success of the Restoration state's efforts at nation-building.

Spanish Anticlericalism in Comparative Context

Spain was not the only nation whose nationalists became increasingly intolerant of other collective identities that interfered with the identity of the nation they championed. Throughout Western Europe, some degree of *ressentiment*[66] over clerical power resulted in new forms of anticlericalism designed to marginalize the Church from the construction of the nation. These anticlerical/clerical battles cannot be considered marginal to the history of Spain and Europe in the nineteenth century, and just as Spain experienced ebbs and flows in the anticlerical/clerical battle, so too did Spain's neighbors. Anticlericalism sprang up as a response to increased clerical activity, which was a response to the context of secularization and modernization. In Italy and Russia, where clerical campaigns lacked money, coordination, and efficiency, anticlerical responses were similarly weak. There, the particularism and weakness of the Church and clergy, as well as the state, posed significant difficulties to the process of nation-building. In Germany, where Catholics were well organized, especially after 1848, anticlericalism took on a decidedly strong and authoritarian response. The result in Germany during the later part of the nineteenth century was that religion became a national identity, which also made building the nation a futile or incomplete exercise. The differences between Catholics and Protestants meant that there were at least two Germanys.

Spain and France saw the most acute manifestations of the battles between anticlericals and clericals during the nineteenth century. That this was the case is testimony to the strength of the two sides in each nation. Unlike Germany, however, the clericals in both France and Spain questioned the legitimacy of the state and of any nation-building project that actively sought to curtail the presence of the Church and clergy. But while the French republicans and anticlericals actually held formal political power at the end of the nineteenth century, Spanish republicans and other anticlericals were often at the margins of political power and they too questioned the legitimacy of their state.

France's nineteenth-century anticlerical/clerical battle actually mirrored Spain's in many ways because the contexts for these battles were similar. Both Spain and France experienced a politically convulsive nineteenth century as liberals and republicans constantly fought the forces that sought to restore the Old Regime. Indeed, the religious question in France pitted two ways of thinking, two political cultures, against each other throughout the nineteenth century. Anticlerical scholars such as Jules Michelet or Edgar Quinet won out and have written the history of France's nineteenth century as if all Frenchmen were excited by the nation's acceleration toward a secular and modern society. However, there were many in France who actively worked against the gains of liberalism, and thus France was locked into its own cultural civil war in the nineteenth century. Each of Liberalism's triumphs in France came at the expense of traditionalist France. These liberal triumphs would be followed by reactionary, conservative, or traditionalist responses such as the Bourbon Restoration, Louis Napoleon's Empire, Boulanger's attempted coup, the Dreyfus Affair, and, perhaps, the Vichy government. Both Spain and France had rich traditions that hoped to undermine the liberal states for introducing secular initiatives perceived as attacks against the Church and clergy.

In addition, both nations' clericalism and anticlericalism ran in cycles: anticlericalism arose to curtail and/or punish a swell of clericalism.[67] This was especially true of the aftermath of the Dreyfus Affair. Because the Church plunged into the Affair and fought what it saw as the united threats of Dreyfusards and the Third Republic, the Church forced the Republic to impose its will on the clergy.[68] In other words, the anticlericalism of 1900–1905, which included the separation of Church and state, can be blamed in part on the conservative character of French clericalism.[69] However, Catholicism in France, while certainly a vehicle of cultural resistance to secularization and republicanism, did not become an instrument through which to express an alternative mass national identity (like in Spain with Carlism or Basque nationalism) despite twentieth-century apolitical efforts to tie the survival of French identity to Catholic culture.[70] Finally, while French republicans tenuously controlled the French government after 1871 and were able to diffuse republican values in civil society,[71] their Spanish counterparts were on the margins of formal political power, struggling within civil society to make their Republic possible.

Although French anticlericalism often sprang up to curb French clericalism, the battle between these two forces was much more complicated. France suffered through the development of two culturally divided conceptions of the French nation: one primarily Catholic and traditionalist, the other liberal progressive, anticlerical, and republican. As in Spain, the rebarbative form of Catholicism preached by French clericals[72] made it increasingly difficult to reconcile the religion with republicanism. This dichotomy transformed the attempted secularization of the nation into an attack by one half of France on the other. Jacques Gadille argues that French anticlericalism's origins can be found in the radicalization of the eighteenth-century gap between "a religious sentimentalism, an evangelism which could take the form of mysticism...and which led to arduous apostolic and missionary principles" on the one hand, and "a rationalist deism, whose God of reason justified the claim of the enlightened state to install a central and national religion" on the other.[73] The confusion between individual religiosity and formal external religion meant that France's modern anticlericalism would be protean in manifestation, torn between attacking religion and protecting freedom of religion, and omnipresent in a variety of political and nonpolitical arenas.

Throughout the nineteenth century, the gap between the religious and those who fought to protect the freedom of religion grew wider, so much that these "Frances" refused to understand the fears of the other. The result was the political radicalization of the battle between clericals and anticlericals.[74] We can gauge the differing cosmos of clericals and anticlericals by studying how each understood important events in France's history. For example, the traditionalist clergy and their following understood the French Revolution as a holy war not unlike those they fought in the sixteenth and seventeenth centuries. The state's imposition of the Constitution on the clergy and the persecution of those priests who refused to become civil servants of the state went beyond political secularization; it was a cultural and personal affront to Catholic identity. On the other hand, liberal-progressive and republican France celebrated the Revolution. In his seven-volume *Histoire de la Revolution*, published between 1847 and 1853, Michelet broke with a tradition of historians who romanticized France's Medieval Christian past by elevating the French Revolution as the most important event in the entirety of French history. To him, the Revolution constituted *the* human triumph over the damaging clutches of a decadent religion. He thereby became the intellectual mentor of French republicanism.[75]

The battle between these two Frances was omnipresent in the nineteenth century, from the political sphere to the variegated forms of literary expression in the public sphere. France, like Spain, was a nation that seemed to be locked in an eternal war against itself, and this war permeated all aspects of politics, society, and culture. The persistence of this battle may account for the French right's enthusiastic embrace of the Vichy regime. If Herman Lebovics is correct in suggesting that the French right abandoned politics for a while after the Dreyfus Affair (that is at least until the 1930s) in order to concentrate on defining "True France" in cultural terms, then it is clear how the persistence of clericalism hampered or made the Third Republic's attempts to build the imaginary French community incomplete.[76]

In Germany, where Catholics were a minority, Bismarck and the National Liberal elites with whom he was allied found the strength of

the Catholic community to be a formidable obstacle to their version of
a unified nation. Jonathan Sperber argues that the German-Catholic
community's strength had grown since 1848, long before—and perhaps culminating with—the formation of the Center Party.[77] The
bourgeoning Catholic political movement of the 1850s and 1860s
feared the "implementation of liberal economic policies, seen as detrimental to the continued prosperity of the rural and small-town petty
bourgeoisie, around which German Catholicism was constructing
an increasingly patriarchal conception of society."[78] The result here
as in Spain was that the battles between the Church and German
state were interwoven with the clash between antiliberal Catholicism
and the liberalism of the propertied and educated bourgeoisie. As in
Spain, where popular and later political anticlericalism responded to
increased clerical mobilization, it was the German-Catholic Center
Party and its enormous electoral success with the third of Germany's
population who professed Roman Catholicism that led Bismarck to
undertake the political anticlerical campaign called the *Kulturkampf*.[79]
Bismarck considered German Catholics *Reichsfeinde* (enemies of the
state) and introduced a series of bills that restricted the clergy's freedom, established civil matrimony, and dissolved religious orders. At
the local level, political anticlericalism was met with both vigorous
displays of popular Catholic support for the clergy and anticlerical
street violence to combat clerical activity. The persecution during
the *Kulturkampf* did adversely affect the clergy, but at the same
time it made concrete the ideology of political Catholicism.[80] The
Kulturkampf was launched to contain the Center Party and curb clericalism; however, the *Kulturkampf* took on ideological and nationalistic dimensions beyond the political. Helmut W. Smith argues
that confessional animosities between Catholics and Protestants in
Germany reflected long historical memories, deep social and political
conflicts: "[these] were not incidental to German nationalism but the
thing itself."[81]

In much the same way as liberal Spain and Catholic Spain fought
to assert national identity during the Restoration, part of the history
of German nationalism was a history of contention over the defini-
tion, and the legitimating effects, of the nation. Of course it is imperative to differentiate between Spanish Catholics and German Catholics
because the latter rarely questioned the legitimacy of the national
state. However, just as Spanish Catholics and especially the most
conservative segments of traditionalist Spain saw themselves as different from and irreconcilable with liberal Spain, German Catholics

constructed national identity differently, appealing to different traditions, separate memories, and another history. By building Catholic identity through the language of a religious culture very distinct from that across the confessional divide, German Catholics "combined religious and national identity and, to a certain extent, wrested German nationalism from its exclusive association with Protestant Tradition."[82]

Anticlericals in Spain would join clericals in stocking their traditions with the historical memory of the abuses and excesses, perceived or real, of their opponents. As we shall see in chapter three, José Nakens, the most active purveyor of Restoration Spain's anticlerical industry, used the history of Inquisitorial torture against the Church and clergy during the Restoration. Because nationalist campaigns are built upon an appeal to the historical memories and experiences of disparate groups within the nation, Nakens hoped to evoke the foul memories of a violent and oppressive early modern Church that prevented the liberation of the individual.

Italy offers another interesting comparison to both Germany and Spain. Like Germany, Italy was a "new" nation in 1870 whose unification came through the military and political accomplishments of nationalist liberals. However, unlike Germany and very much like Spain, almost all Italians professed Roman Catholicism. In addition, while Spanish anticlericals, especially the republicans, defined both the Church and monarchy as enemies, the new Italian monarchy was a rallying point for Italian unification. The popularity of Victor Emmanuel's monarchy created tremendous difficulties for Italian republicans, who were considered subversive by liberal parliamentarians.[83] Nonetheless, anticlericalism was perhaps the most effective force unifying republicans, radicals, and liberals.

Politically, Italian anticlericalism was inspired by the German *Kulturkampf* and anticlerical developments in France, but the Italian state faced little opposition from antiliberal Catholics and often used anticlericalism's unifying power to generate support for itself.[84] At the local level, the battles between clericals and anticlericals resembled those in Spain and Germany as Catholic clubs and guilds clashed with republican and socialist associations, but in general, these battles were not nearly as severe as the ones in Spain, France, or Germany.[85] The struggle between Italian nationalist liberals and the Church and clergy was made more difficult for liberals because of the fact that the Church enjoyed the "home turf advantage." Nowhere else but in Italy could the Papacy be identified as the chief obstacle to the achievement of national unity, especially after 1860 when it became clear that the Church refused to ally with either Italian liberalism or Catholic liberalism.[86] The rivalry between the Vatican and the Italian state, exemplified by the antagonism between Pius IX and Mazzini, served as the backdrop for the late nineteenth- and early-twentieth-century battles over defining Italian national identity and clerical/anticlerical confrontations.[87]

Political anticlerical legislation in Italy was easy to enact so long as the Catholics obeyed the Pope's prohibition against political participation. With no central clerical political opposition like Germany's Center, and with an impoverished and embattled Church, the Italian state had little trouble imposing anticlericalism. The real battle between anticlericalism and clericalism was fought in civil society and the public sphere. Anticlerical caricatures and ridicule were staples in the press, and tensions between republicans, radicals, and socialists on the one hand and clericals on the other ran high.

Lay Catholic organizations and guilds had been increasingly successful after Leo XIII's *Rerum Novarum* in 1891, an encyclical that condemned socialism and the existing state of capitalism, and which called upon Catholics to transform capitalist relationships between Catholic workers and employers. While the Italian state had no problem proposing anticlerical legislation, the ratification or implementation of these initiatives proved much more difficult within a nation that seemed to believe other problems were more important than the clerical/anticlerical battle. As in Spain, anticlericalism in Italy was not simply a diversionary tool designed to channel attention away from political inefficiency, but rather anticlericalism was tied to the reinforcement of progressive, revolutionary, or nationalistic ideologies.

When compared to Spain, France, and Germany, Italian ultramontanism lacked strength. The entire administration of the Church, from the Pope to the local parish priest, was born Italian, and although they opposed the state, doing so did not, in their eyes, preclude them from membership in the Italian nation.[88] The Church was disorganized, inefficient, and impoverished before and after unification, and the Papacy's prohibitions effectively prevented an Italian Catholic party until well into the twentieth century. The lack of a strong clerical movement engaged in political activity until after the turn of the century, and the absence of a clergy pushing a rebarbative faith on the people, explains why Italian anticlericalism rarely reached the acute stages characteristic of French and Spanish anticlericalism. If anything, the Italian case goes a long way toward proving that some form of gradual rather than revolutionary secularization could have held clericalism at bay during the nineteenth century. Furthermore, the Italian case reveals that anticlericalism needed a heightened form of clericalism as a catalyst to unleash its destructive energy.

A similar situation developed in Russia. Gregory L. Freeze argues that Russian anticlericalism was "stunted" and failed to become a major element in political and social behavior.[89] As in Italy, the lack of an aggressive clericalism stunted anticlericalism by not creating the preconditions for anticlericalism to flourish in the first place. Freeze is quick to point out that the weakness of clericalism was not due to "state control" over the clergy in Russia, but rather due to internal weaknesses and a lack of cohesion within the Church itself.[90] The intense particularism of the Russian clergy meant that, in general, social and economic relationships between the clergy and their parishioners varied widely, and there was not the sense, as in Spain, that the clergy had become rich and corrupt at the expense of the rural poor. In addition, the Russian clergy was able to maintain its control over the Russian lower classes, which were seemingly impenetrable to Western-minded urban liberals and anticlericals. The result was that these classes were not nearly as antireligious as Southern Spanish peasants or urban Catalan workers. Thus, while there were a number of anticlerical and pragmatic liberals, their limited influence in political power coupled with the absence of strong clericalism meant the clergy would not have to contend with the systematic discrimination, abuse, and harassment that formed an integral part of antireligious campaigns seen in Spain and France.

*   *   *

Clearly, when Spanish Restoration anticlericalism is analyzed as part of a Europe-wide struggle between liberals and clericals that became acute during the final quarter of the nineteenth century, it ceases to stand out as peculiar. Liberal states, including Spain, stoked the flames of secularization so that they, rather than the Old Regime institutions of the throne and altar, could emerge hegemonic among their citizenry. What made Spain's case peculiar was the relative weakness of the liberal state when juxtaposed with the strength of both clericalism and anticlericalism. The particular context of Spanish clerical/anticlerical struggle provided a uniquely important role for the Restoration public sphere. Anticlerical campaigns during the first half of the Restoration did not come from the state, as in France and Germany, but still anticlericalism does not need formal political support from authorities in order for it to possess a revolutionary dynamism.

In Spain, the movement toward liberalism and the secularization of society triggered clericalism, which in turn sparked anticlericalism. The same occurred in France and later in Germany. The weakness of clerical movements in both Italy and Russia offers a reason for the relative weakness of anticlericalism in those nations: clericalism is necessary for anticlericalism to transform itself from theory to action and/or violence. Still, modern Spanish anticlericalism was more than a knee-jerk reaction to the strength of clericalism. Modern Spanish anticlericalism, especially in the vision of the republicans discussed in the following chapters, formed a fundamental part of the virtuous attempt to modernize—or even rescue from clericalism—the Spanish nation.

José Nakens Within the New Politics and Nationalist/Republican Culture

On the occasion of José Nakens's memorial in late 1926 the editors of *El Debate*, a conservative Catholic newspaper, denounced the numerous eulogies that praised the anticlerical editor of *El Motín*. Their obituary on November 16, 1926 read:

> Now that Nakens's body rests below the soil, the time has come to express ourselves with complete freedom […]. It must be said that those who ascribe extraordinary praise to the recently-deceased writer have undoubtedly forgotten what *El Motín* was…, and *El Motín* was Nakens. *El Motín* was not only a sectarian newspaper. Its anticlerical sectarianism could be curbed with some discrete adjustment through (legal) proceedings. *El Motín*, who would deny it, distinguished itself among the professionals of slander. It systematically slandered the Church, the clergy, the religious orders, including the Sisters of Charity […]. *El Motín* was a vulgarity—(it was) offensiveness embodied. Its style was gutless and indecent; fortunately, our Press—from the Communist to the ultra-right—has abandoned that style. The literature of *El Motín* was an affront to the history of journalism in Spain. And we also do not see it as a glorious page in the (History of the) Madrid Press to laud and give tribute to the disgraceful author of these perversions.[1]

This passage reflects much about the life of Nakens and the anticlerical industry of Restoration Madrid. To some journalists, he had grown from being a thorn in the side of the Spanish clergy to an admirable defender of republicanism and champion of the people. Arturo Mori wrote that "Nakens represented the Spanish liberal nation, a bit ingenious and a bit distracted, (who) innocently fell into the jaws of salivating venom that is reaction."[2] Yet to the staff at *El Debate* and other segments of the conservative population, Nakens's death was ushered in with a chant of "good riddance." This chapter will explore Nakens's role in the "new politics" of Restoration Spain and within Restoration republican culture. I argue that Nakens was a transitional figure between the old conspiratorial and militaristic tactics of Manuel Ruiz Zorrilla and a younger generation of populist politicians who began mobilizing the masses for the first time against the regime. Keeping in mind this book's theme that anticlericalism is one of the most important discourses to understand Restoration republicanism, I argue that Nakens's anticlerical *raison d'être* dovetailed with his critiques and messages to his republican coreligionists.

José Nakens Pérez, the best-known anticlerical ideologue of the Restoration, has never been the subject of a biographical monogram, although Manuel Pérez Ledesma has recently contributed a biographical sketch in a collection of essays on nineteenth-century Spanish agitators and conspirators largely neglected by historians.[3] Relying on Nakens's own autobiographical essays, published correspondence with various Restoration figures, and a 1922 interview with Alfonso Camín, Pérez Ledesma presents a portrait of a tireless and committed lifelong anticlerical republican convinced that Carlism lied in wait at every corner, and whose confrontational and uncouth anticlericalism grated on the tempered tone of moderate republicans. Pérez Ledesma's essay is particularly invaluable for its relation of *El Motín*'s ups and downs during its long life between 1881 and 1926. Pérez Ledesma's work excepted, historians' neglect of José Nakens is peculiar, for he stands out as a bridge in the history of nineteenth-century republicanism and helps explain the transition to the mass politics for that movement. Central to Nakens's bridge role was the cementing of anticlericalism to republican nationalism.

Nakens was more than a Restoration journalist, and his newspaper *El Motín* was significantly different from that of the mainstream republican press. In addition to informing his readers of republican developments, Nakens attacked republicans themselves, especially the movement's old guard. In addition to being a master purveyor of various symbols of an anticlerical nationalism, he was a rabble-rouser who mobilized support through the press. He brought notoriety to his causes by being prosecuted numerous times, especially after 1895 when the Supreme Court ruled that the clergy "formed a specific class of the State" and could appeal for redress of alleged "injuries" (*injurias*) to the courts.[4] Nakens believed he spoke for the anticlerical public, and he insisted their struggle was his. In other words, Nakens's persecution for his anticlerical transgressions became equated with the persecution of a fundamental republican commitment to overcome the Church and clergy's impediments to the nation's regeneration.

Although Nakens shied away from electoral politics, the younger populist republicans who shared in his frustration with old-guard leaders and embraced his rabid anticlericalism followed his lead, making everyday activities such as speeches, demonstrations, and courtroom battles into festivals celebrating the republican *ethos*. José Nakens's contributions are twofold. First, his attacks on the republican old guard created opportunities for the new republican populists to break with the past and create a dynamic form of republicanism. Second, his sustained anticlerical campaign offered the images, symbols, and rhetoric of an alternative political culture diametrically opposed to the conservative Catholic monarchy. Chapter three explores Nakens's anticlericalism in greater detail; this chapter focuses on Nakens himself and his role within republicanism.

It was precisely Nakens's political mobilization through a newspaper that republican populists and radicals built upon to mobilize their constituencies against the regime. Alvarez Junco has shown that Alejandro Lerroux's journalistic career, his Madrid-based networks, and the emotional link he forged among the Barcelona masses through his demagoguery were crucial to his rise during the Restoration.[5] Certainly Lerroux and Vicente Blasco Ibáñez, the subject of similar research by Ramiro Reig,[6] eclipsed Nakens and used their journalistic successes as well as their youth to become major players in Spanish republicanism. However, lost in the history of those energetic leaders is Nakens's similar—albeit on a smaller scale—role in the transformation of republican politics and political culture during the Restoration.

Nakens was a lightning rod of controversy, and, as a result, public opinion about him was divided: there may have been as many people from all parts of Madrid and Spain who hated Nakens for his lifetime of work as there were those who cherished his service. So while I make no claim that Nakens was the principal republican theorist of the nineteenth century or that his articulation of an anticlerical nationalism was representative of the majority of fragmented republicanism, I do maintain he is a particularly important figure who carried on the republican-military veteran spirit of men such as Ruiz Zorrilla and prefigured the mass politics of demagogues such as Lerroux and Blasco Ibáñez. The value of studying Nakens and his sustained attacks against the regime, the clergy, and the old republican guard lies in the fact that he injected the symbolic messages of an anticlerical-nationalist republicanism at a time when anticlericalism offered enormous potential to mobilize much of the regime's opposition.

José Nakens And *El Motín*

One of the best accounts of Restoration Madrid's literary circles is the autobiography of Rafael Cansinos-Asséns. The promising Cansinos-Asséns, who became one of Madrid's most respected literary critics, provides a unique glimpse into Nakens's circle of friends and his enterprise. In 1897 when Cansinos-Asséns, unemployed and seeking work, walked through the doors of *El Motín*—doors that he wrote were always open to all, like those at a Church—he met the "*comecuras*" (priest-eater) José Nakens for the first time. By then, Nakens was an "old republican" with a "solid head, spectacled eyes, an eagle-beaked nose, an already-grayed beard and large moustache, and that split lip, which someone said he himself bit one day when he did not have anyone else to bite."[7] Nakens liked Cansinos' work, happily published it in *El Motín*, and asked for more. Although Cansinos felt *El Motín* was beneath him, he had had little success publishing elsewhere. In time, Nakens grew on Cansinos, and he appreciated Nakens for giving him his start in Madrid's literary circles. Cansinos-Asséns' memoirs provide a view not only of Nakens and *El Motín* but also of transitional republicans who resented the old republican leadership for failing to precipitate a political revolution and who were simultaneously leery of younger republicans who flirted much too closely with the revolutionary working class.

The *El Motín* office was a "chapel in ruins of the cult to the Republic."[8] The old republican editor sat at his favorite chair under a lithograph of a large woman wearing a toga and Phrygian cap, a representation of the Republic. Nakens surrounded himself with his faithful disciples as they all sat around the offices cutting and pasting old articles, essays, or poems that were to be recycled in the next *El Motín*. Among them was José Ferrándiz, who despite being a defrocked priest was called *páter* or *pae*.[9] Ferrándiz was loyal to Nakens because the republican championed him after he blew the whistle on financial discrepancies at the Madrid Church of San José.[10] Ferrándiz saw the hand of the Jesuits in everything and used his columns in *El Motín* and the republican daily *El País* to demand the separation of Church and state. "Claudio Frollo" (pseud. Ernesto López Rodríguez) also joined Nakens each day at the office to malign the bourgeois presence in the republican leadership. He declared himself an anarchist who believed only a revolution could do away with the status quo.[11] "Claudio Frollo" had been Alejandro Lerroux's right-hand man in a number of journalistic endeavors, including *El País*, but the two split due to irreconcilable differences.[12] Pedro González Blanco, translator of Nietzsche's *Thus Spake Zarathustra* into Spanish, hoped for supermen who would shake up Spanish society. The young theosophist, Viriato Díaz Pérez, delighted in exposing the old men's ignorance about ancient civilizations, scientific discoveries, or nature by offering useless trivia or reports on his reading choices.[13]

Each day Nakens's "team" sat around their table, some smoking cigars, shouting loudly (Nakens was losing his hearing) about their disillusionment with republican leadership, the impotence of the republican movement, the corrupt Restoration regime, the influence of the Jesuits and Freemasons, and any number of diatribes against academicians and modernists. Though they resigned themselves to *El Motín*'s poor circulation numbers and the fact they might never see the realization of the Republic, they continued to prepare a journal that promulgated a social *zorrillista*-republican ideal. Nakens himself was involved in the enterprise of publishing *El Motín* for over forty-five years (1881–1926), and at the weekly, he and his friends built a small community that lived by a republican ideal of a community of kindred spirits, or coreligionists. They dedicated themselves to championing meritocracy in virtually all aspects of society, criticizing nondemocratic political behaviors and, most especially, attacking the Church and clergy for hindering the forward progress of the nation.

José Nakens Pérez was born in Seville on December 21, 1841. He wrote that he was born poor and that poverty followed him throughout his life.[14] Very little is known about Nakens's childhood or what incited his anticlerical fervor at an early age. In 1894 he admitted to his readers that he was baptized and may have been confirmed, but that he took it upon himself to fight the growth of clericalism once he discovered that religious dogma and mysticism were not only useless but also directly or indirectly injurious to the nation.[15]

At age seventeen, he volunteered to serve in the Spanish army and rose through the ranks to attain sergeant's bars while stationed in Cáceres. Though Nakens claims he was mystically drawn to Madrid in 1867, in reality he was transferred to the capital in late 1866. At that time Nakens began to dabble in writing anticlerical editorials for the satirical journal *Jeremías*. That short-lived journal, founded by Juan M. Villergas and illustrated by Francisco Ortega, was a model for Nakens's future venture, *El Motín*. *Jeremías* featured text that was peppered with satirical cartoons and various genres of anticlerical literature. As was customary, Nakens wrote under a pen name "El Soldado" (The Soldier). In addition, early examples of Nakens's call for revolutionary democracy and anticlericalism, as well as critiques of the rich, made up the entire section "De puertas afuera" ("Outside looking in") in the fledgling republican newspaper *República Ibérica*.

While in Madrid, Nakens maintained that the Revolution of 1868 came as a big surprise, but he enthusiastically took part in it seeing an opportunity to effect change in Spanish society. He remembered the Revolution fondly and criticized the haughtiness of revolutionary heroes:

> ...I was [one of those] heroes who, risking infinite danger, threw himself into the streets followed by fifty or sixty comrades when we first heard the result of the battle of Alcolea; [I did] no more or less than many others did whom I later saw congratulating themselves and swollen with pride.[16]

In describing himself, Nakens never apologized for being a difficult person to get along with, and he attributed the friction in his relationships with other people to their inability to be true to their beliefs:

> I am affable and kind at times, and at other times, I am ill-tempered and intensely proud depending on the internal organ that secretes my bile and depending on whom it is and what affair it is that I am dealing with at the time. I am insufferable at times. Other times, I am enchanting due to my tenderness. But I am a person who has always adhered to a [specific] line of conduct and will not deviate from that for anyone or anything. Is this what they call self-interest? Is this what they call stubbornness? The fact of the matter is that is how I am.
>
> I [possess] a rare blend of activism and negligence, the most venial of difficulties erects (don't be alarmed!) my mental faculties. Obstacles incite me, impediments do not defeat me, I revel in a fight, I do not surrender in the face of danger, and I can always count on myself for anything. If I have only one strength, it consists in that.
>
> I love well what I love, and I hate well what I hate; and I love, without exception, all victims of injustice and ignorance. And I hate, as well without exception, those who make them victims: the higher up they are the more I hate them.[17]

Rather than adhere to unwritten rules of Spanish status and caste, Nakens partook in the republican spirit of egalitarianism by feeling perfectly free to disrespect anyone or anything regardless of rank.

After obtaining his college degree in 1871, he joined the brilliant republican journalist Federico Moja y Bolívar (his closest friend) at his weekly newspaper called *El Resumen*,[18] which later became the satirical journal *Fierabrás*. These papers eventually folded and Nakens struggled to find a niche in the Madrid press. He was reinvigorated by the establishment of the First Republic in 1873 and claimed that he anonymously contributed more anticlerical and antiaristocracy rants to small publications such as *La Infantíl, Capellanes, Martín*, and *Variedades*. Still, Nakens admitted that as much as he fell in love with the potential of republicanism in the early 1870s, he actually did very little in terms of politicking and held very little influence in perpetuating that political system.

In fairness to Nakens and other republicans, the First Republic was a complete disaster. The leaders of the eleven-month republic contended with a civil war against absolutist Carlists in the North, a revolution in Cuba, cantonist movements throughout the peninsula, and, most damaging perhaps, the complete fragmentation of the republicans themselves.[19] Their infighting, coupled with the chaos that characterized the republican experiment and Cánovas' masterful construction of the *turno pacífico*, essentially discredited republicanism and made a Republic impossible for generations to come. Nakens vowed to make sure that such a situation was never repeated in the next Republic. One of the ways he went about this was by becoming both a literary and a political watchdog after the fall of the First Republic.

Republicanism was a protest against all arbitrary abuse of power, and an early episode in Nakens's literary career illustrated his commitment to fighting injustices. Nakens won great notoriety in 1875 when he publicly embarrassed Ramón de Campoamor for plagiarizing from the works of Victor Hugo. Campoamor was a widely respected poet and a member of the *Real Academia de la lengua española* (The Royal Spanish Language Academy). His literary prestige, his Catholicism, and support for the Spanish monarchs had won Campoamor a political post as civil governor of Castellón. Although Nakens was not the first man to accuse Campoamor of plagiarizing Hugo's *Les Miserables* and other works in the poem "El Tren Expreso" ("The Express Train"), Nakens persisted in his campaign to publicly humiliate the literary titan because Campoamor exploited the creativity of his enemies.[20] The opportunity to embarrass Campoamor afforded

Nakens the opportunity to make a name for himself, to besmirch a member of the political elite, and make a definitive stance on protecting intellectual property.

It should be noted that Nakens was not only angry at Campoamor for appropriating Hugo's words, thereby taking in vain the work of a hero to republicans,[21] but also for being a monarchist. To Nakens, Campoamor's abuses of literary property paralleled the abuses of the monarchy. Republicanism arose because of the exclusion of nonaristocratic Spaniards from formal political circles. The aristocracy's and monarchy's justification of their existence by divine mandate was rejected by republicans at a time when they were inebriated with the concepts of popular sovereignty and social justice. And it is in this context of speaking out against not only political exclusion but also artistic and cultural elitism that Nakens's antipathy to Campoamor should be understood.

From 1876 to 1879 Nakens moved up from being a contributor at *El Globo* to being one of the editors of the literary review. There Nakens may have repeatedly dealt with the paper's most recognized figure, Emilio Castelar, former president of the Republic, who Nakens grew to loath politically and for his refusal to divorce himself completely from Catholicism.

In a style he used throughout his career, Nakens took on the role reserved for priests when he criticized and condemned the clergy for not living up to Christ's teachings. He played up the idea that he was much more scrupulous, noble, and inherently better than the clergy; therefore, he claimed he had the right, the obligation even, to malign the clergy for its greed, lust, and other sins. Likewise, he attacked the old republican leadership out of a self-defined sense of being a better republican than they were. Though his pay was meager at *El Globo*, Nakens claims it was a lifesaver considering that he would have been completely ruined were it not for his post. Upon leaving the newspaper, he founded an unsuccessful drama-literature review called *El Buñelo* before forming part of the original *El Motín* team in 1881.

Perhaps because Nakens was identified with *El Motín*, many observers concluded that Nakens was the sole driving force behind the paper at its inception. Though this may be true of the *El Motín* of the 1890s, it was not the case in 1881. The success of satirical newspapers such as Barcelona's *La Carcajada* and the Madrid-based *Madrid Cómico* and *Jeremías* set the groundwork for Nakens's, Eduardo Sojo's (also known as "Demócrito"), and Juan Vallejo Larriaga's anticlerical-republican review.[22] During a particularly difficult time when *El Motín* was harassed by Cánovas's conservative administration between the beginning of 1884 and the end of 1885, Editor-in-Chief Vallejo found himself incarcerated and the paper cited for eighty-four violations of the print laws and fourteen separate fines of 500 pesetas.[23] In time, however, Nakens assumed exclusive control of the journal and as his contemporaries noted: "Nakens was *El* Motín."

The first *El Motín* appeared on April 10, 1881 and the paper's front page featured Demócrito's cartoon of a number of republican leaders, such as Castelar and Pi y Margall, admiring a bust of Lady Liberty. To ensure there was no doubt that *El Motín* was a satirical journal, Demócrito dressed the republican leaders as peasant women. When *El Motín* first appeared, the newspaper was only four pages long. The middle two pages of the newspaper featured a large carica-ture that was on occasion lavishly colored with expensive chromatic inks and satirized the political regime, the leaders of the republican movement, and/or the clergy. All the center caricatures were not nec-essarily satirical or critical; in late 1883 and early 1884, *El Motín* published a series of handsome lithographs of important republicans in Spain and France, such as Francisco Pi y Margall, Manuel Ruiz Zorrilla, Emilio Castelar, Estanislao Figueras, León Gambetta, and Victor Hugo. Occasionally, *El Motín* magnified the portraits into impressive 77cm x 55cm posters, mass-produced them, and then sold them for three *pesetas*. Anyone who was sympathetic to the messages that Nakens put forth could buy the posters or simply pull out the colorful cartoons and portraits and hang them in a study, workplace, or other visible spots. If Catholics and clericals decorated their homes with crosses, candles, or other religious icons, anticlericals and repub-licans were free to decorate with *El Motín*'s paraphernalia.

El Motín's back page usually included a series of brief news items taken from other newspapers throughout Spain and a brief comment on those items. Eventually, the back page also included a number of advertisements for various items put out by *El Motín*. These included novels (frequently anticlerical in theme and usually sympathetic to republicanism), poetry books, posters, postcards, and other para-phernalia usually of an anticlerical nature. The idea, it seemed, was to flood readers with suggestions for readings that would allow them to share in the anticlerical cosmos of the editors. In 1882 the paper devoted a special section on its back page, called "Manojo de Flores Místicas" (Bouquet of Mystic Flowers). This section, presumably edited by Nakens rather than Vallejo, became a popular fixture in the paper and concerned solely with tearing down religious fanaticism and the influence of the clergy. Nakens printed anecdotes of priests' misconduct from all over the world. The column depended on contributions from the readers and the veracity of the items were dubious, although Nakens maintained that each item was true and verifiable.[24] The "Manojo de Flores Místicas" column as well as the center caricature were usually the sections of El Motín that offended the sympathies of religious Spaniards and invited fines and confiscations.

The first page of the journal included the above-mentioned Demócrito cartoon over the title of the paper and a series of anonymous editorials probably written by Vallejo or Nakens. It was customary that the writers of editorials in Spanish newspapers remained anonymous to avoid fines and court proceedings. Often, El Motín's front-page editorial was a response to an article or an editorial in another newspaper, usually a republican rival such as La Justicia or La República. During the mid-1880s when the Carlist daily El Siglo Futuro grew to become the most dominant of the Catholic newspapers in Spain, El Motín reacted directly to El Siglo Futuro's critiques of Liberalism and its claim that Spanish Catholics suffered persecution. Jesús Timoteo Alvarez has pointed out that picking on El Siglo Futuro or its founder, Cándido Nocedal, became standard practice whenever an editor could not find anything else to editorialize about.[25]

David Ortiz, Jr. has recently pointed to the importance of this intra-press debate that led to the definitions of responsible journalism, made the press more sophisticated than sensationalist, made the competition for readership fairer, and shaped the role of the press in the public sphere.[26] In addition, the front-page editorializing of the Spanish press also made the significant contribution of exposing the injustices of the regime's oppressive press laws, which dictated, among other things, that authorities review contents as soon as it had been printed but before it was distributed and made every paper subject to confiscation and suspension.[27] El Motín was a newspaper that was locked into a debate or dialogue not only with the Carlist and the conservative press but also with other republican organs on a number of issues, including republican leadership and the role of the Church in a rapidly modernizing society.

Though Nakens's anticlericalism would make El Motín famous, the newspaper was not solely about anticlericalism. On the contrary, at its inception, El Motín was designed to troubleshoot the fragmentation within the republican movement and demand the reunification of all republicans; the newspaper's original mission statement promised to admonish those who had and would continue to create factions within the republican movement. The editors wrote:

> With great sadness we admit: there has never been a party that has destroyed itself with as much ire, or that has fragmented into so many minor groupings.
>
> And what for? Because of a disagreement in principles? No, because we are all fundamentally united. (We are divided) because of petty personal rivalries; because of the drive to always be the leader; because of the everyday development of individual cantonism.
>
> But let us be honest; it is not the party that is at fault; the ten or twelve men who aspire to dominate the party, who insult each other and squash each other with every step, thereby sacrificing the triumph of democracy to their own ambitions: they are at fault.
>
> We are here, in the little time that the conservatives allow us, to combat that conduct now that the union of all has been made impossible, and to proclaim that the truth cannot be sacrificed in favor of the interests of any one class.[28]

However, despite the altruistic goal of uniting all republicans, Nakens and his coeditors devoted more energy to tearing down republicans than reconciling their differences. Valeriano Bozal's analysis of the early *El Motín* centerfold caricatures reveals that the editors were primarily concerned with politics, especially republican politics, and shifted their focus toward anticlericalism only in the 1890s (see table 2.1). With the ratification of universal manhood suffrage in 1890 and the decline of old republican leaders, Nakens shifted his energies toward mobilizing the masses to vote republican. He evolved from dabbling in the old politics and began to believe that a military coup

Table 2.1   *El Motín* caricature subject matter in discrete periods*

	I	II	III	IV
Political Issues	34 (73.9%)	44 (74.5%)	49 (71%)	21 (50%)
Economic Issues	4 (8.6%)	5 (8.47%)	3 (4.3%)	4 (9.5%)
Anticlericalism	5 (10.8%)	6 (10.1%)	9 (13%)	11 (26.1%)
Customs/Habits	1 (2.1%)	0 (0%)	1 (1.4%)	4 (9.5%)
The Nation	2 (4.3%)	2 (3.3%)	3 (4.3%)	0 (0%)
Journalism	0 (0%)	2 (3.3%)	2 (2.8%)	0 (0%)
Municipal Government	0 (0%)	0 (0%)	0 (0%)	2 (4.7%)
International Events	0 (0%)	0 (0%)	2 (2.8%)	0 (0%)

*Period I: Apr 4, 1881–Dec 12, 1881; Period II: Jan 1, 1882–Dec 12, 1882; Period III: July 1, 1883–Dec 31, 1883; Period IV: Jan 7, 1893–Oct 12, 1893

Source: V. Bozal, *La ilustración gráfica del XIX en España* (Madrid: Lipal, 1979), 214

would be enough to reinstate the Republic to the charge of a man who would actively seek to create more republicans, especially anticlerical republicans. With the coming of age of King Alfonso XIII, Nakens again turned his efforts to rallying republicans politically under Salmerón, but his role in the 1906 regicide and subsequent imprisonment completely discredited him politically (see chapter five). After 1908, Nakens primarily returned to his anticlerical roots.

Though El Motín would continue to be published well into the Primo de Rivera regime, thus making it one of the longest-running republican journals in Spanish history,[29] observers constantly expected it to fold. The paper's longevity is perhaps tied to its ability to generate a constant sense of turmoil and confrontation with the existing regime and clergy. El Motín's editors believed and conveyed the idea that the Restoration regime could crumble under the force exerted by the mobilized populace. However, the same type of harsh criticism leveled at the regime and Church was also directed at republican leaders, which undermined their authority. Again, it was perfectly acceptable for the editors to suggest that Restoration society was caught in a vortex of constant turmoil. However, Nakens especially must be blamed for that turmoil for overtly offending sympathies under the guise of improving the society through republicanism.

The early years of El Motín were quite tumultuous as Nakens and his coreligionists dealt with repeated fines and confiscations in addition to being embroiled in the infighting within their movement. El Motín prided itself on being the people's newspaper and the editors used their newspaper to attack the old republicans for failing to take the zorrillista social message to heart. I now briefly explore how El Motín attacked the old republican leadership through new visual images and thereby helped the populists break with the past and create a new form of republicanism.

Nakens and his talented political cartoonists were especially hard on the remaining three former presidents of the Republic (the federalist Estanislao Figueras died in 1882). Emilio Castelar was maligned specifically for disingenuousness in moving away from Republicanism—albeit possibilist republicanism—to a type of Liberal Catholicism.[30] In the December 18, 1881 cartoon in El Motín, a republican Castelar (wearing a Phrygian hat) stands with his arms outstretched and about to be executed by a death squad composed of many Castelars while Lady Liberty [a representation of a woman in a Roman toga] weeps. The sketch was derived from Goya's famous 3 de Mayo, which depicts the French executions of Madrid rioters on the morning after their

1808 uprising. In the January 29, 1883 issue of *El Motín*, Demócrito depicted Castelar frightened by his own shadow of his republican past. By 1889, *El Motín* had given up hope in Castelar; in the January 13, 1889 cartoon, Castelar is depicted as a large mastiff protecting his master, President Sagasta, from Pi y Margall, Salmerón, and Ruiz Zorrilla. Nakens's attacks on Castelar were often gendered, more so than those he directed at Pi or Salmerón. For example, in the January 15, 1888 issue, Nakens questioned Castelar's manhood when he wrote that he failed to understand why republican men still embraced Castelar when *even* Spanish women know to reject men who lack virility.[31] As Castelar gravitated more toward the right, Nakens once called him a "male prostitute" for delivering a sermon at a cathedral.[32]

El Motín was equally if not more hostile toward Francisco Pi y Margall. Its antipathy toward Pi stemmed from the fact that the former president was a federalist. Federal republicanism, which advocated an American type of decentralization, was particularly strong in Catalonia and Spain's east coast, and although Pi never called for a separate Catalan state, *El Motín* grew frustrated with Pi's reluctance to have a pact with centralist republicans such as Ruiz Zorrilla and Nicolás Salmerón. In the same autobiographic sketch that Nakens offered his readers in 1889, he ended by writing that Pi y Margall's "effeminate haughtiness was matched by Nakens's virile indignation" toward federal republicanism.[33] Nearly the entire September 29, 1889 issue of *El Motín* was dedicated to attacking Pi, and Nakens denounced him as a representative of "hate, perturbation, and disunity."[34] Soon after, an editorial in *El Motín* questioned Pi's commitment to republicanism and accused him of seeking to prevent any revolution that would obliterate the *status quo*.[35] The anti-Pi campaign picked up steam in late 1889 when the pragmatic Pi's doubts about what would be gained if the republic could unseat the monarchy in that year were interpreted by Nakens as outright betrayal.[36] The cartoon in the January 19, 1890 issue of *El Motín* depicts Pi about to club Ruiz Zorrilla in the head as the exiled radical reaches out to pick up a tattered and downtrodden allegory of the Spanish everyman. Nakens only tempered his attacks on Pi y Margall in the beginning of 1890 after he visited Ruiz Zorrilla living in exile in Paris and was presumably asked by Zorilla to curb his attacks on other republicans.

However, no sooner had Nakens and *El Motín* relaxed their campaign against Pi than they turned their attention to Nicolás Salmerón. Neither a possibilist nor a federalist, Salmerón was considered a hypocrite not solely by *El Motín*. Committed to slowly evolving toward a Republic, Salmerón favored allying with political groups and working within the political system. At times, he made the wrong decisions, and his numerous about-faces irritated the republican faithful.[37] For radical republicans such as Nakens, Salmerón's conciliatory politics were not pragmatic but acts of self-interest and betrayal. On February 16, 1890, Nakens accused Salmerón of a number of acts of treason to the Republic, including inaction to save the Republic when it was in crisis, facilitating General Pavía's coup d'état that ended the First Republic, and publicly doubting if Spain was ready to be another Republic.[38] The *El Motín* stand on Salmerón was illustrated best in the center caricature of its February 30, 1890 issue. Titled "Lealtad Filosófica" (Philosophical Loyalty), Salmerón "allies" three times: with Pi in 1873, Castelar in 1874, and with Ruiz Zorrilla in 1890. As he enters into a pact with Pi he saws off one of the legs of the chair the federalist sits upon, as he enters into a pact with Castelar he is about to club Castelar in the groin, and as Salmerón hugs Ruiz Zorrilla, he prepares to plunge a dagger into the radical's back.[39]

Although he may have been hurting the republican movement by undermining the old-guard leadership, Nakens was engaged in a new form of politicking. While he realized that *zorrillista* militarism was not an option during the Restoration, he still held out hope for the social and national messages of his hero. Through the constant barrage of anticlerical, antimonarchical, and antirepublican leadership propaganda, Nakens was providing and manipulating the visual images of his specific idea of the Spanish nation and Republic. His attacks on the former republican presidents were tied to asserting a strong centralized republic, devoid of compromises and federalist or possibilist adjectives, which would move quickly toward repairing the nation's problems. It was his belief that the images in his newspapers could stir the masses emotionally on behalf of Ruiz Zorrilla, at least while Ruiz Zorrilla was alive.[40] But Nakens was also laying the groundwork for the successful radical republicans of the 1890s with the tone and intensity of his disrespect for the clergy, Church, monarchy, regime politicians, and even the republican old guard.

The New Politics: The Production, Manipulation, and the Meanings of Political Ritual and Symbolism

Part of the Europe-wide processes of liberalization and secularization initiated by the French Revolution was to move toward involving more people in the political process and replace allegiances to established institutions with an allegiance to the people and its general will. In most nineteenth-century republics or constitutional monarchies, worship of the people meant worship of the nation through nationalism. This shift of allegiance was accomplished through a new politics that sought to express the unity of the general will through the creation of a political style, which became a secularized religion.[41] Whether it is the invention of tradition or the imagining of community, the new politicians throughout Europe attempted to draw the people of their respective nations into active participation in the national mystification of the people *themselves* through rites, festivals, and the edification of monuments or other symbols that gave a concrete expression to the general will.[42] In theory, this Rousseau-inspired general will[43] was incapable of self-expression without democratic and selfless political leaders, and this function was what many nineteenth-century politicians and journalists considered to be their mandate.

Taking a page from the chaotic years of the French Revolution, which left no village unaffected by the spontaneous explosion of symbols and rituals employed in the making of a secular or civic religion of modern politics, nineteenth-century Spanish republicans recognized that political power always requires symbolic practices.[44] During the Revolution, symbols made political positions possible, and thus also made adherence, opposition, and indifference possible by politicizing the symbols of everyday life.[45] Revolutionary France taught Europeans that differences and distances—defined in the broadest sense: from political to geographic to economic—could be bridged through the manipulation of symbols and ritual. Festivals and the symbols involved in the revolutionary festivals were the way through which people could be linked with an idealized concept of the French nation.[46] The identification of the local with the larger national community could only happen through the use of symbols and rituals that identify one with the other and can recast peoples' notions of space and time.[47] Political rites are thus important because "political power relations are everywhere expressed and modified through symbolic means of communication."[48]

The manipulation of symbols is an important way by which those in positions of political power could reinforce their place, especially in the age of the new politics. For example, David Cannadine suggests that the lavishness of twentieth-century British royal rituals does not constitute a continuation with age-old traditions. Rather, these elaborate rituals and the splendor of the monarchy were the product of a nineteenth-century attempt to update the monarchy and regain its popularity among the English.[49] The orchestrators of royal rituals embellished the royal pomp for the masses at a time when mass mobilization posed new challenges to the state, and the empire needed a symbol of authority to unite the colonies. The splendiferous elaboration of royal ritual conveyed stability and a sense of belonging to a grand imagined community. In this way, ritual and symbolism are necessary for rulers and ruling regimes to maintain their grasp on political power.

However, the use of ritual and the manipulation of symbols can also create solidarity among those seeking power. Through an eclectic exploration of political rituals throughout the world and history, David Kertzer shows that ritual defined the individual's relationship to his or her society and created new realities, new perceptions of society, and new loyalties, rather than merely reflecting the existing hierarchies and understandings. All revolutionaries, for example, use rituals and symbols first to delegitimate and then to overthrow monarchs and other established authorities. Kertzer argues, "the political elites employ ritual to legitimate their authority, but rebels battle back with rites of de-legitimation. Ritual may be vital to reaction, but it is also the life blood of revolution."[50] Thus, political ritual and symbols constitute a common terrain through which both those in formal positions of political power and those seeking to ascend to formal political power battle to either control or mobilize the masses.

Rituals and symbols themselves are politically multivocal, which means that they facilitate a sense of communion with others without necessarily revealing the participants' inconsistencies or differences of opinion, class, race, or gender. Kertzer argues that "ritual builds solidarity without requiring the sharing of beliefs. Solidarity is produced by people acting together, not by people thinking together."[51] The ambiguity of rituals and symbols means that those that are created in one context can be appropriated to mean a completely different thing for different people. For example, in his analysis of the Festivals of German National Unity, Jonathan Sperber demonstrates how common symbols of national unity in 1848–1849 meant the affirmation of the rule of German princes in Cologne but meant a rejection of princely rule in the Rhineland.[52]

The modern collective representations of the nation in Europe were founded on not only the use of linguistic supports but also with visual symbols.[53] The "new politicians" used these signs and rituals as mediums of communication and collective action. Symbols created meanings that helped unite people and their projects and also consolidated collective identities. Even today, symbols possess a measure of "marginal utility" that consists in simplifying and abbreviating political messages.[54] Political discourse, supported by the linguistic or the visual, could be used by its broadcasters in order to foment specific emotions among the audience, and indeed much of the projected symbols of the Spanish republican movement was designed to strike an emotional chord with those frustrated with the regime.

Since Ferdinand VII abandoned the liberalization program at the start of the nineteenth century, many left-of-center liberals and nationalists were unable to see the monarchy as an ally in the nationalization of the Spaniards. While Spanish Liberalism was able to win out by 1840 and establish a constitutional monarchical tradition for the rest of the nineteenth century, those liberals who pushed for democratization found themselves on the margins of formal political power. These so-called democrats, who would become the forerunners of Spanish republicanism, were impoverished and unable to reshape the political institutions and culture of Spain.[55] Spanish democrats in the mid-nineteenth century were isolated mainly in urban political centers removed from the rural and Catholic populace, and for this reason they were particularly concerned with a new form of political mobilization that sought to generate enthusiasm for an alternative modern and secular vision of the nation. One of the hallmarks of the republican movement was anticlericalism. In order for the political discourse of anticlericalism to be efficacious, republicans employed any number of linguistic and visual tools that seduced their audience into believing that the liberation of the nation could come about through anticlericalism.

Nationalists (the imaginers) knew that the national identity (the imagined) is constructed and furnished through the manipulations of political ritual and symbols (nationalism, or the imagining of community). National identity is something that must be made and reworked on constantly in order for it to continue to mobilize the masses behind a nationalist project. As we shall see, radical republican populists were also keenly aware of the need to reshape the Spanish imagination.

Spanish Republican Culture

Just as in France, one of the new political forms in Spain was republicanism.[56] If republicanism had merely been a political movement in

Restoration Spain, then it follows that it would have died out along with the dynastic parties by 1923. The movement was paralyzed by infighting and was unable to secure much of an electoral following before 1890, especially among the Spanish working class.[57] Even the regime considered the republicans too weak to pose much of a threat, too divided to combine forces, and too demoralized by Manuel Ruiz Zorrilla's exile in France.[58] However, as the movement's most prolific historian José Alvarez Junco argues: republicanism was more than a political movement because it constituted "a total conception of the universe, an ensemble of beliefs about the destiny of humanity, both past and present."[59] Radical republicanism became a dynamic form of the new politics, blessed with visionaries who ushered the Spanish masses into political participation and mobilization for the first time. José Nakens himself represented a clear example of a republican who conflated his patriotism with the cause of the republic, and he employed his journalistic resources to promulgate that nationalist-republican vision.

Ironically, late nineteenth-century republicanism was devoid of a discernable political platform. This was no different from republicanism at the beginning of the Restoration when the republicans failed to coalesce into a unified movement. Instead, republicans formed into local intellectual circles primarily in the nation's periphery.[60] In fact, republicans such as Lerroux and Nakens disparaged formal political programs and concrete forms of government, as their intentions could not be synthesized into one program. Lerroux, for instance, felt that the necessities and collective problems republicans faced, as well as the political conduct necessary to confront them, were self-evident to honorable patriots, and he did not invite rigid proposals.[61] Thus, nineteenth-century republicans called for economic modernization, but none had any concrete plan for agrarian reform and resolving land tenure inequalities.

Geopolitically, republican goals revealed that many of these men lacked pragmatic sense as some were obsessed with reuniting Portugal and Spain, allying with autocratic Russia, or uniting the Latin world for France.[62] What really mattered were not concrete programs so much as the fundamental philosophy and the temperament, talent, and morality of those who were going to revolutionize Spain. Despite amorphous political platforms, perhaps because of them, the republicans were remarkably successful at securing a constituency late in the nineteenth century, but only in Spain's large cities. The radical republicans, especially men such as Lerroux, were not averse to political linkages with the revolutionary left if the timing and terms were to their benefit.[63]

Spanish republicanism constituted a culture complete with a political aspiration as important to its people as any heavenly aspiration found in the Bible. Alvarez Junco suggests that Spanish republicans saw their world and history in moralistic, if not religious, terms of Paradise Lost/Paradise Regained.[64] They extolled as paradisiacal the virtues of Medieval Spain when religious tolerance defined the nation. In their view, the Austrian Hapsburgs and their religious intolerance caused the once vibrant Spanish nation to rot. The social, political, cultural, and religious problems that afflicted the Restoration state were rooted in the decaying process begun with the Catholic reconquest. In the republican mind-set, redemption or paradise regained was only possible through a Republic that "incarnated all of the virtues that were the opposites of the vices inherent in the monarchical regime."[65]

Intellectually, Spanish republicans were children of the Enlightenment and most considered the American and French Revolutions as paradigms of sweeping political, social, and cultural changes Spain desperately needed. Republicans were enamored with the idea of a revolution, a sudden shift to polyarchy brought on by granting universal suffrage and the rights of political participation and opposition. Because the American and French Revolutions were followed by dramatic advances in both industry and agriculture, republicans believed that the economic regeneration of their nation could be initiated through a dramatic transformation of the status quo.[66] Nakens firmly believed in a rapid transition to a Republic, and much of his criticism of the republican ex-presidents was grounded in his perception that they were dragging their feet by not fomenting a revolution. A revolution was essential for the purification of the Spanish nation and for creating the necessary conditions for the most sacred of political forms: the Republic.

For republicans, the Republic was the embodiment of the general will and the true and just way to order everyday life. Republicanism arose as a reaction to the processes of exclusion from formal politics that were already in place in the governments that preceded the Restoration.[67] Republicanism held that social stability, economic modernization, and meritocracy proceeded from democracy, and republicans were adamant about allowing only the brightest and most moral visionaries to ascend to the leadership of the nation, regardless of their social status.[68] While in exile, Manuel Ruiz Zorrilla, the leader of the Progressive Democratic Party from which emerged the radical republicans, advised Spanish republicans on matters of recruitment with the following words:

> In choosing those who will form (our) popular base of support, you should try to select those who have honorable credentials; who identify with the cause of the Republic; who have, at least, a part of themselves already committed to (the cause) of universal suffrage...[69]

Ruiz Zorrilla grew obsessed with a sudden radical military-initiated change in the Spanish government during the Restoration, and his sense of urgency, aggression, and nationalism filtered into the writings of men such as Lerroux and José Nakens.[70]

Of course, to republicans the members of the oligarchy that controlled the government during the Restoration were not those who deserved those ranks. So long as the majority of the population lived in rural settings and the oligarchy's network of *caciques* could rig elections, the republicans were denied the opportunity to halt the process of Spain's decay. To the republicans, the once proud Spanish people were being crushed by the moribund manifestation of its Catholic and ultratraditionalist past. Luckily, this condition was temporary. The rhetorical appeals of republican journalists and leaders, especially those of the republican populists after 1895, promoted the image of the nation as a redeemer or a messiah, and they looked forward to the time when the nation rose up against the state in the name of Reason and Progress.[71]

What the Republic would look like when it came about, as well as the path to that Republic, was a matter of derision. Some sought a federal organization of the Republic, one that resembled the United States, while others insisted on a centralized Republic rooted in Madrid. Some embraced the radical and complete reorganization of society that Jacobins initiated during the French Revolution, while others were unwilling to make overtures to the public, given the threat of the revolutionary left. These divisions crippled Spain's first experiment with republicanism in 1873–1874, and it persisted throughout the Restoration. Indeed the deep divisions within republicanism cannot be ignored because they characterized the outward political appearance of the movement. However, the republican project was special because it was as much an effort to mold minds and bodies culturally as it was a political movement. Republicans were most concerned with building a modern secular Spain at a time when no one in formal political power was open to doing so. Building a modern secular Spain necessitated making republicans out of the Spaniards, and that task fell to republican journalists such as José Nakens.

Between *Zorrillismo* and Populism

Republicanism was also a project in transition during the Restoration, and Nakens is considered a bridge between the old and new republican politics. The republican movement that emerged from the First Republic had a number of structural difficulties preventing it from building a popular base of support. Republicanism was an elitist and highly personalistic political culture led by intellectuals such as Francisco Pi y Margall, who led the federalists, and Emilio Castelar, who led the possibilists. Although they concerned themselves to some degree with the social problems of the nation, most republicans were unwilling to allow their critique of political system to be taken up by the revolutionary left. The republican leadership felt more at home in the Senate, a classroom, or at an athenaeum than at a workers' club or neighborhood pub. Thus, Pi, Salmerón, Castelar, and even Ruiz Zorrilla toed a fine line between reforming the political system gradually and allowing their movement to get rapidly out of their hands and into the hands of a proletarian revolution.

Nakens was first and foremost a *zorrillista*: his political views as well as his patriotism were informed by his admiration of and belief in Manuel Ruiz Zorrilla. Nakens adopted the social messages of his hero and wrote to, and for, the Spanish people who would bring about a republic with the assistance of enlightened military leaders angry with the regime. However, Nakens's personal decision not to engage in formal politics, as engaged in by the populists Alejandro Lerroux and Vicente Blasco Ibáñez, set him apart from younger republican hotheads. Indeed, by the time *lerrouxismo* and *blasquismo* were changing the political landscape in Barcelona and Valencia, respectively, Nakens was well into his fifties and content with printing his small anticlerical newspaper. Still, the *zorrillista* tendencies of the populists, their break with mainstream republicanism, their emphasis on emotional appeals to the masses, and their intense anticlericalism were all hallmarks of José Nakens.

A part of this background is found in the career of Ruiz Zorrilla and his influence on Nakens. Although Ruiz Zorrilla's biographers went to great lengths to suggest otherwise, it is difficult to disassociate this hero of the 1868 Revolution from a well-documented obsession with political power.[72] Exiled to Paris by the regime, Ruiz Zorrilla was consumed with the thoughts of returning to power and orchestrated military coups to that end.[73] He underestimated the talents of the *turno pacífico*'s architect Cánovas del Castillo, who corralled political support from stable civilian sources. By putting his faith in an old-style military *pronunciamiento* to topple the oligarchy, Ruiz Zorrilla believed in a political solution that actually was not be viable between 1875 and 1923. Still, it could be argued that Cánovas erred by exiling Ruiz Zorrilla and placing him far from the Spanish "arm" of Justice.[74] For the next fifteen years, Ruiz Zorrilla was a thorn in the regime's side as he tried to disrupt the monarchy on a number of occasions, especially with the creation of his Republican Military Association (ARM) that repeatedly conspired to plot military coups in the 1880s.[75]

Ruiz Zorrilla's conspiratorial propensities were coupled with a tendency to flatter and cater to the military; a large and centralized military was one of his priorities. In 1876, he joined forces with Salmerón in rejecting the federalist republican goal of replacing the Spanish army with popular or regional militias. Instead he advocated a united republic with a strong military fed by the compulsory military service of all Spanish men.[76] By resisting a military draft, Cánovas missed the opportunity to create Spaniards loyal to Spain and to invent Spanish tradition. This has led Núñez Seizas to conclude that the military "never fulfilled in Spain the unifying role it played in other European states where military service was mandatory of all citizens."[77]

Still Ruiz Zorrilla's continued obsession with triggering a military revolution from above not only drove a wedge between him and peninsular republican leaders but also further anathematized the military in the regime's circles. Given that Cánovas and the oligarchy had struggled for so long to establish a sense of order in Spain after 1876, Ruiz Zorrilla actually hurt the republican cause by setting back any attempt by the constitutional monarchy to move toward a truly liberal-democratic polity.[78] Perhaps more important than Ruiz Zorrilla's popularity within the Spanish officer corps was that a wing of the republicans, mainly radical republicans led by Alejandro Lerroux, inherited his militant tendencies.

In addition to its militarism, Ruiz Zorrilla's republicanism included a number of socialist-inspired concessions. For example, the 1876 pact he signed with Salmerón complemented calls for a centralized republican government and military with calls for universal manhood suffrage, trials by juries, religious freedom, and a commitment to a proportionate distribution of wealth and a reduction of the work week. He also ambitiously envisioned a strong state that would build homes for the workers, back agrarian banks to assist the peasantry, and manage free and mandatory secular schools.[79] A common theme in the political writings and speeches of Ruiz Zorrilla was that of the abandoned or forgotten Spanish working class. He ripped the neo-Catholic political elements in his native Burgos because "they never concerned themselves with the apathy that corrodes the entrails of the part of our society that is less-educated."[80] Perhaps more out a fear of socialism than anything else, Ruiz Zorrilla advised republicans that if they wanted to prevent a frightful "social problem," it was necessary to concern themselves with pressing multiple social questions that the working classes must see as being solved by republicanism.[81] Certainly, Ruiz Zorrilla's language showed a concern for appealing to the masses, but in practice he never followed through on his rhetoric. The next generation of radical republicans did tap into his populism and vision.

As a man of the 1868 Revolution and as a military veteran himself, Nakens always admired Ruiz Zorrilla and never lost hope in a sudden military takeover by republicans. In January 1886, while Ruiz Zorrilla and republican elements within the military plotted a coup, Nakens lamented the belief that the Republic would come about by peaceful means.[82] In his famous *La dictadura republicana* (The Republican Dictatorship), Nakens outlined the parameters of a republican dictatorship in which Spaniards would temporarily sacrifice their rights to a military strongman who would teach them to be free.[83] In general, however, while never fully rejecting *zorrillista* militarism, Nakens picked up the social and nationalist messages of his hero and promulgated those messages when asserting that republicans must promise social gains to the masses to win them over. From the very beginning of *El Motín*, Nakens began not only to attack old-style, elitist, and federalist republican traditions but also tried to demonstrate to the masses how the Republic represented Paradise Regained.

Unlike Ruiz Zorrilla, Nakens lived in Spain and could attest that the political and social climate of the nation had changed significantly since 1868. Neither the state nor the military were the same because the regime was built in such a way that two stable parties shared political power and worked together to keep the military out of politics. This system replaced the old pattern of various weak political parties taking over whenever they could convince the military to launch a *pronunciamiento* on their behalf, or at least in the name of change. Rather than changing society through a top-down revolution, Nakens, Lerroux, Blasco, and others realized the value of a significantly more popular approach to politics than Ruiz Zorrilla ever had in mind.[84] Taking advantage of the Liberal Press Law of 1883 and universal male suffrage in 1890, Nakens and the other radicals sought to mobilize the masses politically in order to topple the regime, and in Nakens case he did so through his newspaper. Most importantly, he used anticlericalism as a link to the working classes. In the process, his role was to provide the populist republicans with both language and a set of images, especially anticlerical ones, which resonated with those opposed to the regime.

Spanish Republican Populism

In time, Nakens's style of anticlerical imagery, language, and political style was picked up by charismatic politicians who ran newspapers themselves and who became the political bosses in Spain's burgeoning urban neighborhoods. The study of populists and populism poses a number of challenges to historians and political scientists accustomed to investigating regimes, movements, or intellectual trends through their legal or ideological texts and institutions, such as the state bureaucracy. Populists were rarely inspired by doctrinal works and hardly offered any concrete plans for the reorganization of their societies, they rather issued vague manifestos through impassioned oratory. They rarely controlled purely representative and stable institutions, although they freely associated with powerful elites.[85] Despite these apparent deficiencies, they were successful at securing a broad and diverse base of support. Populists also exhibited a number of similar tendencies and characteristics, especially in Spain and in Latin America.

First of all, populism sprang up in the later part of the nineteenth century, usually in large modernizing urban settings. In Barcelona, for example, the rise of populism, specifically *lerrouxismo*, followed that city's expansion and development after the fall of its medieval walls in 1857.[86] Migration from the Catalan countryside into the city made it necessary for planners to design the *Eixample*, where numerous residential communities temporarily absorbed the city's population overflow. These new communities, composed of an amalgam of lower-middle-class and working-class elements, were often crucial to supplement the success *lerrouxismo* enjoyed in the working-class suburbs of the city.[87] Similarly, Valencia's demographic and commercial expansion in the late nineteenth century provided the backdrop for the birth of mass politics under the charismatic republican Vicente Blasco Ibáñez.[88] By the turn of the twentieth century, radical republicanism had generated a broad base of political support in these provincial capitals precisely because they were provincial capitals and *entrepôts* for the displaced rural population.

Populists flourished in the rapidly modernizing urban setting, and after striking nostalgic, premodern chords with their following, they wholly embraced modernization. The urban setting allowed populists to take advantage of the fact that modernization, migration, and urbanization created a new constituency that experienced profound *anomie*. Such people were predisposed to resent the state for prompting their dislocation and for preventing them from formal political participation. The novelty of the rapidly modernizing urban environment necessitated that populists appeal to the masses in new ways so as to differentiate themselves from the governing oligarchy. In the case of Barcelona, Mosher suggests that *lerrouxismo*

> was a political expression of the modernization of Spanish life. It mobilized elements of the proletariat and the petite bourgeoisie, formerly unrepresented within the Spanish political system, into a potent political movement that blended protest against the social injustices accompanying economic change with a vision of a modernized future in which Spain would realize great economic and social progress under a strong, efficient republican government.[89]

The same is true of Valencian *blasquismo*, and radical republicanism in Madrid. Like the revolutionary left movements, radical republicanism was one of a handful of Restoration political movements able to overcome the general apathy of the Spanish people toward politics and attract mass support for their amorphous ideas in the principal cities. Populists in Spain emerged from a professional class that included journalists, professors, lawyers, and middle-class politicians who saw themselves as a modern enlightened alternative to the traditional oligarchy.[90]

Lerroux and Blasco Ibáñez, the most renown of a number of republican populists, parlayed successful journalistic careers into local and national political careers. Their anticlericalism, especially, but also the sharp criticism of the monarchy and the old republican leadership that characterized their newspapers, mirrored the contents present in Nakens's *El Motín* since 1881. The press allowed the populist republicans to generate a following that crossed class barriers between them and their ideology. In a modern and industrialized world the importance of written culture and the media of communication are multiplied, and mobilization is impossible without a comprehensible message. Because the one and only general will cannot express itself without representatives who know they are not above popular sovereignty, it follows that populists emerge as "Jacobin-Bonapartist" embodiments of the nation's will to topple the oligarchy.[91] Many populists took advantage of their privileged positions as newspaper editors to become mouthpieces of radical republicanism and to justify their leadership over the masses.[92]

Perhaps the most important element of nineteenth- and twentieth-century populism was its attempt to mobilize the masses. Observers of Hispanic populists note similarities in their rhetorical appeals to the people. Populists often played up their charismatic personalities by portraying themselves as servants or saviors who have taken up the burden of liberating the people from the oligarchy.[93] Simultaneously then, the populist was both a leader and a follower. The fact that populists often belonged to the petty bourgeoisie class meant they could draw support from that class by addressing important issues such as state intervention in commerce or the obstacles foiling the bourgeois' path to an administrative post. However, their appeal to the marginalized working class also won them support from below. Their interclass appeal often involved a rhetoric of nationalism as they called on the nation (*pueblo* or *nación*), the repository of morality and social justice, to mobilize against the oligarchy.[94] Alvarez Junco, for instance, showed that when populists such as Lerroux were not presenting themselves as possible Messiahs, they often lauded the people as redeemers.[95]

Populist discourse in Spain echoed the contents of Nakens's work since the early 1880s and hammered home the message that the Spanish people were at war with their corrupt and decadent state. In Spain, this appeal to the masses was a new form of politics, which bore no resemblance to the politics of the oligarchic dynastic parties. Rather than maintaining a depoliticized populace controlled through local political bosses who "fixed" elections, radical republicans in Spain's major cities actively sought to mobilize the masses. As part of an infrastructure of meeting houses, neighborhood cultural and political associations, and face-to-face grassroots politics, Spanish populists tried to mobilize the masses through their seductive political rhetoric as well as through the manipulation and production of symbols.

Although there is the temptation to link *zorrillismo* with Spanish republican populism (*lerrouxismo* and *blasquismo*) in a seamless development model, I maintain that Nakens and his brand of anticlericalism and politicking represented an intermediate step between these political phenomena. Nakens had been mass-producing anticlerical cartoons, books, poems, posters, and other paraphernalia in the hopes of making the masses feel aggrieved by the Church and clergy long before Lerroux sat at Ruiz Zorrilla's death bed in 1895 and decided that anticlericalism offered a way of mobilizing the people. And although anticlericalism and appeals to the working class were nothing new to republicans, the intensity and volume of Nakens's campaigns offered the Spanish populists the tone and symbols of an effective new politics.

Reconciling Republicans and Republicanisms

Nakens made one final attempt to reconcile the old republican leadership with the new mass constituency he was trying to build. In the spring of 1902, the Spanish republican movement sank to one of its lowest points. The unthinkable had occurred: the Republic did not come about before Crown Prince Alfonso XIII came of age. The great republican ex-presidents had begun to pass away. And while Lerroux and Blasco Ibáñez were tremendously successful in republicanizing Barcelona and Valencia, respectively, their local victories were not significant at the national level.[96] Rather than participating in the annual republican banquets that commemorated the anniversary of the Declaration of the First Republic, Nakens interjected his annual condemnations of these feasts that he said resulted in nothing but vain nostalgia.[97]

So on April 12, 1902, the sixty-year-old Nakens reprinted an important article in *El Motín*, in which he criticized those who deluded themselves into thinking that a republic could be possible given the disparity of the republicans themselves.[98] Although he blasted such doubts regarding the Republic in the past, Nakens foresaw stagnation without some sort of significant behavior modification, deep reflection about the future of the party and its relationship with the masses, and a reunification of the factions. He wrote:

> Let us appear dignified now at the moment when we are impotent. (…) Let us return to being a serious party, one that is not demoralized by setbacks but rather learns from experience. Let us reject the

many practices that have resulted insufficient or ineffective for attaining what we seek. Until now we have trudged along without a plan, a [group] devoid of prudence, energy, and resources; let us hoard these in order to accumulate them in large quantities, and apply them dutifully at the precise moment. [Let there be] fewer speeches that pass away and more actions that make an impact. When we speak to each other, let us do so to face to face. In a word: more seriousness.[99]

That these words came from the republican who had been the thorn in the republican leadership's side was significant and effective to some degree. The *zorrillista* old man who saw the value of appealing to the masses had suddenly switched his efforts toward delivering the republican masses to Salmerón.

One of Nakens's visions for the movement was the creation of a National Assembly of the Republican Union. In the beginning of 1903, the political weight of the leading republican daily *El País* was essential in bringing about Nakens's Republican Union, which invited to Madrid republicans from all over Spain in order to simplify the republican message under the leadership of Salmerón. On February 14, 1903, Nakens, Fernando Lozano, who was the long time editor of *Las Dominicales del Libre Pensamiento*, and Miguel Morayta, the Grand Master of Spanish Freemasonry, led an assembly of the republican leadership in order to begin planning a plenary meeting of all republicans in Madrid on March 25, 1903.[100] For his efforts, Nakens received word from Vicente Blasco Ibáñez that he had selected both Nakens and Salmerón to represent Valencian republicans in the *Cortes* (the national parliament). While the self-satisfied Nakens publicly acknowledged that he deserved such an honor, he turned down the seat arguing that he would be more effective and helpful behind the scenes as an independent journalist than as a public official.[101] Rather than believing that change could only be brought about from the top down, Nakens saw his niche not so much in leading the republican movement but rather in *making* republicans for the republicanism. This dedication to making republicans is Nakens's unique part as a transitional figure between *zorrillista* militarism and republican populism.

Although more republicans flocked to the Teatro Lírico in Madrid on March 25, 1903 than Nakens and company could have ever imagined, the National Republican Assembly went down in history as a mere pep rally, or as the conservative newspaper *La Epoca* wrote: "A lot of noise for nothing."[102] The Assembly agreed that Salmerón was the sole leader of the movement and that all republicans were to support him in the movement's quest for a democracy devoid of demagoguery and class struggle. True to form, however, nobody detailed how the Republic would come about. Nakens suggested that the republicans conquer the state "by any means" because the monarchy impeded popular sovereignty, and Salmerón echoed the Lockean justification of force as a duty to restore popular sovereignty when those in political power engage in repeated abuses against the people. But again, these were the demagogic rants characteristic of leaders faced with the uphill task of destabilizing the well-entrenched regime.[103]

The enthusiasm and optimism of that large republican pep rally was short-lived. Although many republican candidates, especially at the local municipal level, were successful in the April 1903 elections, Salmerón proved unwilling to couple electoral successes with the intervention of the remaining republican elements in the military to bring about the Republic.[104] Younger republicans such as Lerroux, who had never fully abandoned *zorrillista* conspiratorial tactics, began searching for ways to destabilize the monarchy and bring about the revolution, while not severing ties with the Republican Union. As Alvarez Junco has demonstrated, the charismatic Lerroux found a kindred soul in the anarchist pedagogue Francisco Ferrer, who was also quite close to Ruiz Zorrilla, and together they conspired to precipitate a revolution (see chapter five).[105]

Two years after the Assembly, Nakens reverted to criticizing Salmerón for the stagnation of the movement. In an open letter to Salmerón, Nakens reminded the ex-president that he could count on Nakens's support so long as the party progressed toward the realization of the Republic.[106] However, Nakens accused Salmerón of purposely allowing the enthusiasm generated by the Union to fizzle, of prolonging the life of the moribund oligarchical regime by not lending his support to provincial republican candidates, and of doubting the utility of the Union that afforded him leadership. Although Nakens maintained that he was breaking the silence by uttering the grievances of the entire republican movement, he was sharply criticized for constantly destroying whatever he built up. He was also defended for speaking the truth. The Sevilla-based *El Baluarte* wrote that Nakens's only mistake is his foolhardy insistence on using "old and corroded materials" (read Salmerón) to build on the aspirations of the movement.[107] As the Republican Union deteriorated due to factionalism, Salmerón abandoned ship the summer prior to the September 1905 elections. At the national level, republicanism gradually faded away between 1905 and 1931, despite two spikes in popularity in 1906 and 1909.[108]

In his impatience and disgust with formal political programs, Nakens had finished trying to deliver constituents to the old republican leadership. Because he himself never lost hope in a *zorrillista* solution to Spain's political and social problems, Nakens began to ruminate about a "Republican Dictatorship" replete with an iron surgeon who would force Spaniards to be free.[109] It should be noted that he did not advocate a totalitarian twentieth-century dictatorship so much as a strange amalgamation of the authoritarianism of Caesar Augustus during the Ancient Roman Republic and Rousseau's notions of defending the general will. Making republicans was not enough if there were no dynamic and capable leaders, which Salmerón was obviously not. Alejandro Lerroux, on the other hand, was talented, innovative, and popular, and Nakens embraced him as a viable leader of the movement.[110] In the process, without him wanting it, Nakens's frustrations with Salmerón and the Republican Union attracted elements of the radical left and revolutionary left to him. Ironically, the more illiberal and undemocratic Nakens became, the more successful he was at gaining a loyal following among those who would never consider republicanism under Salmerón an option.

It is in this political context that we can better understand Nakens's clashes with the old republican leadership as well as his relationships with *zorrillismo* and republican populism. Nakens realized that a military coup would not suddenly deliver the Republic, and he was willing to give Salmerón a try while building an anticlerical-republican culture. His conflicts with Salmerón as well as Gumersindo de Azcárate were motivated by his perception that the energy contained within the 1903 Republican Union was enough to deal the death blow to the regime. Republicans, in his opinion, had squandered the chance to regenerate the nation because they were led by an evolutionist and elitist Salmerón who refused to acknowledge and harness the revolutionary pulse of the people.

José Nakens and Republican Anticlericalism: Making an Anticlerical-Nationalist Tradition

Until the demise of the Republican Assembly, José Nakens' anticlericalism intersected with republicanism in its abortive revolutionary form. As old-style, conspiratorial republicanism lost its political potential, anticlericalism took on increased importance in the development of radical republican nationalism. This centrality of anticlericalism to republican nationalism, especially in the life and work of Nakens and other radical anticlericals, is the focus of this chapter. Alvarez Junco has elsewhere shown how nineteenth-century republicans linked their nationalism with anticlerical ranting and also analyzed the major themes of Spanish republicans, but it was the neglected Nakens who best conflated anticlericalism and nationalism.[1] He completely invested in developing an industry full of anticlerical images and symbols to instill the message that Spain was a backward nation because of Catholicism. In addition, he served as a populist model for younger republicans such as Lerroux and Blasco Ibáñez. Thus, I argue that Nakens played a unique part in constructing a republican anticlerical nationalism during the Restoration, a process that would hold important consequences for republican culture in subsequent decades. This chapter is intended to be a discursive analysis of Nakens's anticlerical-nationalism synthesis.

Perhaps no other group in Restoration Spain was as concerned with the state of the nation and its regeneration as the republicans. The possible exception was the current of social-Catholicism or national-Catholicism that emerged in civil society rather than high political circles as a response to the *anomie* created by modernization. However, unlike social-Catholicism, burdened with a lack of consensus over how to act publicly or politically,[2] virtually all republicans were committed to curbing clerical presence in political and social life. In the radical republican imagination, the clergy represented an obstacle to solving Spain's national problem because the clergy was committed to stopping the forces of progress.[3] Curtailing clerical influence went hand in hand with the liberal-democratic vision of the republicans, and anticlericalism was essential for Spain to become a modern nation. The nationalistic discourse of Spanish republicans has been well-documented,[4] but the centrality of anticlericalism to republican nationalism, I believe, less so.

This chapter sketches out the multivalent forms of anticlerical discourse and symbols developed by Nakens and other radical republicans in their attempt to discredit the Catholic Church, its clergy, and the state on behalf of the exploited nation (*pueblo*). Nakens' project involved the mass-production of anticlerical messages in a deliberate attempt to turn people against the Church and clergy. The messages themselves constituted an evaluation privileging a secular and anticlerical-republican vision of Spain over any conservative, oligarchic, or clerical vision.

Nakens updated a long anticlerical tradition and blended it with a modern Europe-wide obsession with nationalism. With his anticlerical campaign between 1881 and 1926, he developed a range of symbols with which many Spaniards identified. His newspaper, plays, collections of essays, cartoons, posters, postcards, almanacs, and more were part of a desire to make tangible his vision for the nation and provide emotional flashpoints evoking more complex ideas. Anticlericalism was particularly useful for Nakens because it offered a unifying cross-class appeal; all who felt aggrieved by the opulence of the Church and clergy could join Nakens in imagining an alternate community. At the root of the anticlerical imagery and discourse was a fundamental belief that the forward progress of the Spanish nation could only come through a significant alteration of the relationship between the clergy and the state. In a recent historiographical essay on anticlericalism, Pérez Ledesma intersperses his own commentary with Nakens's own words:

> [W]hat he [Nakens] was really interested in was "undermining the authority of the clergy," for a fundamentally political reason, "because I saw and see in the clergy (and ever more so in the friars) the logical incarnation of absolutism," that is to say because priests continued to

be the firmest supporters of Carlism and therefore the greatest threat to the freedom of Spaniards.[5]

Like the populist republicans who followed his lead, Nakens focused on republican morality and honor rather than class status. In this way, he appealed to everyone opposed to the Restoration status quo. This republican quality of *rassemblement*—appealing to and uniting all who sought to end the oligarchy's reign—was very powerful, but necessitated the skillful manipulation of discourse in order to maintain a following among people from different classes and occupations. One of the most powerful unifying forces for the Restoration regime's opponents was anticlericalism, and Nakens was a master at purveying and mass-producing its symbols.

Again, rather than interpreting anticlericalism as an anachronistic or premodern phenomenon, the mass-production of anticlerical symbols and discourse in this era of Europe-wide nation-building made anticlericalism integral for republican nationalism. At a time when the Restoration regime refused or was unable to address Spain's national identity crisis, radical republicans such as Nakens tried to establish an anticlerical-national identity through the proliferation of anticlerical imagery, symbols, and even the ritualized reading of anticlerical texts. To Nakens, indeed to all republicans, Spain was deteriorating, and the once-proud nation was losing its honor. By contributing to the Restoration anticlerical "industry," Nakens engaged in the "new politics" by mobilizing the masses to revolutionary action that would restore Spain's honor. More prominent figures such as Lerroux and Blasco Ibáñez later echoed and magnified the intensity of Nakens's anticlerical campaign.

José Nakens and Anticlerical Nationalism

Clearly Nakens and *El Motín* were not exclusively about anticlericalism. Nevertheless, Nakens's major legacy was his anticlericalism between 1881 and 1926. Newspaper historians María Cruz Seoane and María Saiz write that *El Motín* was "the anticlerical journal *par excellence* and more concretely the principal representative of the most extreme and uncouth popular anticlericalism."[6] Today, leading historians of the period often look through the pages of *El Motín* or the books and pamphlets produced by Nakens for provocative passages on clerical misconduct or the relationship between clericalism and national degeneration. This anticlerical paraphernalia was nationalist at its core, with its message that the clergy was detrimental to the Spanish nation and, thus, essential to the ideological triad of radicals: republicanism, nationalism, and anticlericalism.

It is difficult to estimate the size of Nakens' audience. In addition to weekly written selections and the books put out by *El Motín*, Nakens's anticlerical pamphlets and essays were often reprinted in the mainstream republican press and in the revolutionary working-class press. Pérez Ledesma estimates that Nakens's words reached 10 percent of the Madrid reading public.[7] He was also a frequent contributor to the literary magazine *Vida Nueva*, which featured political-social and anticlerical articles from Spain's greatest writers.[8] It is equally difficult to assess the effectiveness of his anticlerical propaganda. His caustic and offensive anticlericalism did not lead to the type of sweeping anticlerical violence that he encouraged readers adopt into their repertoire of protest. One wonders who exactly were his audience; *El Motín* was a mixture of the high anticlericalism of Catholic and Protestant critics of the clergy and the low insulting anticlericalism reminiscent of early modern peasants. In practice, Nakens' special role in the new politics bridged intellectual rebels and disgruntled workers through the power of anticlericalism, blurring the traditional distinctions between the "high" cultured anticlericalism and the "low" popular anticlericalism of the masses. Because of this, Nakens is an important "missing link" between cultured anticlericalism and the spontaneous, violent, urban anticlericalism, like the one that exploded in 1909, for example.

Although many scholars are aware of Nakens and his anticlerical campaign, no one has explored the nationalist dimensions within Nakens' anticlerical discourse. By no means, however, do I claim that Nakens' anticlericalism, which was driven by a decided atheism, spoke for all Restoration republicans. Gumersindo de Azcárate, an extremely pious man who assumed leadership of the moderate republican movement alongside Salmerón after 1903, insisted on respecting all religions and forms of religiosity so long as this did not interfere with the functions of the state.[9] Nonetheless, republicans—even those critical of Nakens, *El Motín*, and other anticlerical endeavors—were united in their commitment to some degree of anticlericalism, or at least secularization.[10] The power of Nakens's and radical republicans' visceral and populist anticlericalism meant that anticlericalism's political terrain went beyond discussions among the republican leadership and Parliamentary debates to include quotidian spaces such as alleys, streets, and newsstands.[11]

Nakens was a man who dealt in symbols, and much of the mythical lore that surrounded him was created by his opponents. For example, Nakens embraced the "priest-eater" (*comecuras*) image in the clerical press when he published an 1883 cartoon that represented two large, filthy, bearded men with rat tails who gobbled up clergymen. In the illustration, one figure stabs at a dead priest's chest in order to hold the body steady while he slices at the priest's leg. The other man is about to eat the head of a priest whom he scooped out of a bloody broth.[12] Nakens was not a priest-eating monster, but he heartily embraced this image and enjoyed shocking the readers almost as much as he enjoyed attacking the clergy. This image was also embraced by those seeking to limit the scope of the clergy's influence in Spanish society at the same time that it was used by Catholics and conservatives to generate public condemnation of Nakens and anticlericalism.

Republicans were particularly excited by the significant gains made by the Liberal revolutionary successes of the 1830s that subsumed the clergy under state control, and they genuinely felt that the replacement of the religious with the secular was humanity's greatest accomplishment. However, because the nineteenth-century state did not sever its ties with the Church and allowed the Church and clergy to make a financial and cultural comeback during the Restoration, republicans believed the regime held back the forward progress of the nation. Nakens himself was critical of the state's financial obligations to the clergy as well as the fact that the clergy charged fees for sacramental services, and he once suggested the Church finance itself by charging for each Eucharistic host it doled out.[13] None of Church's perks was significant enough to return the Church's income back to its ancien régime levels, but the perception that the Church was stronger than ever before was common among republican populists.[14] The state was able to curb the clergy's financial powers (such as money lending and investment) as well as end the clergy's role in censoring newspaper content, but it remained too weak or unwilling to disrupt the Church's education monopoly to assert itself over the international religious orders (especially the Jesuits). Perennial debt as well as structural difficulties in raising money over the nineteenth century meant that state funding for elementary education was below 2 percent of public expenditure in 1900.[15] To republicans, Spaniards were enslaved in a cultural morass created by centuries of Catholic dominance, and the clergy was free to strip the Spanish nation of honor. The state could no longer defend national honor because its weakness and identification with Catholicism were part of the national problem. Thus, it was up to republicans to fight for Spain's honor.

Since the republicans were more than a political movement, they were particularly concerned with the cultural hegemony of the Church and clergy. They believed that the Church was indoctrinating Spain's youth to perpetuate the fanaticism and traditions republicans believed choked the nation. An illustration from a 1910 issue of *El Motín*, for example, depicts a rotund priest happily pouring crucifixes, rosaries, and demons into funnels protruding from the heads of small children preparing religious compositions. The caricature's caption reads: "How clericals prepare children's brains for civilization."[16] The role of the clergy and Church was thus a lightning rod in the debates prevalent in the press and in popular literature between progressives and traditionalists, between Catholics and republicans, between those who were nostalgic and those who embraced modernity.

Nakens's anticlericalism could not have existed in a vacuum. Anticlericalism in Spain was a by-product not only of the fundamental differences between progressives and traditionalists over the essence of Spain but also the perceived advances of clericalism after its defeat in the 1840s. According to Timothy Mitchell, the first boom in anticlerical publishing came in the mid-1840s, coinciding with rapid growth in the publishing industry and an increase in various forms of religious literature produced by prominent clergymen.[17] This spurt was closely associated with the translation into Spanish of popular French novels whose anticlericalism was patent. Spanish Liberalism's shaky and incomplete triumph led to a number of grassroot clerical movements that used the pulpit to criticize the government and the press. Other examples included the Nocedal Law, which exposed anticlerical journalists to court proceedings if they offended Catholic dogma, the resurgence of Carlism in the 1870s, and Queen Isabella II's confessor's mass-production of religious and clerical pamphlets and other paraphernalia.

These movements were as much political as they were cultural. For example, the mass-production and distribution of scapulars (small cloth squares joined by shoulder tapes and bearing a religious image) to parishioners during the 1880s took on highly charged meanings. For Catholics these scapulars were symbols of the wearers' commendation to God. However, because these scapulars were quite popular with Carlist troops (who were told they warded off enemy bullets), republicans suggested that scapulars were symbols of defiance toward liberal and modern Spain.[18] By the middle of the nineteenth century then, religion and irreligion, clericalism and anticlericalism, had become not only political activities but also exercises in asserting national identity.

Images of a Tired and Embattled Spain

Perhaps one of the best starting points for an analysis of Nakens's anticlerical propaganda is how he and other republicans represented the Spanish nation. In the case of *El Motín*, Spain, Castile, the Republic, and Lady Liberty were all portrayed as women. *España* or *La República* was no different from other European embodiments of the nation, such as France's *Marianne*, Germany's *Germania*, or England's *Britania*.[19] In the images, these female allegories wore long white togas or dresses and brightly colored shawls, usually red and gold. The allegory of the Republic usually wore a Phrygian cap, while that of Spain wore a granite crown alluding to the castles of Castile. In Spain, as in France and Germany, the woman as a national symbol represented the "continuity and immutability of the nation, the embodiment of its respectability."[20] She represented everything that men fought to protect and she was honor personified. Sarah White has shown that these allegories of the nation, the Republic, and Liberty were particularly prevalent during the Revolutionary Sexenium when Spain switched from a monarchy to a republic and back to a monarchy.[21] During those difficult political transitions, the once-proud allegories were constantly manipulated to convey the national visions of the men behind political changes. Thus, the nurturing image of the Republic when she was installed in 1873 was rapidly transformed into a promiscuous whore after Pavía's *pronunciamiento* in 1874. White demonstrates how the allegorization of the nation and the republic was inextricably tied to long-established Spanish codes of masculinity and honor: the promiscuous Republic was dishonorable and a threat to the nation, and it was up to honorable men to put her and the nation in their place.

The same tradition of female allegories and its link to masculinity was present in *El Motín*'s imagery. However, unlike the regal and positive representations of Marianne and Germania, *España* and *La República* in the pages of *El Motín* were often tired, in jeopardy, and besieged. Both wanted to stand tall and proud, but the conditions of Restoration society precluded that. *España* and *La República* were under attack from the regime's politicians, from the clergy, and from international threats such as socialism, or the Papacy. At times, it seemed that some combination of these forces worked together to strip her of honor. For example, when Germany tried to claim the unoccupied Caroline Islands from Spain, the centerfold cartoon to the October 14, 1883 *El Motín* depicted Spain, wearing the granite castle crown and carrying a Spanish flag, being pushed down (by governing elites) to prostrate herself in front of an indignant Chancellor Bismarck.[22]

Much of the language and imagery of Nakens's enterprise dealt with how the Spanish nation was smothered, tethered, or otherwise restricted by the clergy. The centerfold cartoon to the May 19, 1898 issue of *El Motín* depicted a fat friar sitting on *España*. Not only the monk's girth but also the large sacks of coins he holds crushes Spain.[23] The idea behind much of the imagery dealing with *España* was to make Spaniards angry at her dishonor as represented by that embattled and exhausted woman and impel them to fight for her. *España*'s honor could only be restored by replacing those premodern institutions—the monarchy, the elites, the Church and clergy—that besmirched her each day.

The themes of an exhausted Spain who needs the help of virile republican men to fight her battles and of a Spain under constant attack from the clergy were repeated every week in some form or another in the pages of *El Motín*; this is detailed further in chapter five. Of particular interest is how Nakens blended anticlericalism with nationalism because he assumed that a degree of anticlericalism could unify a varied spectrum of the regime's opponents. The central organizing principle of Nakens's anticlericalism was the belief that the clergy, above all else, represented the most significant obstacle to the sudden and no less magical resolution of the Spanish national problem.[24] His discourse affirmed that the clergy kept Spain from transforming herself into a modern nation.

According to Nakens and many republicans there were signs that Spain was falling apart, that rot had become endemic. To them, this national degeneration was rooted in Catholicism, which was far from a moral religion but rather an immorality that allowed crimes and abuses to go unpunished. According to *El Motín*, the Crime at Fuencarral Street—a case not involving the clergy, but rather a young woman who was murdered by a jealous male relative who in turn framed a poor servant—was symptomatic of a society "that celebrated prostitutes who happened to spend an hour at mass each day or burglars who doused themselves with holy water once in a while" to cleanse themselves of their sins.[25] Nakens's anticlericalism stemmed from his perception that the Church and clergy—in the name of God and Christ—enjoyed economic, political, and cultural monopolies over the Spaniards that allowed religious justice to trump civil justice.

Nakens's anticlerical nationalism also reflected a larger European concern with degeneration. Over the course of the nineteenth century, scientists, especially physicians and anthropologists, explored the complex relationship between the progress of civilization and the prevalence of sickness.[26] Ironically, as European societies rapidly progressed toward modernity, its burgeoning cities seemed to trigger social malaise. The increases in crime and mental illness were symptomatic of this unfortunate paradox. Rather than condemn Spain's modernization, Nakens and radical republicans embraced it so long as the individual could find political, economic, and cultural freedom unencumbered by Catholicism. The Church and its clergy in this vision were premodern, stagnant rather than progressive, and incompatible with modern Spain. Whether he depicted priests and nuns as unclean or diseased or morally deficient in some way, Nakens's anticlericalism also shouted that the Church and clergy were unhealthy for the nation; the clergy had to be extricated for Spain to recoup her health and honor.

The embattled and tired woman was but one image designed to suggest that Spain's honor was threatened. Other dark and animalistic images of the Church and clergy were designed to identify those who were anti-Spaniards. Nakens built upon the anticlerical models of the past and amplified modern anticlericalism both in quantity and intensity. He took not only from the 1840s French-inspired boom in anticlericalism—the anticlericalism of Michelet and the anti-Jesuitism of Eugene Sue, for example—but also from early modern forms of Catholic anticlericalism.

Although it seems that Nakens never made much money from his anticlerical industry, he constantly offered readers new forms of anticlerical discourse. In addition to the newspaper, the occasional posters, his collection of essays or *El Motín* excerpts, and selected novels from French and Spanish republicans, Nakens also offered readers anticlerical postcards and almanacs. In the summer of 1887, for example, Nakens was particularly enthused about offering the *Testimonio* (Last Will and Testament) of Jean Meslier, an eighteenth-century Roman Catholic priest from Champagne who published a scathing atheistic, anticlerical critique.[27] In December of 1910, Nakens offered readers ten color postcards, each demonstrating "how much heed the clergy gives to each of God's Commandments." Of course, these post-cards depicted any number of examples of clerical sloth, abuse, and exploitation.[28] Also in 1910, *El Motín* printed a series of cheap sheets of paper (*hojitas*) with anticlerical messages on them, which were inserted into the weekly editions. One could also purchase anticleri-cal postcards, which were sold in four collections of 10 cards each for 50 *céntimos* (cents). Sold separately, these were 10 céntimos each, and discounts were offered based on the number of postcards ordered. In 1910, *El Motín* itself cost 10 *céntimos* an issue, 1.50 pesetas per trimester in Madrid (1.60 pesetas in the provinces), or 5 pesetas for a year paid up front (6 outside of Madrid, and 10 pesetas internation-ally). There were so many *El Motín* publications that Nakens divided the collections into: (1) the Library of the Inquisition, which included Pey Ordeix's biography of Miguel Servet; (2) the Anticlerical Muse, which included anticlerical poetry, imagery, and other "lighter" works printed in the form of cheap pamphlets that sold 10 for a peseta; and (3) Collection of clerical festivals, whose pamphlets were much more cerebral in subject matter.

Still, something more than the pursuit of profit was behind Nakens' obsession with anticlerical production. He was engaged in the "new politics" and was determined to strike an emotive chord with the masses to make them think in terms of being a nation and protecting that nation from the immoral clergy and state. He was most concerned with flooding his readers with alternate images of the nation that were designed to tear away at the Church's cultural hege-mony. These were images that turned the world upside down, images designed to inject urgency into the struggle over national identity. A number of the *El Motín* illustrations altered national and regional her-aldry with anticlerical images. For example, the cover to the June 8, 1911 issue of *El Motín* replaced the Royal Crown of the National crest with a Bull's Head, a series of clergymen's hats, a couple of acoustic guitars, and an assortment of bottles of alcoholic cordials.[29] The cracked and weakened pillars along the escutcheon represent "Catholicism" and "Disaster," and are inscribed with the words Jesuitism, Immorality, Nepotism, Servileness, Separatism, Bossism, Terror, Hypocrisy, Clericalism, Emigration, Hunger, Sloth, Illiteracy, Vagrancy, Mendicancy, National Debt, and Criminality. In place of the symbols of Castile and Leon, and the Kingdoms of Aragón and Catalonia on the escutcheon, are images of the Inquisition and Carlist wars, a mangy dog, rosaries, crucifixes, and scapulars. These were powerful images of a seemingly omnipotent but decadent Church and clergy that in Nakens's eyes had to be eliminated for the good of the Spanish nation.

Images of the Anti-Spaniards: The Clergy

The heroine of perhaps the most successful anti-Jesuit novel ever written, *Le Juif Errant* by Eugène Sue, declared herself unable to think of the Jesuits "without ideas of darkness, of venom and of nasty black reptiles being involuntarily aroused" in her.[30] Although animal allegories of humans or Gods have been present in Western literature dating back to antiquity, anticlerical animalism such as that in Sue's novel exploded during the aftermath of the French Revolution. It was not, however, without its early modern European precursors; these were prevalent throughout the Reformation when "animal allegories were a stock part of the Protestant propaganda repertoire."[31] The pope, priests, and even Humanist scholars such as Erasmus, who refused to break with the Papacy, were often depicted as wolves or foxes with a reputation for slyness, cunning, and violence. Satirical caricatures of the clergy and other pillars of the *Ancien Régime* had already formed a part in shaping the imagination of French society prior to the Revolution.[32]

But with the convulsive efforts by the French state to assert its authority over the Church and clergy after 1789 came any number of campaigns to dehumanize those who refused to swear loyalty to France. This was especially true of the Jesuits who were often portrayed as beasts of prey, reptiles, insects and arachnids, and mythical beasts (such as the hydra).[33] While an expansion of anticlerical animalism in Spain did not occur until around 1868, these French and Protestant German precursors gave Spanish anticlericals, such as José Nakens, symbolic models for his own attacks.

It was very common for Nakens and his staff to represent the clergy as insects, serpents, spiders, or crows that prevented allegories of Spain from greater things. A particularly poignant example of the dehumanized constrictive clergy image appeared in the center cartoon for the May 31, 1885 issue of *El Motín*. In it, a female allegory representing either Spain or education is constricted by a large python with a Jesuit priest for its head. She is gagged by tape that reads *Syllabus*—no doubt referring to the Syllabus of Errors of 1864—while a raven wearing a Carlist beret prepares to claw at her. Rather than allowing her to study a modern curriculum, she is forced to read religious and theological texts.[34] In the accompanying comment, *El Motín*'s editors wrote:

> Today the mystical black serpent and the devout snake slither around
> on Spanish soil penetrating throughout, coiling wherever they can and
> fleeing wherever they are driven back. [They] first spew their venom
> to see if they can poison what they have not been able to destroy under
> any circumstance.
>
> What is most disgusting about the orgy that we are presently wit-
> nessing is to see these reptiles become infuriated because the nation
> does not willingly allow itself to be swallowed whole, and wipes off
> their drool with indefatigable energy.[35]

The intended message behind the symbol of the serpent was relatively obvious. Although Cubitt suggests that reptiles in French anti-
Jesuitism represented subtlety, slipperiness, and venom,[36] they meant
more than that. Serpents, especially snakes, were associated with
Satan ever since a snake duped Eve to eat of the forbidden fruit in the
Garden of Eden. To associate the clergy with evil rather than virtue
was part of a larger process by anticlerical republicans to turn the
world upside down: to suggest that the world is not right so long as
those who are evil rule over the virtuous nation.

Similarly, the central cartoon in the Christmas Day 1887 *El Motín*
depicts a situation in which the Jesuits control all aspects of society.[37]
A Jesuit priest whose body has taken on the form of a large spider
lords over large sacks of money while his legs—each armed with razor
sharp claws—menaces a young couple, overpowers a young damsel,
and takes the life of a sleeping old man (figure 3.1). In addition, representations of a factory, a peasant working the land, a large Church
and school house, a naval vessel, a bank, and a locomotive all lie on
the spider's web. In 1887, Nakens wrote:

> The black spider completely imprisons the Spain of '20, of '35, of '54,
> and of '68. And wherever it can plant its disgusting and innumerable
> legs, it hatches a seminary, quashes activity, or prays a rosary.
>
> It persecutes, maligns and excommunicates in the name of religion,
> and it works silently, but tenaciously, to resuscitate the ignominious
> decade of 1823–3.[38]

The most accomplished and most widely read novelist among the
anticlerical republicans, Vicente Blasco Ibáñez, himself picked up
the theme of the omnipresent and omnipotent Jesuits in his *La araña
negra* (The Black Spider, published in 1892). Like the work from which

Figure 3.1   "The Black Spider," February 3, 1910 *El Motín* cover

Blasco plagiarized, Eugene Sue's *Le Juif Errant*, the Jesuits in *La araña negra* murder, rape, and steal as they conspire to dominate the world. They have a complicated network of *agents provacateurs*, they hate progress and the idea of human dignity, and they consider religion pure farce.[39] Because the state prosecuted press offenses against the Church, clergy, or Catholic dogma, it too was considered to be caught in the web of the clerical spider.[40] When an insect is caught in a spider's web, it is virtually helpless and will soon be consumed by the much larger and crafty arachnid. It is that bug's sense of frustration and impending doom that Nakens and Blasco tried to convey to their readers: Spaniards were entangled in the web of the clerical "predators." Hans Bierdermann suggests that the spider has represented the opposite of what the bee has represented. Whereas the bee is usually portrayed as industrious for its honey, spiders have represented the sinful urges that suck blood and vigor from humanity.[41] Cubitt argues that the web imagery in anticlerical propaganda could be very flexible: it could simultaneously convey the idea of a society hopelessly caught up in the clerical web and also the notion of a tight-knit network of Jesuit organizations or agents.[42]

Perhaps the most common animal used to represent the clergy was the crow or raven. For example, on August 3, 1884, *El Motín* printed a colorful centerfold cartoon in which *España*, wearing a red and golden yellow toga, is harassed by an ugly raven wearing a Jesuit's hat. The editors wrote:

> No, do not be afraid, Spain: that repugnant *pajarraco* can do nothing against you. Stand up proudly and shout out "Long Live Liberty!" and you will see how it flees back to the Kingdom of Darkness.
>
> I know that your attitude is not of fear, but rather of indignation and surprise: All the more reason why you must stand up valiantly because a moment of your doubt and vacillation could lead to it becoming more audacious, and splash the blood of your children onto your gown.[43]

On June 15, 1911, *El Motín*'s central cartoon juxtaposed a modern France with a premodern Spain. The left half of the centerfold depicted a female allegory of France wearing a Phrygian cap and standing confidently as she observes airplanes flying overhead. In the background, an upright crowd applauds France in front of the Eiffel Tower (itself an important modern architectural and communications accomplishment). The right half of the illustration, however, features a female allegory of Spain attempting to shoo away a swarm of flying crows and ravens all wearing the clergymen's hats. Churches make up the background of the picture, and here the mostly male audience kneels in prayer. The illustration's caption reads: "In France: Aeroplanes!= In Spain: Priests!"[44]

Spaniards are not the only people to have had a long and combative history with ravens and their smaller bird brothers, crows. According to Greek mythology, the crow or raven was originally a lovely white bird that Apollo entrusted with watching over his beloved Coronis. When Coronis gave herself to an Arcadian prince, the enraged Apollo killed her and punished the bird by turning it completely black.[45] Athena replaced her raven with an owl because she deemed the former untrustworthy for indiscreetly revealing secrets. The raven has been berated in Christianity for not reporting to Noah that the flood waters had receded (Genesis 8: 7). According to Biederman, the raven became a symbol of those who are so caught up in worldly pleasures that they keep putting off their conversion to Christianity: it is a bird of procrastination who cries *cras cras* (in Latin: "tomorrow, tomorrow").[46] In German anti-Protestant propaganda, Luther was usually presented as a type of demon or the Antichrist, and often with a diabolical raven on his shoulder.[47] Even today there are a number of very common Spanish proverbs that speak to the sinister nature of these birds; one such proverb warns:

Cuando un grajo	(When a crow)
vuela abajo	(flies below)
hace un frío	(cold winds blow)
como un ¡carajo!	(like the Dickens!)

Yet another speaks the ravens' ungrateful nature: "*cría cuervos / y te pican los ojos*" (Raise ravens/and they'll peck your eyes out).[48] Nadia Julien maintains ravens came to represent the deadly sin of gluttony in the Middle Ages and ravens are considered miserable parents who neglect or abandon their young.[49] Ravens are scavengers whose very existence depends on stealing grain from farmers as they undermine the hard work and hopes of peasants. An Icelandic superstition mandated that children not use raven feathers for quills or for drinking straws because of the risk that they would grow up to be thieves themselves.[50] That ravens also feed on carrion led to them being viewed as harbingers of misfortune, disease, war, and death.[51] Clearly the symbol of the raven had many connotations, very few of them positive, and while it would be conjecture to suggest priests as ravens meant priests were thieves in Nakens's eyes, portraying the clergy as crows and ravens was obviously an attempt to offend the clergy, make dubious their virtue, and turn notions of good and evil upside down.

From these raven images as well as many others like them that dehumanize clergymen, Nakens's and the *El Motín* staff's anti-sacerdotalism was indisputable: their anticlericalism went beyond ideology. To anti-sacerdotalists, clergy members become symbols or representatives of an opposed institution, and the common garb and training of any one priest allows for the anti-sacerdotalist to equate the one with the many.[52] In addition, as Cubitt suggests of anti-Jesuitism in France, the animalism in the anticlerical imagery had the cumulative effect of reducing clerical behavior to a "comportment governed by animal instinct, incurable by morality and reason, unassimilable [sic] to human civilization, and fit only to be opposed by a facile intransigence."[53] If Spain were to progress and modernize toward becoming a wholly liberal democracy governed by morality and reason, then the clergy—these representatives of backwardness and obscurantism who all wore black, like the ravens—were incompatible with the nation's regeneration.

The Attack on Clerical Opulence: National Comparisons

The number of anti-sacerdotalist images like those just referenced paled in comparison to the number of articles, editorials, and essays asserting that Spain's backwardness could only be explained by clerical machination, greed, and wealth. In 1901, Nakens wrote an open letter to Luis Bonafoux, a well-respected libertarian journalist, saying:

> Everything is becoming ruined slowly in Spain; only the Church grows more powerful. All cry, only the Church sings.[54]

Around that same time, Nakens would write:

> Convents are raised up everywhere while there is no broth in the hospitals, households are perturbed by the clergy's lack of want; fathers of daughters with dowries must take great precautions so that they aren't kidnapped; mothers of beautiful daughters desperately search for them around religious asylums; the seminarians and apprentices of the friars find themselves exempt from military service.... Today this nation does not breathe except through the lungs of friars, clergymen or nuns; today one can only read orations (that are) insults to liberty.[55]

In times of acute military crisis, such as protracted conflict in Cuba, Nakens was fixated on the national budget from which the clergy were supported. After studying the budgets, Nakens argued that the Church's wealth came at the expense of the nation, and perhaps most unforgivable was that an opulent Church and clergy stood in the way of Spain's military victories. For example, he was quick to point out that Spain did not have the navy it so dearly coveted because of the huge amount of money extracted from the state by the Church. In the period when England, Germany, and the United States raced to build the world's biggest navy, Nakens suggested Spaniards could simply point to the clergy and say: "There is our navy."[56] In 1896, *El Motín* maintained that over the course of the Restoration, one billion *reales* (between 200 million and 250 million *pesetas*) of the nation's treasury had been spent on construction of religious buildings; another billion funded the religious orders; and one could assume the Jesuits managed another billion *reales* for their "noble, dignant, and saintly arts." In comparing Spain with the United States, the editor(s) wrote that 3,000 million *reales* earmarked for the Church and clergy could have endowed the army to "teach those pigs of the United States a lesson without subjecting the country to new taxes." He would also add, "And thus, you can see how the permanence of the religious orders can be the principle cause of the loss of Cuba and the complete ruin of the nation."[57]

The veracity of these figures was less important than the goal of making the *El Motín* readership feel aggrieved by the opulent Church, and the decadent state that supported it. Particularly important about throwing out these figures was that anticlerical republicans played up the widely held belief that the Church had made a financial comeback during the Restoration. In responding to criticism about the March 18, 1886 *exposé* on the Bishop of Madrid's financial records, *El Motín* sarcastically acknowledged that the Bishop's supporters were correct in suggesting there was a direct relationship between the Bishop's income and charitable works. Since there were so many poor and "unredeemed" citizens of Madrid as well as a great deal of suffering within the city, this clearly meant that there was no possible way the Bishop could earn 27,000 *duros* per year. If the Bishop had the money he'd most certainly help the poor.[58]

The often self-pitying tone of the anticlerical diatribes in *El Motín* were just as often complemented with articles and images presenting other nations, particularly France, as modern secular success stories. The close ties between French and Spanish republicans meant the latter were celebratory toward, if not envious of, the victory and apparent permanence of the Third Republic after 1871. While the Spanish clerical press worried that the entire French nation would be condemned to damnation because of the Third Republic,[59] anticlerical radicals argued that France's government and anticlerical policies, including Waldeck-Rousseau's expulsion of the religious orders, were precisely what would regenerate Spain. According to Nakens, France no longer saw civil wars between ultramontane elements and the Republic since General Lazare Hoche violently put down the royalists of the Vendée uprising, and Nakens implied that vicious repression be directed against the Spanish clergy.[60] France represented an idyllic community: a land of free speech, secular education, and, given the failures of Boulanger and the anti-Dreyfusards, France represented a nation in which clericalism would never be victorious.[61]

Unfortunately, according to Spanish republicans and anticlericals, while France did the right and progressive thing, Spain merely demonstrated how backward she was by taking in the French clergy exiled in 1901. In the republicans' eyes, Spain was enslaved by the Vatican. The center illustration in the March 27, 1887 *El Motín* juxtaposed another image of the Pope bowing in deference to the allegory of the French Republic with an image of the Pope stomping on the back of a shocked, confused *España*. Similarly, the centerfold illustration for the January 26, 1890 issue depicts a long train chugging from Spain toward St. Peter's Basilica. The train's boxcars, which are labeled "E á R" (*España a Roma*, Spain to Rome), are filled with sheep, all wearing Carlist berets and clergymen's hats. The final car has a couple of rotund friars sitting on sacks of enormous sums of *duros*.[62] For Nakens, the situation was intensely shameful because Spain "prostrated at the feet of Rome."[63]

The loyalty that the clergy held toward their "monarch," the Pope in Rome, meant the Church represented a supranational or internationalist threat to the Spanish nation and attempts to establish a modern secular Spanish identity. In many ways, the Church and clergy were no better than the socialists who posed internationalist threats to the building of the nation. For this reason, the clergy were depicted as unpatriotic and not the least bit concerned for the health and progress of Spain.[64] At the outbreak of the Spanish-American War, an incensed Fernando Lozano asserted that the Vatican's declaration of neutrality was proof that the Church and clergy worked to destroy the Spanish nation.[65] In another one of its center cartoons, *El Motín* juxtaposed those "who give their lives for the nation"—injured and dismembered veterans from the Cuban campaign—with those "who sacrifice their nation for their lives" (fat drunken friars).[66] Priests were not only noncitizens but also anti-Spaniards. According to radical republicans, since the Restoration state was an accomplice in furthering the goals of the Church, it followed that the state was also a curse to the nation.

Clerical Immorality and National Morality: The World Turned Upside Down

By far the most common message of Nakens's anticlericalism was that the clergy was immoral; the clergy betrayed the gospel of Christ. According to republicans, the Spanish nation was fast becoming culturally impoverished, and the spiritual decadence of the clergy was largely to blame for this rot. To illustrate this state of affairs, republicans linked their moral language with a racial or biological language of national degeneration, which itself was part of a prevalent set of nationalist anxieties throughout *fin-de-siècle* Europe.[67] Inextricably tied to both the racial/biological and moral degeneration languages were the mass-produced images of a degenerate clergy. This section briefly explores some of these images of moral and biological degenerates in order to demonstrate the novelty of Nakens's anticlericalism.

Dozens upon dozens of the illustrations in *El Motín* resurrected the theme of a hypocritical clergy that turned their backs on the teachings of Christ and their vows. For example, the caricature on the front cover of *El Motín* on October 6, 1910 depicts a Bishop spearing the side of the crucified Christ. As gold coins flow from Christ, a mob of friars, Jesuits, and other priests scramble eagerly to get their hands on the money.[68] This immoral clergy critique went beyond suggesting the clergy had a penchant for gold; the clergy was morally bankrupt, hypocritical, perverse, deviant, and filthy. Rather than preaching the Gospel of the Lord, or love and charity, the center illustration to the January 10, 1884 *El Motín* depicts a priest throwing out muskets, rifles, pistols, and Carlist berets to his congregation.[69] Political issues were framed in moral terms for republicans and, thus, an attack on clerical morality *was* a political attack.

Images of the immoral clergy were often juxtaposed with images of hardworking, impoverished Spaniards who were noble in spirit. The cover to the April 14, 1910 *El Motín* splits the page between those who "preach abstinence,"—priests (a bishop flanked by monks, friars, and Jesuits) sitting down to enjoy a large banquet—and those "who practice it" (a hungry family of five huddling in the cold) (figure 3.2).[70] Elsewhere, an *El Motín* cartoon features a priest so obese that he requires a wheelbarrow for his giant gut.[71] In another illustration, a monk kicks a tiny boy and his even tinier sister for having the audacity to beg for alms from the bishop.[72]

Indeed, clerical demands for fees to perform religious rituals even from the poor were proof to *El Motín* that the clergy did not have the

Figure 3.2   "Those who preach abstinence and those who practice it," April 14, 1910
El Motín cover

people's deepest and most personal needs in mind. In 1882 the news-paper ran a firsthand (albeit likely apocryphal) account of a priest who refused to bury a couple's child without first seeing a baptis-mal record. The priest held onto the corpse while the impoverished couple found the documents. After performing the funeral, the priest charged them for the service and the storage of the corpse, adding that no warehouse business or docking company offers space for free.[73] In October of 1884, *El Motín* began publishing a series of articles detailing clerical misconduct in Puerto Rico, including the clergy's refusal to bury a child in a Catholic cemetery without first receiving a fee, and an account of clerical body snatching of the child's corpse when he was buried in a civil cemetery. The clergy often withheld religious services from those considered to be lapse in their faith. In 1879, for example, a priest in La Coruña refused to bury a man in a Catholic cemetery because he had allegedly stopped attending Mass. In May of 1882, María Theresa Folch de Amigo's cadaver decomposed for a protracted period of time while friends and family battled with a priest who refused to give her a Christian burial because she did not complete her "Easter obligation" and was an alleged member of a different faith. In the late summer of 1882, villagers from San Pedro de Eume (La Coruña) appealed to their civil governor about their parish priest who refused to perform services or administer the sacraments to them unless the villagers made donations to the Church beforehand.[74]

The clergy was depicted as so morally perverse that they celebrated diseases such as cholera, which in striking down citizens brought them more money in the form of fees for funeral services. In the summer of 1885, an *El Motín* caricature depicted numerous priests and monks singing, dancing, drinking, and carousing with women. One young altar boy takes the opportunity to look up a woman's skirt while a priest kneels in front of the altar and raises his cup to toast the grim reaper of cholera.[75] *El Motín* never believed that the clergy existed to comfort the sick and poor, but if service was its alleged mission, the editors delighted in pointing out how the clergy failed to live up to their duties. During an 1884 cholera outbreak, *El Motín* found it surprising to have to inform the clergy to leave their religious convents and monasteries and attend to the scores of sick and dying.[76] Because the clergy enjoyed cholera epidemics, they were not only sick, but rather sickness embodied. They were a contagion, a cancer, a plague that destroyed the social body from within.[77] They eroded the national vigor and the national honor by ravaging the nation like a virus wrecking its host. Here again we see that one of the most novel and important qualities of this new republican anticlericalism was its nationalist message, replete with images of the degenerate clergy, which linked a language of moral degeneration with a language of biological degeneration.

Although the biological language of degeneracy in other parts of Europe moved toward condemning miscegenation, especially when the heightened concern with race blended with anti-Semitism, Joshua

Goode has shown that some Spanish intellectuals actually believed that the Spanish race had been strengthened by miscegenation.[78] However, just as race was a central part of the nationalizing project elsewhere, in Spain racial fusion offered a tool through which to construct a basis for national unity. The republican obsession with science when applied to racial thinking allowed them to imagine a Spain that was secular, democratic, and rooted in a fusion of groups that each contributed elements to the nation. Spanish national strength had begun to erode with the imposition of intolerance and homogeneity during the Catholic *Reconquista* of Spain. Political and cultural separatist movements such as the Carlists and the Basque and Catalan autonomists—all, incidentally, deeply concerned with safeguarding a conservative and Catholic way of life—were a result of an incomplete racial fusion.[79] The nationalist implication of this degeneration of the Spanish alloy was that it left the possibility of national unity in doubt.

For republicans, politics was a moral endeavor because it offered the path to redeeming the nation by curbing the immorality of the clergy through a Republic. If the republicans were in a position of political power, they believed that they could also do something about the racial-biological degeneration of the nation through controlling the whole population of priests and nuns, the principle agents of the nation's demise. The Spanish populace's political apathy *vis-à-vis* the Church and clergy's abuse of power was unacceptable, and anticlerical propaganda was designed to expose clerical immorality to awaken the public's sense of morality and engage them in the moral endeavor of political participation. To this end, transforming the society necessitated turning the entire world upside down; it necessitated an inversion of the normal state of affairs to replace national dishonor with a reign of virtue.

One of the most common ways Nakens tried to turn the world upside down was by using religious imagery in order to construct a mirror image of republicanism. In January of 1885, *El Motín* set up a hypothetical Diocese, called the Diocese of Common Sense, because the editors said Spaniards only understood issues when presented in a religious mode. "Friar Motín, the Bishop of the Religion of Work in the Diocese of Common Sense" promised religious documents in the form of newspapers, books, posters, and medallions that addressed the stupidities and dogmatic absurdities of those whom (Leon) Gambetta called "the enemy."[80] Because the clergy failed to live up to the teachings of Christ, they were summarily excommunicated by the Diocese of Common Sense, and instead of Beatitudes which read "Blessed are the poor...," the Diocese's prayers read: "Damned be their (the clergy's) properties, may trichonosis befall their pigs, pip their chickens, epizootic diseases to their lambs, glanders their horses, locust their seedlings, and phylloxera their vines."[81] Elsewhere, Nakens turned the afterlife upside down; Satan was a moral champion of social justice who inflicts any number of Dantesque punishments on the clergy. Because Nakens's work on earth as a critic of the sinful clergy was exemplary, Satan offered him the chance to be his first lieutenant before he awoke from his dream lamenting that he could not stay in Hell forever.[82] Perhaps to shock more than anything, in 1889 *El Motín's* editors established the United Brotherhood of Lucifer, which was dedicated to expose, judge, and condemn unpardonable clerical crimes.[83] By contrast, Jesus Christ, in another of *El Motín's* publications, was portrayed as an imbecile who failed to understand how his teachings were misconstrued by the clergy to take advantage of the poor and sick.[84]

Similarly, *Las Dominicales del Libre Pensamiento* co-opted religious imagery and language in its newspaper. Rather than being followers of St. Dominic (Dominicans), the Freemason journalist Fernando Lozano and his coeditor Ramón Chiés were devotees of Free Thought. Their newspaper included a column that juxtaposed religious texts, such as Scripture and Catholic dogma, with the "Gospel (The Good News) of the Republic."[85] Together with Nakens and *El Motín*, they attempted to "moralize" the immoral clergy throughout the Restoration.

The "Manojo de Flores Místicas" (Bundle of Mystical Flowers) column of *El Motín* was perhaps the most widely read of all, and it offers the best examples of Nakens's sustained effort to turn the world upside down. On the back page since 1882, the "Manojo" column was chock full of clerical transgressions ranging from child abuse to accounts of women beating their priests for abandoning them with children.[86] The items included news of clerical misconduct from as far away as Detroit[87] as *El Motín* became a depository for gossipy accounts, truthful or not, about the lives of the Spanish clergy. From time to time, Nakens had so many anticlerical stories to tell that he published an entire four-page supplement containing just the "Manojo de Flores Místicas" section.[88] This anticlerical superabundance speaks to its enormous popularity as only a full "Manojo" collection could supplant the weekly cartoon. In 1883, Nakens transcribed highlights from the "Manojo" section and published them in *Espejo moral del clérigo*, which he said offered accounts of priests who are "gamblers, embezzlers, drunks, forgers, thieves, simonists, scandal mongers, physical abusers, including of children, grave robbers, murderers, assassins, patricides, adulterers, practitioners of incest, kidnapers of young girls, and pederasts who had victimized 248 children under the age of thirteen."[89] The book offered yet another forum to paint the clergy as dirty, lascivious, and immoral.

The national conflict between clericals and anticlericals extended into the realm of sexuality, and republicans such as Nakens were determined to assert their notions of respectable sexuality won over the alleged sexual dysfunction of priests and nuns. As described in detail in chapter five, Nakens's sexualized and gendered his attacks on the clergy, which was a technique employed by many late-nineteenth-century nationalist movements.[90] Nakens's sexual anticlerical attacks were motivated by a desire to shape the sexuality of Spain for the well-being and honor of the nation itself. If the state was unable to halt the sexual immorality of the clergy, then it followed that republicans, defenders of national honor, should dictate appropriate and honorable sexual comportment. The sexuality of the clergy was a constant theme throughout *El Motín*'s existence, and, though modern, it also tapped into a long anticlerical tradition of sexual jokes about the clergy, reminiscent of Dante and Rabelais. Playing up the idea that priests and nuns were making love and having families was an important component of a message designed to label the clergy hypocrites. However, these anticlerical tropes were updated with a wider concern for the biological and moral degeneration of Spain.

Nakens was particularly enthusiastic about the pseudoscientific work of Dr. Gaétan Delaunay, a French phrenologist who claimed that religiosity was usually a characteristic of the weak.[91] This confirmed Nakens's vision that the members of the religious orders were of a different "race" or of a different time; the clergy was anachronistic and incapable of fitting into the modern world. Because the religious orders grouped themselves into monasteries and convents as well as lived like hermits, anticlerical republicans hypothesized about what went on inside those cloistered spaces. One of *El Motín*'s earliest essays on Franciscan Friars claimed that they were dirty and lice-infested: a civilization of moles.[92]

The secrecy that surrounded the Jesuits and their networks led to a number of publications claiming to expose how they were taught to be evil. In the 1890s, *El Motín* printed *Mónita secreta*, which was a fabricated manual that taught young Jesuits how to control the world.[93]

A cartoon on the cover of the October 20, 1910 *El Motín* illustrated the anticlerical fantasy of what went on inside the religious monasteries. Over the caption reading "Holy asylums of peace and chastity," a nun breast feeds her baby as she watches a dozen of her colleagues preparing chemical explosives and bombs.[94] Republicans may not have known what went on in the cloistered homes of the religious, but clearly the message was that they were up to no good. For radical republicans, these signs of the times necessitated the closer investigation and even segregation of the whole population of clergymen and clergywomen. The goal of portraying the clergy as animals, as sexual predators, as hermits, and so on was to suggest that the Church and clergy were incompatible with the liberal polity that republicans were moving toward.

The Struggle for National History

Over the course of the nineteenth century in Europe, there was a preoccupation with popular understandings of the past as nation-states endeavored to inculcate "patriotic" values in their citizens. National histories were centrally relevant to ideologies of nationhood and national identity and many states attempted to shape national history in order strengthen their base of support.[95] The Restoration regime, however, differed from many nationalizing states and did relatively little to impose a national history.[96] The weak regime chose to stay out of important issues such as establishing an educational curriculum in order to prevent politicization from either the left or the right. Nonetheless, the state's abandonment of national history did not signal a shortage of attempts to assert a national history in civil society.[97]

If Catholicism was consubstantial with Spanish history for Menéndez Pelayo, who was the conservative titan among the Spanish historical profession, the then republicans such as Nakens took it upon themselves to recapture and recast national history in such a way as to present Catholicism working against Spanish nationalism (figure 3.3). To this end, and through humor and gravity, Nakens conflated clericalism with the antinationalist and traditionalist Carlists.[98] In addition to his newspaper and the images therein, Nakens attempted to appropriate history to meet his own ends. In 1912 and 1913, for example, Nakens and Segismundo Pey Ordeix, another disgruntled ex-priest who had assumed a great deal of responsibility at *El Motín*, offered Carlist and Inquisitorial almanacs.[99] The Carlist almanacs

Figure 3.3 "Preaching the extermination of liberals," January 27, 1910 *El Motín* cover

were primarily composed of a series of 1897 articles in *El Motín* called *Los crímenes carlistas* (Carlists Crimes), in which Nakens provided detailed accounts of bloodthirsty Carlists during their civil wars with the Spanish state. In addition to graphic descriptions of civil war events, Nakens added nineteen illustrations of atrocities from past issues of the newspaper. Nakens maintained that he considered it his duty to remind Spaniards of the barbarity and depravity of the Carlist soldiers precisely because the liberals and republicans no longer considered the Carlists a threat.[100] Of course, Nakens made sure that the clergy's role as soldiers, accomplices, and passive bystanders was central in these almanacs to show that in the Carlists the Church had both political leaders and a standing army ready to disrupt the forward progress of the nation.

Rather than continuing with the somber and macabre body counting of the 1912 Almanac, Nakens published a comical Carlist Almanac in 1913 designed to poke fun at the Carlists for being the most absurd of peoples. To complement an assortment of anti-Carlist and anticlerical poems, articles, and satirical biographical sketches of the Pretenders, Nakens printed some sixty cartoons not only from *El Motín* but also its predecessors: *Jeremías, Gil Blas, La Flaca*, and *Cañón Krupp*.[101] Included among these were a series of cartoons that *Cañón Krupp* had put onto the covers of matchboxes in the 1870s, and which Nakens had placed on the cover of the August 4, 1910 issue of *El Motín*. The illustrations depicted a fat musket-wielding Jesuit volunteer in the Carlist infantry (figure 3.4), an armed rotund priest who volunteered in the Carlist cavalry weighing down a donkey, an armed priest interrupting the confession of a young woman, saying: "Hurry up, sister, the battalion is waiting for me," and a priest who had lost a leg and the use of one eye because he "preached religion by gunshots."[102] Although only a minority within the Spanish clergy participated either directly or indirectly in the Carlists Wars, no institution offered radical republicans such ample evidence of clerical persecution of the nation's citizens like the Inquisition did.

The Tragic Week of 1909 and the subsequent execution of Francisco Ferrer had many in the international community convinced that the Black Legend of Inquisitorial Spain was alive and well.[103] It is in this context that Nakens and Pey Ordeix published an Inquisition Almanac for the year 1912. On January 4, 1912, Nakens and Pey Ordeix announced that they had been doing a great deal of research at the National Historical Archive where they uncovered a cache of fifteenth- and sixteenth-century Inquisitorial documents, which they

Figure 3.4 "Recurring Fashions," August 4, 1910 *El Motín* cover

transcribed on the cover of *El Motín*.[104] That same issue of *El Motín* bore a seventeenth-century public announcement of the men and women who were tried, sentenced, executed or absolved in a Toledo *auto de fe*. These transcriptions made their way into the Almanac, which Nakens dedicated to the tens of thousands of Inquisition victims.[105] In addition to body counts, the almanac also published Papal Bulls that established jurisdictions and the logistics of the Spanish Inquisition, a history of European Inquisitions, a running commentary that reminded readers that despite the violence of the Inquisition the Church still preached loving thy neighbor; and most importantly, graphic descriptions and depictions of Inquisitorial torture.

Nakens and Pey Ordeix explained in graphic detail how the Inquisition tortured alleged sinners in order to secure a confession. For example, in the "tormento de cuerda" (torture of the rope), a sinner was stripped completely naked, tied with her arms above her head with rope counterweighed and strung through a pulley. The person was left suspended in the air with her feet just above the ground. The sinner's humiliation was accompanied by tremendous pain when additional weights were strapped to her ankles so that she was pulled apart from her extremities.[106] In the "tormento del fuego" (torture by fire), the victim was again stripped naked, strapped to a chair, feet locked in stocks over a cauldron or a pan of sweltering coal or burning wood. The sinner's feet were held over the heat as the torturer stoked the fire with bellows.[107]

A dozen different types of tortures were described in this almanac, and wherever possible Nakens included the cold, dry, and monotonous language with which the Inquisitors used to interrogate and condemn. Their cruel irony was captured in a passage in which a torturer beats a naked sinner and tells him: "If we holy men motivated by our love of God treat you in this manner just imagine what they would do to you in hell!"[108] Of course, no work of Nakens and *El Motín* was complete without a series of graphic illustrations of these tortures. These illustrations first appeared on the covers of various editions of *El Motín* in 1911. On June 29, 1911, Nakens offered for sale the mass-produced illustrations of torture, which he claimed sold out in a matter of weeks.[109]

Again, the idea behind the *Almanac of the Inquisition* was similar to that of the Carlist almanacs: Nakens appropriated the history of the Church to meet his ends. Nakens used the bloody history of the Church and clergy against them during the Restoration in order to completely discredit them. By linking the Church's Inquisitorial atrocities with the execution of Francisco Ferrer in 1909, Nakens hoped to offer a series of poignant examples of how the Church and clergy posed a danger to Spanish citizens during the Restoration. Nakens suggested to readers that the Inquisition was not a thing of the past but rather an ongoing process designed to perpetuate the Church's dominance in Spain. Most of all, Nakens hoped to justify, if not expedite, the coming about of the Second Republic in the future by besmirching the present Church with its past history.

* * *

This journey through the messages in the anticlerical industry of radical republicans led by José Nakens reveals a number of factors that should be kept in mind. First and foremost is that the anticlerical industry was nationalist. The production of anticlerical discourse was motivated by a concern for the nation and its regeneration. It was a product of a perception that the Church and clergy had made a financial, social, and cultural comeback at a time when secularism was supposed to be triumphing over religion. In addition, it was a product of a self-pitying belief that Spain was falling behind in the modernizing international community.

Second, republican anticlericalism was very much a modern phenomena because it blended their politics of morality with a Europe-wide language of racial or biological degeneration. Republicans such as Nakens were obsessed with controlling the Church and clergy because they considered them to be agents of the nation's moral and racial/biological degeneration. While clerical elements tied degeneration to secularism and modernity, anticlerical republicans separated national degeneration from the history of progress. Closely tied to these languages of morality and degeneration is the idea that an anticlerical-republican conception of good government and social justice should be privileged over those of Catholics, the clergy, and the oligarchs. Only republicans—who conceptualized politics as a moral endeavor rather than a means toward social control— knew what Spain ought to be like.

Third, the terrain in which the clericals and anticlericals fought out their battles was as much cultural as it was political. These battles took place not so much in the rarified circles of formal politics but rather in the press and other avenues of the public sphere in which Spaniards discussed the common good. Finally, Nakens's sustained anticlerical campaign and mass-production of anticlerical propaganda was a form of the "new politics." Nakens's manipulation of symbols was crucial for the anticlerical republicans because not only did anticlerical symbolism simplify and abbreviate their message but also served as way to reach the masses emotionally and increase the chances of mobilizing them. Appeals to anticlericalism were thus very much a central part of the discourse of populists such as Blasco and Lerroux because anticlerical rants allowed them to secure a following without having to present a concrete plan or strategy for bringing about the Republic.

As the man who spoke for the *pueblo* (nation) against the abuses of the clergy, and the man who was obsessed with distributing anticlerical paraphernalia for the good of the nation, Nakens was one of the primary inventors of an anticlerical-republican culture. His anticlerical production sought to break the almost hypnotic control the clergy maintained over Spaniards. It was an attempt to, as Timothy Mitchell has put it, "override the old scripts" of the Church and clergy.[110] Nakens sought to flood Spaniards with the symbols of an alternative vision of Spain, and the constant and repetitive nature of anticlerical themes constituted an effort to get Spaniards to think in anticlerical ways. The anticlerical industry was an effort to unite opponents of the regime through their hatred for a common enemy and thus define the nation through those who were excluded, namely clergymen. People feel like a community the most when they think alike and are engaged in similar activities. Anticlerical discourse provided the regime's progressive opponents such a social glue. In many ways, anticlericals from all facets of society fought their own anticlerical battles vicariously through José Nakens. His frustrations with the theorization of republicanism and over the waning possibility of a Second Republic in his lifetime were their frustrations too. Anyone who came in contact with *El Motín* was engaged in the process of evaluating, rewarding, or discarding the anticlerical-republican vision of Spain.

Republicanism, Anarchism, Anticlericalism, and the Attempted Regicide of 1906

On May 31, 1906, King Alfonso XIII and his new bride, Victoria Eugenia of Battenberg, were off to the Royal Palace after their wedding when a bomb hidden within a bundle of flowers exploded as they passed Calle Mayor, 88. The Royals were not hurt, but twenty-four spectators and soldiers were killed and over one-hundred others were wounded.[1] The scene was tremendously macabre. Guy Windham, a British colonel who observed the royal procession and claimed that he was among the first to get to the royal carriage, mentioned that he was relieved the King and Queen were safe and sound. However, just a few feet away there were "such horrible things, as awful as those that could be seen in the war."[2] When the smoke cleared, security officials could see that one of the horses pulling the royal carriage had its belly blown open splattering blood onto the Queen's white gown.[3] The Count of Romanones, Alvaro Figueroa y Torres, who as Minister of the Interior (*Gobernación*) was in charge of the security detail for the wedding wrote that he would never forget the blood splatter, the cries of anguish and pain, and the acrid smell of the explosive materials used for the bomb. Romanones suggested that what nauseated him most in the room was the bitter smell of the explosives mixed with the smell of medicine the assassin took for a venereal disease.[4]

The police traced the bombing to a young anarchist from Barcelona named Mateo Morral, who had managed to escape the scene in the commotion that ensued after the bombing. As the investigation unfolded, it was revealed that Morral had ties to the renowned anarchist pedagogue, Francisco Ferrer. In addition, the assassin decided to seek out the republican journalist José Nakens for help after the attempted regicide, which seemed particularly curious given the fact that Nakens, like many republicans, was antipathetic to anarchism and certainly anarchist terrorism. However, as I show in this chapter, the aftermath of this attempted regicide suggests a great deal about how anarchists looked to anticlerical republicans for entertainment, knowledge, and perhaps even leadership. Despite Nakens's vehement cries that he was not an anarchist—indeed, that he hated anarchists—his career leading the anticlerical vanguard attracted rather than repelled the radicalized workers. Thus, this attempted regicide of Alfonso XIII provides another window into the existence of anticlerical culture beyond republicanism and beyond the Restoration, as demonstrated in other studies.[5] It also demonstrates republicans' unique and powerful potential to arouse popular emotion in support of their policies by injecting drama into the political life of a nation that was disillusioned with formal politics.

At the same time, the assassination attempt and its aftermath exposed the significant rifts within the republican movement, between left or radical republicans (especially the "young republicans" such as Lerroux and Blasco Ibáñez, but Nakens as well) and moderate republicans (such as Gumersindo Azcárate and Nicolás Salmerón). The gulf between these factions widened and left the republican movement with a political identity crisis. Though the actions of radical republicans seemed to elicit universal condemnation and to usher in a victory for moderate republicans, the attempted regicide of Alfonso XIII would live on as a moment in which the revolution seemed only seconds away.

The Worst Wedding Day in the History of the Spanish Bourbons, May 31, 1906

Mateo Morral was a very troubled soul, and he was a pawn in a much bigger anarchist conspiracy against the Spanish monarchy. He was the son of a textile manufacturer in Sabadell and had studied abroad and traveled a great deal as a representative of his father's firm, but his affiliation and financial support of *Librepensadores* (a radicalized segment of republicans and Freemasons) forced him to sever ties with his father. In 1905 he moved to Barcelona with some send-off money from his father, where he met and befriended Ferrer, the anarchist pedagogue and founder of the *Escuela Moderna*.[6] According to Ferrer, who after sixteen years in Paris had returned to Barcelona in

1901 to propagate the rationalist education of workers, Morral was so excited with Ferrer's project that he offered him some 10,000 pesetas for whatever was necessary to help the school.[7] Ferrer claimed that he declined the money but did employ Morral as part of the Modern School's library staff. During the police investigation of the attempted regicide, Ferrer tried to give the impression that he was not close to Morral, that he did not know Morral was in Madrid, and that he had no idea that Morral was even a revolutionary.[8] However, Ferrer had introduced Morral to leading radical republicans in Barcelona, such as Lerroux, and evidence suggests not only that Ferrer and Lerroux actively conspired to kill the King in the hopes of precipitating a dramatic revolution but also that Ferrer introduced Morral to an explosives expert who would provide him with the bomb.[9] As the director of Ferrer's library, Morral was constantly exposed to a treasure trove of anarchist and revolutionary propaganda.

Morral's troubles began when he developed romantic feelings for Soledad Villafranca, the young and beautiful director of elementary studies in Ferrer's school. Though Ferrer was twenty years her senior, Villafranca took up residence with him and she was probably his lover—a reality possibly unbeknown to Morral.[10] When Morral privately declared his love to Villafranca, he was crushed to find that she did not feel the same way about him, and this set in motion the chain of events that ultimately destroyed him, and nearly destroyed the Spanish monarchy.

The angry and desperate Morral wanted to make a name for himself, perhaps to impress Villafranca. While he was in Madrid, Morral sent Villafranca a series of postcards in which he expressed his continued love for her, as well as stating that he felt alone in the world.[11] On May 20, 1906, shortly after being rejected by Villafranca, Morral said goodbye to Ferrer, reporting that he was ill and wanted to travel in order to recoup his health. Morral traveled to Madrid, walked all over the city, and attended a few *tertulias* (or roundtable discussions), at which the anarchist novelist Pío Baroja remembers seeing Morral, before settling in at a *pensión* on Calle Mayor, 88.[12] He gave his birth name, requested a room facing Calle Mayor, and gave the proprietor 500 pesetas up front for his stay. He also told the proprietor that he loved flowers and asked her to buy him some each day. On the morning of the 31st of May, Morral informed the lady that he had a rough night due to some stomach problems. He asked for some bicarbonate and asked not to be disturbed. When the afternoon wedding procession began, he got up and looked out his window, waited until the royal carriage approached, and then threw down the bomb concealed within a bundle of flowers.

Ironically, Romanones believed that there would be an attempt on the King; the wedding was just the type of large public event that anarchist terrorists used to make their so-called propaganda by deed (*propaganda de hecho*).[13] His suspicions were echoed by the French *commissaire* in charge of the surveillance of Spanish anarchists in France. Monsieur Bonnecarrère speculated that he was

> almost sure that the anarchists would attempt something against the King during the festivities in Madrid. What an occasion this royal wedding offers someone who is sick of this world, and imbued with subversive ideas! All the heir-princes of the reigning houses (and) all the representatives of the bourgeois republics will be reunited at one capital and, at times, reunited at the same place![14]

Although anarchists, radical republicans, and regional opponents to the Restoration regime challenged the legitimacy of the Madrid-based monarchy and government, the state did indeed reside in Madrid, and events and decisions made in Madrid affected the entire nation. Madrid again was more than a political and administrative center; it was a symbolic center that came to represent all that was wrong with Spain in the eyes of dissidents. Numerous nineteenth-century military coups in Madrid had demonstrated that revolutionary action in the Capital could destabilize the government, and destabilization was precisely what the anarcho-republican plot against the King had as its goal. Romanones believed that if there were to be an act of terrorism it would occur in the Iglesia de San Jerónimo where the couple took their vows. He was partly correct as Morral did originally intend to bomb the Church, but the killer was frustrated with Romanones' concentration of policemen and guards there.

Romanones rushed back to his office overlooking the Puerta del Sol when the wedding ceremony ended without incident, and he was relieved when the King and Queen safely came down Carrera San Jerónimo, and crossed the Plaza, also without incident. Romanones was exhausted and had just laid down to rest when he was telephoned with the awful news that an attempt had been made on the Royals and that there were massive casualties along Calle Mayor.[15] The King and Queen were rushed to the Royal Palace while Morral was able to escape the scene by using the panic in the streets as his protective decoy. The Count was despondent and he put up 25,000 pesetas of his own money for information leading to the assassin's capture. The manhunt was on.

Morral ran to Plaza Dos de Mayo in the Malasaña neighborhood of Madrid. Of all the possible republicans, socialists, and anarchists living in Madrid, Morral may have specifically sought out José Nakens whom he admired for much of his adult life.[16] Alvarez Junco maintains that Morral had no premeditated plan for his escape, and that he sought out Nakens because he remembered that Nakens had befriended Michele Angiolillo, the Italian anarchist who assassinated Cánovas in 1897. I am not convinced. As we shall see below, it is quite possible that Ferrer tried to bribe Nakens into believing that he owed a debt to the anarchists just days before Morral appeared at the republican's printing shop. Determining what a dead man did and thought on his last day alive can be foolhardy at best, and we may never really know if he purposefully sought out Nakens. However, it very well could have been that Ferrer had told his troubled follower to specifically seek out Nakens.

Morral stepped into the printing offices of Nakens's *El Motín*, identified himself to Nakens as the perpetrator of the atrocities, and said that he recalled that Nakens had befriended Angiolillo. When Morral asked for Nakens's help, the editor reluctantly agreed. He left Morral hidden in the *El Motín* office while he stepped out to enlist the aid of his friends. Nakens returned some ninety minutes later to pick up Morral and take him to the home of a friend where he was to spend the night while Nakens sought a way to transport him out of Madrid. Morral was suspicious that Nakens's friend would turn him over to the authorities, so he spent that night fleeing Madrid.

The next day, Morral made his way to Torrejón de Ardoz where he sought food and shelter. The villagers figured out who he was based on his handsome but visibly soiled clothes, his sudden appearance in a rural locale, and his Catalan accent and features. Rather than confront him, they sent one of the townsmen (Benito Reyes) to Madrid to report that Morral was in Torrejón. On the 2nd of June, Fructuoso Vega and a couple of village militiamen confronted the Catalan with the intention of detaining him for the authorities, but Morral pulled out his revolver and shot Vega in the face, killing him instantly, before fatally shooting himself in the chest.[17] His body was sent back to Madrid, identified by witnesses, and the Count's reward money went to Vega's widow.

It was not until pictures of Mateo Morral appeared in the pages of the June 4, 1906 issue of *El País* that José Ródenas Colomer, a watchman in Madrid's Parque del Retiro, recalled an incident a week earlier. According to Ródenas, a concerned citizen named Vicente García Ruipérez informed him that two men had carved threats against the King on a tree's bark along the Paseo de Lamas.[18] According to García Ruipérez, one of those men was Mateo Morral who had whittled, "Alfonso XIII shall be executed on the day of his betrothal," and signed it "an unfulfilled one" (*un irredento*).[19] There were also two crosses carved into the bark along with the word "dynamite." Although Ródenas had brought this to the attention of his supervisors, it appears no further action had been taken before the Royal wedding.

The Legal Aftermath for Nakens and Ferrer

While Alejandro Lerroux denied that he had anything to do with the assassination attempt, or even the slightest bit of knowledge of the plot, his most important biographer has shown otherwise. On the afternoon of the wedding day, Lerroux and Ferrer sat at the same Barcelona café—at separate tables, of course—without speaking to each other. Both eagerly waited for news from Madrid, and Lerroux had his lackeys armed and ready to take the fortress at Montjuich.[20] In addition, Lerroux had fallen on very hard times in the Spring of 1906. He had lost control of his popular journal *La Publicidad*, and his inroad into the middle class had been reversed by the new political alignments of *Solidaritat Catalana*, which favored the measured and restrained Salmerón over the revolutionary Lerroux. Though Lerroux was in financial difficulties before the attempted regicide, he suddenly found himself quite wealthy afterward. Ferrer had arranged for Lerroux to control his financial resources while the case against him was being built. Lerroux used some of the money to hire a legal defense team led by Federico Urales (a.k.a. the anarchist, Juan Montseny) and to start various republican journals devoted to freeing Ferrer and Nakens. According to Urales, Gumersindo de Azcárate was asked to join the legal team. However, Azcárate told Urales that he could not defend Ferrer unless he was certain of his innocence. When Urales showed Azcárate the preliminary findings, Azcárate was more convinced than ever that Ferrer was responsible for the attempted regicide.[21] Still, if anyone should count his blessings and profited from the attempted regicide, it was Lerroux.

In the June 2, 1906 issue of *El Motín*, Nakens condemned the attempted regicide, although he did not reveal his role in the events or mention Mateo Morral's name. Nakens said he hated all terrorists but was especially antipathetic toward those cowardly anarchist assassins who were in the business of indiscriminately "killing in bunches."[22] He maintained that he had not devoted his life and his fight to further the cause of these assassins who hid behind their ideology. When he argued that he would feel the same way if leaders of a hypothetical republic (rather than royals) were the objects of assassination, he may have been trying to diffuse some of the intense anger that was sure to come his way once it was discovered that he helped Morral.

Perhaps out of a guilty conscience or perhaps out of a need to grab the national spotlight, Nakens prepared a full confession of his part in the events in an open letter, which appeared in *La Correspondencia de España* and in the Republican daily, *El País*.[23] The irascible Nakens may have dug a bigger hole for himself when he argued that he helped Morral primarily out of a concern for his fellow man and that he was not thinking straight, given how fast the events unfolded. He maintained that he was not sympathetic to the anarchist cause, that he thought Morral was a coward for his actions, and yet he felt obligated to do something for Morral. Nakens added:

> …if tomorrow we were in a Revolution, and if the King, held prisoner and condemned to death by my vote, escaped and sought my help, I would save him from the execration of the people. Do I know what I did is wrong? I do, and though it may not have been the right thing to do, it is what does not cause anguish to my spirit, or perturbation to my conscience. If I had reported that anarchist, I would never be able to fall asleep, and if I could sleep, I would forever have nightmares of a man hanged more as a result of my accusation than for his crime.[24]

The case against José Nakens, who was arrested on June 6, 1906, was a clear-cut and easy one to make. At Nakens's sentencing hearing a year later, Judges Albaladejo, Ortega, and Serantes admonished the journalist for his comportment vis-à-vis Morral, which they argued led to the murder of the Torrejón villager.[25] They did believe that Nakens had never met Morral before he came to him that fateful day, but rejected Nakens's claim that he was not thinking straight because he left Morral alone in his office for ninety minutes while he devised a plan to help the assassin. For his aiding of a criminal, José Nakens was sentenced to nine years of prison, and ordered to pay heavy indemnities to the Royal House, the military, and a fund for the families of those killed or injured in the blast.

Building a case against Francisco Ferrer proved much more difficult. In attempting to prove that the regicide attempt was purely the brainchild of Ferrer, the prosecution played up the schoolmaster's close ties with French and Spanish Anarchists. Prosecutors at Ferrer's trial presented a variety of anarchist and revolutionary propaganda seized from Ferrer's apartment and school.[26] The judges believed that Ferrer encouraged Morral's revolutionary anarchist leanings and felt that Morral directly sought out Nakens because Ferrer had lauded Nakens's newspapers, works, and ideology.[27] In fact, Morral must have come into contact with many of Nakens's works because Ferrer bought anticlerical publications put out by Nakens.

In late 1905, Ferrer had heard that Nakens was in financial difficulties, and he offered to purchase as many books as Nakens could send him for his library and those of his colleagues in Barcelona.[28] The prosecution's case included a series of letters that Ferrer had sent Nakens just prior to the regicide attempt. Ferrer sent Nakens a promissory bank note for 1,000 pesetas and a letter asking him to write a series of curriculum books for the Modern School. Nakens received this mail on May 26, 1906, while Morral was in Madrid. Nakens was deeply puzzled. Despite his constant call for revolution, he considered himself an outspoken enemy of the anarchists, and though he had maintained a cordial correspondence relationship with Ferrer for some fifteen years, he considered Ferrer to be an anarchist agitator. Nakens wrote Ferrer back to tell him that he would not write books for the Modern School, he declined the 1,000 pesetas, and he told Ferrer that it was inappropriate for an enemy of anarchism to write books for Ferrer's enterprise.[29] On the May 31, 1906, the day Morral tried to kill the King and Queen, Nakens received a response from Ferrer, in which Ferrer wrote that if there were no books to be written then there were no books to be written, but that Nakens should still hold onto the money to fund his important journalistic endeavors.[30] We probably will never know if Ferrer tried to bribe Nakens into believing he owed Ferrer a favor and/or to predispose Nakens to aid the troubled Morral on the day of his violent crime.

The prosecution hoped that these letters would be the smoking guns that would send Ferrer to prison for sixteen years for conspiracy to commit regicide. However, the Judges were not convinced. They ruled to exonerate Ferrer on the crime of conspiracy, arguing that all evidence pointing to him as the mastermind behind an anarchist plot was circumstantial. However, the Judges did take the opportunity to publicly attack Ferrer's character, reputation, and project. He was called a dangerous anarchist whose so-called Modern School's curriculum "taught children in such a way as to undermine the fundamental values toward the State, Religion, the Family and the Fatherland (*Patria*)," and they maligned Ferrer for financially supporting periodicals that were offensive to the Regime, such as *El Motín*.[31] Though Ferrer and his theories were called morally reprehensible by the Judges, they determined he never went beyond the bounds of freedom of expression and conscience dictated by the Constitution.

Although Ferrer was released after having served a year and eighteen days in jail, Nakens and his friends Bernardo Mata and Isidro Ibarra were not so lucky. Only half of the time served between their arrest in June of 1906 and the sentencing on June 24, 1907 was allowed to be counted against their sentences. The despondent Nakens maintained that he could not stomach reading any newspapers for the first four months of his incarceration.[32] He was not aware of any campaign among republican newspapers demanding a royal pardon for him.

The campaign to pardon Nakens, who was sixty-five in 1907, picked up momentum when he became a vocal advocate for prison reform. Beginning with an October 1906 article in *El País*—the republican daily that had offered Nakens unlimited space so that he could discuss his life in prison—Nakens drew attention to the squalid conditions of the majority of the penitentiary's prisoners.[33] Although Nakens himself enjoyed a small (albeit larger than his office at *El Motín*), clean, and comfortable cell in the Cárcel Modelo in Madrid, he wrote that many of the prisoners suffered from disease, malnourishment, cold, and demoralization.[34] Conditions were made worse by the abuses and neglect of underpaid prison guards and by priests who offered neither religious services nor comfort to the prisoners.[35] Although he maintained a solemn tone throughout his column, anticlericalism continued to be Nakens's *raison d'être*, only that now anticlericalism was meshed with his call for making incarceration more humane. He echoed earlier calls among prison authorities that envisioned a secular prison system, devoid of a clerical presence, and which emphasized rehabilitation over punishment and proselytization.[36] In many ways, the "Honorable Delinquent," as Romanones called Nakens,[37] was able to win back many of the people who were angry and disillusioned with him and by his role in the assassination attempt.

By November of 1906, the campaign to have Nakens pardoned became multifaceted: not only were the republican papers calling for his pardon, but appeals by prison officials suggested that Nakens was a model prisoner, who was resigned to his long sentence, and clearly a reformed individual.[38] The campaign continued as the prime minister and the cabinet members received daily letters from journalists, politicians, and other supporters—both Spanish and international—demanding Nakens's pardon. Eventually, the campaign worked; based on recommendations from President Antonio Maura dated May 8, 1908, King Alfonso XIII granted Nakens, Mata, and Ibarra their pardon and they were free to go some ten days later. Because "he was as impoverished when he came out of jail as Robinson (Crusoe) was when he washed up on an island," Nakens was unable to restart *El Motín* until October of 1908.[39] However, when it resumed, Nakens made clear that he was going to return to the paper's roots and offer constant attacks against the clergy and its supporters.[40] Ever more radicalized, Nakens put it simply upon his release:

> I warmly salute the liberal press from that of the conservatives to that of the anarchists.
>
> And I spit on the clerical press.[41]

With radical anticlericalism as its primary focus, and its low point during Nakens's incarceration behind it, *El Motín* continued to enjoy a small yet constant presence well into the Primo de Rivera dictatorship.

Unpacking the Lessons of the Attempted Regicide

There are many lessons to be learned from the day anarchism collided with republican anticlericalism in Spain. First of all, this episode reminds us there was a broad anticlerical milieu that crossed political and class lines. While republicans, especially the radicals, had been dealing in anticlerical imagery since the beginning of the Restoration, anticlericalism was not the exclusive domain of the republicans. Instead, anticlericalism was a remarkably unifying force for numerous elements of the opposition to the regime. Because anarchism was very much committed to the destruction of the existing society in order to construct a new, organic society devoid of hierarchical institutions, and because anticlericalism was an effective form of mobilization for the revolutionary left, the radical republicans' expert manipulation of anticlerical imagery and their criticism of the Church's power in society provided a link between republicans and the revolutionary left.

Of course, I do not mean to exaggerate the influence Nakens and other republican intellectuals exercised over other opposition movements, least of all the multifaceted Spanish anarchist movement. The anarchists' antistatist and antireligious views were shaped by a diverse group of thinkers, including Bakunin, Kropotkin, Comte, and Nietzsche, whose works appeared in both anarchist and republican journals.[42] As we shall see, the collaboration that an anarchist pedagogue such as Ferrer sought with Nakens was indicative of the libertarian movement, and thus it was not uncommon for the writings of freethinkers and republicans such as Nakens, but also Francisco Pi y Margall, to be published in anarchist journals and newspapers. Furthermore, scholars have demonstrated that anarchist antinationalism can be vastly overstated given the importance of their community, a *patria chica* (a mini-Fatherland), as that which makes possible the self-improvement of the members of that community, and given that collaboration with political forces, even with state institutions, could also spring from anarchist apoliticism.[43] Thus, while not responsible for providing anarchists with the ideological structures they needed to articulate their anticlerical and antimonarchist beliefs, republicans such as Nakens, and later on Lerroux, contributed to the very fluid and diverse melting pot of Spanish anarchist ideology.

As case studies of Restoration urban centers reveal, radical republicanism's vitality and support came from people's adherence to its cultural vision.[44] In the republican mind-set, the regime, clerical and monarchical in essence, represented the type of backwardness that the nation had been trying to slough off since the beginning of the nineteenth century. In order to regenerate the Spanish nation, the pillars of the regime (that is the monarchy, the clergy, and the oligarchy) had to be vanquished so republicans could replace old Spain with a modern, secular, and democratic version of the nation.[45] Getting there, of course, as established in chapters two and three, was made difficult by the fact that republicanism never operated successfully at the national level during the Restoration. Traditional republican strongholds in cities and regions like Barcelona, Madrid, Valencia, and Asturias were dominated by local political leaders who were often not tied to a national party. Repeated efforts by some republicans, such as José Nakens in 1903, to unify the movement were thwarted by entrenched regionalism and political rivalries. Notwithstanding these setbacks, the fact that republicanism never articulated a concrete plan during the Restoration and that republican politicians were prone to populist demagoguery as well as the dramatization of everyday life did not hurt the movement. Republicanism was the only movement that attracted sizeable segments of the nonsocialist, non-anarchist working class, as well as the petite bourgeoisie, and blended protest against social injustices with its vision of a modern Spain. The republican rhetoric of purifying Spain, fixing the injustices present in Spain, and destroying the power base of the clergy, monarchy, and aristocracy also allowed republicans to win over, or at least influence, segments of the revolutionary left.

Nakens himself was not a politician, but in the nature of his appeals he prefigured Lerroux and Blasco Ibáñez. This new generation of radical republicans injected vigor into the republican message through anticlericalism and making overtures to social revolutionaries, as well as through an organizational machine that mobilized the masses. Nakens was identified with anticlericalism more than anyone else in Spain. Though he was the driving force behind the failed attempts to unify the republican movement in 1903, his anticlericalism defined him. Thus, while Nakens lacked the organizational talents that Lerroux and Blasco were blessed with, his style of propaganda helped establish the rhetorical framework for bringing in a broader constituency to the republican movement.

Anarchists were themselves divided between forming a coherent libertarian ideology and embracing the dynamism of the "new politics" offered by radical republicans. But it is important to keep in mind that anarchism was, at this time, tremendously fluid in its philosophy.[46] The same type of anticlerical-republican fantasy or utopia that Nakens, Lerroux, and Blasco pontificated about was easily subsumed into a wider revolutionary anarchist ideal. Our understanding of the relationship between republicans, anarchists, and socialists, who all had to contend for the same political spaces in order to spearhead mobilization, has been enriched by the above-mentioned historiography, and clearly there were many ways in which the radical republicans helped establish networks between these three major opponents of the regime.[47]

Libertarian/anarchist literature during the Restoration often talked about a "nefarious trilogy" of capital, religion, and state, which anarchists dedicated their lives to toppling.[48] In that order, capitalism was the first and foremost of exploitative forces to overcome, but it was also linked to the other two as it was widely believed by the revolutionary left that the role of the clergy was that of agents who reinforced the economic and political exploitation of the people.[49] Anarchist propaganda, like that of Nakens and other radical republicans, often blamed the Church and clergy for Spain's deficiencies. The libertarian intellectual José López Montenegro writing in the anarchist journal *Los Desheredados* illustrated this point:

> The tremendous Inquisition
> prevented the lovely flight
> with which the nation's knowledge
> had already taken off toward the skies:
> burned at the stake, without compassion,
> were the sages of yore,
> and the country of Cervantes,
> with its glorious possibilities,
> was humbled by those loathsome,
> miserable Jesuits.[50]

Here, the attention to the Inquisition is not at all different from Nakens's attempts to appropriate history in order to discredit the contemporary Church and clergy through the proliferation of almanacs and ephemera detailing the tortures used by the Inquisitors on the "infidels."

Anticlerical anarchist cartoons also mirrored many of the themes present in the radical republican press. A cartoon on the cover of the December 26, 1890 issue of the Madrid-based *La Anarquía* (Anarchy) depicts a bishop, flanked by a priest and a bourgeois on his right and a monk and a military officer on his left, sitting at a dinner table and about to eat duck, ham, and lobster.[51] The depiction of gluttonous clergymen was a common theme in the republican press and even that of the left-liberals of the Glorious Revolution of 1868. For example, the May 23, 1869 issue of the Barcelona-based *La Flaca* included an illustration of inebriated nuns and monks gorging themselves with food and even more wine under a painting of Charles VII, the ultramontane Carlist Pretender to the Throne.[52] The cartoon in the July 5, 1883 issue of Nakens's *El Clarín* (*El Motín*'s temporary name in the summer of 1883) juxtaposed three fat priests enjoying a bottle of wine while a peasant works the nearby fields.[53] The cover of the March 11, 1904 *Tierra y Libertad* shows a corpulent man in a top hat and fine clothing squeezing a naked and impoverished worker until he spits out gold while civil guards stand by.[54] This illustration harkens back to another one in the April 19, 1885 issue of *El Motín*, in which a villager, reduced down to his skeleton, hands over his skin to Cánovas (the representative of the state) while the civil guards reinforce the prime minister's authority.[55] Nakens's very popular *Cuadros de Miseria* (Scenes of Misery)—a collection of essays from *El Motín* centered around the theme of exploited and impoverished Spaniards juxtaposed with rich, corrupt clergymen—was warmly received by the Madrid-based anarchist journal, *La Voz del Cantero.*[56]

These common themes in both anarchist and republican literature— both in written and illustrated form—demonstrate the presence of the broad anticlerical milieu and the fine line that separates radical republicanism from anarchism. Clearly, support for property rights separated republicans from anarchists, and that would constitute the single biggest obstacle to true collaboration between them. However, the shared discourse, vocabulary, and symbolism of anticlericalism bound radical republicans to the revolutionary left. For socialists and anarchists, Nakens's special brand of insulting, sarcastic, and genuine hatred of the clergy in Spain was more important than his republicanism. Nakens's anticlericalism became their anticlericalism, and anticlerical members of all classes could vicariously insult priests and nuns in their lives through Nakens's constant attacks.

Initially, the socialists were indifferent, if not hostile, to anticlericalism. Spanish socialists believed that the Church, like the state, would disappear with the social revolution. Their tendency toward materialism led them to regard anticlericalism as a "halfway measure, more attractive to the middle class than to the proletariat."[57] In fact, Pablo Iglesias, the founder and longtime leader of the Socialist Party, once wrote that "to excite the proletariat into directing its activism and energy against the clericals rather than their bosses is the worst error to which those aspiring to end human exploitation can fall victim."[58] However, as trade union membership declined, the movement shifted its attitudes. Because the anarcho-syndicalist trade union (the CNT), and to a lesser extent Catholic labor syndicates, posed serious threats to socialist recruitment, local socialists often found themselves in tenuous alliances with middle-class republicans on the issue of anticlericalism. Certainly socialists saw the utilitarian value of anticlericalism to further their own goals, and as Joan Connelly Ullman reminds us, anticlericalism "crossed class borders as few other issues could do."[59]

The assassination attempt and its aftermath also remind us that a common vocabulary of anticlericalism and revolution among anarchists, republicans, and socialists was transmitted through common practices or rituals. Restoration newspapers were not read in the same manner that we read newspapers today. Although the majority of the Spanish population was illiterate throughout the Restoration, and although the regime depended upon a depoliticized populace in order to maintain itself in power, it is not at all unlikely that many of the illiterate Spaniards were exposed to a multiplicity of ideas and movements presented in the press. Very often small newspapers like *El Motín*, whose circulation may not have exceeded 12,000 copies each week,[60] were read aloud to crowds at pubs, athenaeums, or meetings. Sometimes the articles and criticisms within *El Motín* were read out loud to family members. In his memoirs, the prolific literary critic Rafael Cansinos Asséns recalled that his republican uncle read aloud the pages of *El Motín* prompting his wife and Cansinos' sisters to cover their ears.[61] It follows that Nakens's brand of anticlerical discourse could have been subsumed into the cosmos of the revolutionary left. At the very least, the revolutionary left was exposed to Nakens's work and ideas, and the circulation of these ideas went beyond the reading public.

Despite the fact that nearly two-thirds of the total Spanish population could not read at the start of the twentieth century, Nakens's anticlerical messages did make their way not only to the educated middle classes but also the illiterate working classes.[62] Ramiro de Maeztu, one of the pillars of the literary Generation of 1898, described a reading in the November 28, 1901 issue of *El Imparcial*. He wrote:

These books, pamphlets, newspapers, are not read in the same manner that others, such as the bourgeoisie, read, nor do they end up the same way. The bourgeois' book…once read, passes onto the library where it shall sit untouched and dormant, until his sons and daughters rediscover it, should they become curious when they grow up. But, the reader of an anarchist and worker book in general does not have a library nor does he buy books only for himself. The writer of this article has been present during the reading of *La conquista del pan* (Kropotkin's *The Conquest of Bread*) in a worker's home. In one room, illuminated only by a candle, up to fourteen workers would meet every winter's night. With difficulties, they would read to one another, and listen. Only the crackling of the candle's flame would interrupt the silence when the reader stopped at a period. I have also been present at the reading of the Bible in a puritan family's home; the sensation was the identical to that in the other home. The same can be said of the press. They read an infinite number of bourgeois newspapers, but (within them) current events dominate […and] the interest they awaken is purely fleeting. The same does not happen with anarchist newspapers. What current events are related in these—almost always about the conflicts between capital and labor— merely represents one third or one quarter of the issues and the rest is dedicated to questions of doctrine. The issue is stored and the influence of these publications will survive beyond death. I know of many people that conserve the complete collection of these newspapers. How many weeklies can we say the same thing about?[63]

Of course, *El Motín* was not all text, and its very popular anticlerical cartoons did not require a literate audience to invoke a response.

Roger Chartier reminds us that "it is important to remember that no text exists outside of the support that enables it to be read; any comprehension of a writing, no matter what kind it is, depends on the forms in which it reaches the reader."[64] That Maeztu chose to equate the reading of anarchist newspapers with the reading of the Bible is also very telling. This nightly mass-ceremony of sitting around a candle listening to the reading of a newspaper became a very powerful way of transferring knowledge, because it served as a substitute for prayer; the printed materials encouraged silent adherence to causes whose advocates addressed an invisible public from afar.[65] Just as the Spanish-bourgeois newspaper reader who saw others of his same class reading the same newspapers and thereby felt assured that his imagined community was also theirs, members of the illiterate working class—be they anarchists, socialists or republicans, themselves—could share in the radical republicans' imagining of national community through the common print language of the press.

It is true that neither Ferrer nor Morral was illiterate. However, before Morral came to work with Ferrer, the young terrorist engaged in the spreading of propaganda among the workers in the form of libertarian and radical republican pamphlets and posters.[66] Thus, it was not only well-educated libertarians such as Morral who had access to republican or radical messages. These messages often filtered down to the anarchist, socialist, and republican workers through the assistance of men such as Morral. In the case of the attempted regicide, Ferrer, an *El Motín* subscriber living in Barcelona, passed on his copies of the tiny Madrid-based newspaper to his close friend who might have decided, on the basis of reading them, that Nakens would be sympathetic to his cause. Keeping in mind this ancillary reading quality of Restoration newspapers should also remind us that José Nakens was one of many important Restoration journalists whose words went beyond the eyes, ears, and hearts of his targeted audience.

Many anarchists, socialists, and republicans counted on Nakens's weekly dose of wicked anticlericalism for a variety of reasons. Some may have wanted to be entertained, some may have been blindly loyal to the charismatic Nakens, and some may have believed that Nakens's vision of a radical and anticlerical republic was the imagined community in which they wanted to live. Lily Litvak's impressive survey of anarchist literary culture demonstrates that Nakens was well-received among anarchist readers. Often his columns appeared in anarchist newspapers such as *Los Desheredados* (The Disinherited) from Sabadell, which, incidentally, was Morral's home town.[67] Within these articles and many like them in the pages of *El Motín*, Nakens addressed issues that were of tremendous importance to the anarchists.[68] In "El hambre y la deshonra" (Hunger and Dishonor), Nakens addressed the injustices of the political and economic systems that, for example, allegedly forced women into prostitution so that their children or siblings could have bread to eat. Nakens lacked any evidence and never delved deeply into the socioeconomic origins of prostitution of the times. Whether it was true or not that the Restoration regime forced Spanish women into prostitution is not nearly as important as the utility of Nakens's language in bringing together aggrieved republicans and libertarians. In the Restoration public sphere, republicans were especially successful at "structuring attention" in order to win acceptance of their own institutions, symbols, and values with the ultimate goal being the obliteration of the hegemonic Catholic culture. This campaign was not ignored but rather embraced not only by anarchist leaders such as Ferrer but also by the rank and file. Even a small newspaper such as *El Motín* reminds us of the powerful impact that the press had in describing events and defining community among republicans, socialists in Madrid, and even Catalan anarchists.

Yet the existence of the anticlerical milieu and of a widely shared language of anticlericalism among republicans, socialists, and anarchists did not constitute a shared vision of the nation. Despite the fact that anticlericalism was a powerful discourse, it could not completely unify the republicans amongst themselves, and it could not completely reconcile republicanism with everyone on the left. While Nakens's anticlericalism was part of his nationalism, which was very much central to all republicans, anticlericalism could have no such nationalistic connotations for members of the revolutionary left who favored *patria chica* conceptions of their community over such bourgeois categories as "nations." Nakens failed to realize that there is an important distinction between a common discourse, on one hand, and the uses to which that common discourse is put, on the other. While the anticlerical language and symbolism of radical republicans was linked to an alternate vision of the Spanish nation, they attracted members of the revolutionary left who were not interested in republican nationalism because they were not interested in the orthodox, bourgeois-inspired, conceptualizations of nations.

Despite becoming a hero to some anarchists, Nakens fought very hard to distance himself from them. Part of his defense strategy at the attempted regicide case was to submit to the court a series of anti-anarchist articles that he had written over the course of his career. Among the articles he listed was an *El Motín* open letter to Blasco Ibáñez, Lerroux, and two other republican leaders, which lamented that there were so many Spanish workers who adhered to political movements and doctrines that were not based on the tenets of the French Revolution.[69] Another essay berated radical members of the republican movement who attended socialist demonstrations and meetings.[70] Yet another essay offered a patriotic and pro-military speech replete with jingoistic overtones.[71] Nakens may have chosen this particular article entitled "O con los unos, ó con los otros" (Either with one or with the others) in order to ingratiate himself with the authorities because in it he argued that one could not simultaneously be loyal to the internationalist-revolutionary workers and the military. Because many of the casualties of Morral's assassination attempt were soldiers and guards, he believed he could only do well if he distanced himself from the anarchists.

Nakens even supplied the court with a series of letters written in September of 1902 between himself and the then minister of the Interior (*Gobernación*) Segismundo Moret.[72] In these letters, Nakens writes about rumors that Moret's agents had been spying on him. Nakens inquired about this surveillance, and Moret assured him that the Ministry was not spying on him, saying:

> What has happened is that someone very close to me, who is righteous and of high social standing, has told me about EL MOTIN, praising the valor and clarity with which you attack the excesses of the anarchists, who cause so much harm to the working class. We naturally talked about the indirect benefit that your newspaper and its work is doing for the interests of the conservative classes.
>
> With this in mind, we would like to facilitate the circulation of your newspaper, especially in Barcelona, where so many obstacles to the working class becoming familiar with your valiant affirmations present themselves. And this person indicated to me the possibility of acquiring a considerable number of copies so that we can distribute them for free.[73]

With Moret's compliments in mind, we can see how Nakens deluded himself into thinking he was an enemy, even an officially sanctioned enemy, of anarchism. Indeed, Nakens had complemented his anticlerical attacks and his antimonarchy rhetoric with frequent written misgivings about the growth of the revolutionary left. During his tenure at *El Motín,* Cansinos Asséns recalled that Nakens was quite hostile to the working-class movement:

> ...The workers!—shouted Nakens....The workers are fine. You're telling *me,* who has to struggle with them constantly....They are only motivated by their interests..., the eight hour work day and a wage increase....They have no ideals....The other day I fired an apprentice, a real snoop, who came to me with some grievances....Look son,—I (Nakens) said—, you know a lot about accounting....Take your cap and scram![74]

Nakens was also quite hostile to Pablo Iglesias, the founder of the Spanish Socialist Party, who was revered as an almost Messianic figure by his constituency. Since the late 1880s, Nakens impugned Iglesias as a man who never got his hands dirty yet aspired to lead those who did so for a living.[75] Nakens saw both the Church and the internationalist working-class movements as supranational impediments to his imagined community. As a *zorrillista* and a military veteran himself, Nakens resented attacks directed at the army by members of the revolutionary left, and he often waxed poetically about the role the military would have in safeguarding the coming Republic.

Clearly there was a deep gulf between the way Nakens intended his work to be read or understood and how it was actually received by members of the revolutionary working class. That this was the case speaks to an inherent paradox within Republican circles: many republicans were eager to increase their constituency among the Spanish working classes, but they were also afraid of them and hostile to revolutionary left forms of mobilizing workers. While Lerroux seemed particularly adept and comfortable at drawing workers to him and navigating through anarchist circles, older mainstream republicans avoided and discouraged allying with the revolutionary left. Nakens, it appears, was neither fully in one camp nor the other and for that he became political roadkill as a result of his role in the attempted regicide's aftermath.

In addition, the gulf between Nakens's intentions and the reception of his ideas demonstrates the tremendous flexibility and fluidity of anticlericalism, because his, particularly, was simultaneously a high-brow and cultured offering as well as a lowbrow, comic, base, and popular offering. The fact that the work of a staunchly anti-anarchist republican was so popular among the anarchists forces us to recognize the fluid circulation of shared symbols and discourse that crossed social boundaries during the Restoration. It seems everybody among the revolutionary left was bound to each other through shared anticlerical symbols. However, while these symbols were linked to nationalism for Nakens and perhaps republican workers, they were not necessarily so linked for anarchists and socialists. This ambiguity of the symbols themselves explains Nakens's confused position between republicans and anarchists, and it points to the weaknesses of anticlerical nationalism.

Despite anticlericalism's unique power to cut across social, economic, and political demarcations, it was too powerful for any one group to control. Anticlericalism was multivocal: it offered too many messages. Because it could not automatically be tied to a nationalist project, as Nakens hoped, it did not function as a particularly cohesive discourse of national identity. The reader with a rudimentary education who read or listened to a reading of El Motín gained knowledge from the recurrence of coded forms, from repetition of themes, and from the newspaper's images. After all, what the most learned of anticlericals wrote and mass-produced had been incorporated into the "cultural style" of those groups that would engage in future anticlerical riots. These writings informed, convinced, and encouraged those forms of anticlerical violence.[76] However, the same reader or listener did not automatically believe what Nakens believed, nor did he suddenly understand anticlericalism to be anything but a step toward the obliteration of the oppressive capitalist system. We can see, with hindsight, that Nakens was tremendously naïve to think that his message, which praised progress, egalitarianism, and democracy as well as calling for immediate political and cultural revolution against the regime, would not attract those to him whom he considered his enemies. The same can be said of his messages that juxtaposed the avarice and wealth of the aristocracy and the clergy with the misery of the people (el pueblo español), and which was presented with a plethora of cultural images and symbols.

The attempted regicide of 1906 exposed deep divisions within Spanish republicanism during the Restoration. Nakens's caustic anticlericalism and reiterated calls for a revolutionary republican government found wide popular acceptance, but they were also a source of discord with more mainstream republican leaders such as Salmerón and Azcárate.[77] To these men, Nakens was an embarrassment rather than an asset. Azcárate's relationship with Nakens had grown hostile ever since Azcárate refused to help Nakens distribute anti-Carlist propaganda, which led Nakens to call Azcárate a clerical sympathizer.[78] On the religious question, Nakens and Azcárate could never agree. Azcárate's correspondence with Nakens bears this out:

> When it comes to religion, I have said, and I will continue to say what I, myself, personally think is completely clear. But when it comes to political-religious questions, when I speak as a man of our party, my slogan is this: Religion is one thing and theocracy is another; Catholicism one and the other ultramontanism; the clergy one and clericalism the other. The republican party has nothing against Religion, nor Catholicism, nor with the clergy; but it has to be, by necessity, a resolved and decisive opponent of theocracy, ultramontanism and clericalism because these form political parties whose juridical and political principles are incompatible with democracy.[79]

Unlike Azcárate, Nakens was unwilling or incapable of divorcing his anticlerical convictions from a broad agenda of republican nationalism; Nakens refused to let go of his Manichean view of the nation divided between clericals and anticlericals. Though Nakens was much older than the *republicanos energéticos*,[80] the so-called energetic republican generation that included Lerroux and Blasco Ibáñez, Nakens prefigured their impatience and constant tugs-of-war with the traditional republican leadership in Madrid over the direction of the republican movement.

In 1905, with the collapse of the Republican Union—the organization that Nakens helped bring about in 1903—Nakens began to attack Salmerón, one of the most respected republicans in the nation and the only remaining ex-president of the First Republic. On June 17, 1905, Nakens crystallized his anger and impatience with the old generation of republicans when he wrote an open letter to Salmerón in *El Motín*. In it, Nakens demanded that Salmerón explain to the republican party how he would help further the revolutionary cause. Nakens maintained that there was discontent within the republican movement and he made a vague threat about a rank-and-file mutiny against Salmerón's ineffective leadership.[81] Men such as Salmerón and Azcárate were gradualist republicans who tried to work within the Restoration regime, tempered their anticlericalism, and were panic-stricken at the idea of a mobilized and out-of-control working class.

At the Madrid republican assembly of July 15–16, 1905, Salmerón angrily attacked the impatient element within the party "that felt it was possible to accomplish a revolution within two years when Spain had been unable to produce one for the last thirty years and not even after the humiliating disaster of 1898."[82] He refused to serve as Nakens's "republican dictator" whose mission was to organize a military revolution, and maligned as morally repugnant those who took part in the 1905 attempted assassination of Alfonso XIII in Paris.[83] So long as the Madrid-based leaders collided with revolutionary republicans such as Lerroux, Blasco, and Nakens, the movement could not proceed as a truly viable mobilizing force.[84]

Nakens's tragedy is poignantly highlighted in his difficult decision to hide and assist an anarchist who had tried to kill the King, a decision that reflected his peculiar position between republicans and anarchists. Nakens's actions meant that he would forever be discredited in republican circles, which seemed to prove Salmerón and company right; Nakens and his followers were a problem to the republicans, and if his supporters included Lerroux and Blasco, then they too were dangerous. At best, Nakens would be considered an "honorable delinquent" or crazy grandfather by his peers from that point on, and this signaled a temporary victory of the gradualist republicans over their revolutionary brothers. The attempted regicide showed that Nakens was a man trapped between a following of the revolutionary left that he did not desire and a republican movement that he could not completely win over.

The Gendered Language of Republican Anticlericalism

In many ways the *machista*, often misogynist, attitudes in the work of José Nakens illustrate those same attitudes in a number of republican men during the Restoration whose anxieties were piqued especially with Spain's humiliating defeat to the United States in 1898. Relatively new research demonstrates that some elite and educated women were present alongside their republican brothers in political groups, clubs, and activities since the middle of the nineteenth century; however, a gendered language that cut down women and publicized stereotypes of the sexes persisted during the Restoration.[1] This book gives pride of place to the importance of symbols and representation in the construction of collective identities and how these are manipulated for political purposes. This chapter will focus on the gendered language of republican anticlericalism, which was an instrument designed to unify men in the attack against the Catholic Church and clergy, and in the quest for a Second Spanish Republic. That the gendered language of anticlerical nationalism was replete with pornographic, homoerotic, comic, and misogynist undercurrents suggests this discourse was limited and divisive.

This chapter illustrates that the anticlerical-nationalist message of radical republicanism was gendered because republicans, certainly radical republicans such as Nakens, Lerroux, and Blasco Ibáñez, understood the clergy to be the single most significant threat to the ideal patriarchal family. José Alvarez Junco's biography of Lerroux pointed to the importance of gendered language, specifically Lerroux's manliness, in cultivating his image as a mover, a shaker, and a leader.[2] For Lerroux, generating support was not the only reason for gendered language; it also built upon gendered understandings of women, men, and priests to potentially unite disparate groups of Spaniards. Nakens demonstrated that languages of nationalism need not be exclusively sober and serious. Sexual jokes and reveling in misogyny were important avenues by which some Restoration republican males bonded and worked to exclude women from leadership positions of their movement.

Anticlericalism was not just a central plank in republican ideology, but also the most desirable and natural discourse in the criticism of what republicans considered premodern and irrational relations between men and women, state and society, and the public and private spheres. Anticlericalism featured a gendered component for both practical and ideological reasons: not only had the Church held tremendous influence over education, finances, and law, but also its views of celibacy, sexuality, marriage, and masculine and feminine ideals were anathema to republicans. Over the course of the Restoration, the republican press created and promulgated a discourse on sexual anxiety, arguing that as Spain continued to languish, so too did the power and virility of Spanish men. For this reason, the republicans were consumed with curbing the religiosity of Catholic women who were supposedly under their priests' thumbs. This was particularly crucial because of their belief that Catholic women colluded with priests in order to turn Spanish children against Liberalism, and specifically, Republicanism.

The central organizing principle of radical republican anticlericalism was the belief that the clergy, above all else, represented the most significant obstacle to the sudden and no less magical resolution of the Spanish national problem.[3] With Spain's humiliating defeat in the Spanish-American War, the republicans had ample proof their nightmare of an emasculated Spain run by priests controlling their sexual resources (women) had become a reality. The once proud nation that dominated one of the largest empires the world had ever seen under Philip II was exposed as decrepit and dysfunctional when parvenu America stripped Spain off Cuba, Puerto Rico, and the Philippine Islands. Spain was ill; Spanish men watched as the Church and clergy threatened and undermined home and family, the building blocks of the nation.

The republicans' search for explanations and solutions was shaped by anticlericalism and gender ideology, which linked women and the clergy as potent enemies not only of the rationalization of human relations but also the republican family ideal and the forward progress of the Spanish nation.[4] Spanish republican men of the Restoration were particularly concerned with what went on in the confessional between their mothers, wives, daughters, sisters, and the priests; the hypersexuality or dysfunction of both women and priests; the "emancipation" of women; and the honor of the once proud and virile Spanish nation sapped of its vigor by the Church and clergy and its hold over Spanish women.

Borrowing from the French Republican Traditions

One of the most salient elements of Restoration republicanism was their profound admiration for the French Third Republic as a model of good government. Though the Third Republic was notoriously insecure and unstable, to Spanish republicans France was a land that had synthesized good citizenship with empire, and social modernization with strong political unity. To Spanish republicans France was where intellectuals were listened to, where women were prettier, and where the people had been nationalized into being partners in secular, civic-minded education and the fight against the Church.[5] Despite the deep divisions that arose within the Republican movement after the spectacular failure of the First Republic and the fact that more often than not they lacked concrete political platforms and goals, there were terrains of thought and society in which Spanish republicans were in agreement. Most republicans were united in their Francophilia because the Third Republic was the polity that encapsulated their resolve to rid their own nation of the monarchy, regenerate a dying popular spirit, and curtail the central role of the Church and clergy.

As great admirers of the Third Republic, Spanish republicans often absorbed the political ideologies of brothers to the north of the Pyrenees. Alvarez Junco's analyses of Spanish republican culture revealed that they were "fetishists" not only for scientific knowledge that often collided with traditional Catholic dogma, but also for the often anticlerical cultural ethos and aesthetic of men such as Renan, Hugo, Dumas, Tolstoy, Rousseau, Diderot, Taine, Proudhon, Balzac, Anatole France, Ibsen, Bakunin, Lamennais, Michelet, Flaubert, Stendhal, and Vigny.[6] The thoughts and writing of these men appeared most frequently in the pages of the Spanish republican press, which also serialized novels by Eugène Sue, Dumas, Balzac, Hugo, and Lamartine, among others. Rousseau was particularly important to republicans on both sides of the Pyrenees, and Spanish republicans romanticized France as the land of Rousseau's Social Contract: the nation where men enjoyed equality, a participatory democracy, and were no longer beholden to the patriarchal authority of the king.

In addition to their enthusiasm for the Third Republic's intellectual traditions, Spanish republicans also absorbed French gendered assumptions about the nature of men and women, Rousseau's especially. His obsession with sexual differences led him to assert that women were incapable of justice and civic participation and should serve the Republic as mothers, instillers of civic values to their children, and objects of men's delight. In the "Discourse on the Origin of Inequality," Rousseau writes of a constant tension between men and women, who privilege sentimentality and abstraction to the point of establishing "their hegemony and mak(ing) dominant the sex that ought to obey."[7] Rousseau's Republic has a place for women because they possess tremendous power to socialize man through sexual relations and demarcating public and private/home life.[8]

The formulation of separate spheres for the sexes became embedded in most of the political ideologies of the nineteenth century, not just French republicanism. Idyllic forms of the social contract in which individuals exchange the insecurity of the state of nature for equality before the state, as well as ideals of male and female behavior, companionate marriage, and a patriarchal family structure as the cornerstone of the nation were diffused among Continental liberals after the French Revolution.[9] However, as Rousseau assumed that women were naturally inferior to men even in the state of nature and thus incapable or ill-suited to participate in political life, so too did many European republicans who were inheritors of his tradition.

Underneath the social contract—underneath all social contracts—argues Carole Pateman, lies an unstated sexual contract among men that equates sexual difference with political difference, establishes that political life and creativity comes from men, and subjugates women.[10] The Western Europe-wide attempt to construct an ideal nuclear family and establish the role of women as devoted mothers and obedient housewives in the nineteenth century was threatened by new pressures such as industrialization. In France, especially, republicans were active in promoting social programs, such as education reform, that would provide women with the skills and knowledge necessary for them to perform their gendered functions and remove women from the control of the Catholic Church.[11] In this way, women could contribute to the modern industrialized society and make a quantum leap from premodern orders or lifestyles. Just as in France, ideals of Spanish women as industrious homemakers were cherished, and though there were efforts in both countries to reform the status of women—for instance granting them access to education—these were informed by an ideological concern for consolidating the sexual division of labor, perpetuating the gender system, and guaranteeing the traditional public/private asymmetry between the sexes.[12]

In both France and Spain, the Republic as understood by republicans was the creation of Reason and the best political plan for the rationalization of human relations.[13] More than a simple philosophy or a current of public opinion, republicanism was a conceptualization of the universe that privileged scientific knowledge and mechanistic explanations for the world while disparaging premodern, fanatical, and superstitious mentalities. Republicans did not question their gendered expectations of men, women, and families because they simply believed their assumptions reflected the proper interaction between the sexes that allowed both sexes to do what their specific nature oriented them toward and ensure men had a space wherein they could be public, political, and intellectual in pursuing the common good. Thus, Demófilo's 1883 article "La Familia" in *Las Dominicales del Libre Pensamiento*, in which he argued that the proper state of affairs for the republican man was to have a loving helpmate stay at home where she filled the household with her "waves of love," is but one of the many examples of domestic bliss in the republican and Masonic press.[14]

As one of the main (albeit disorganized and marginalized) voices of opposition to the constitutional monarchy, republicans condemned the Restoration regime for its illiberalism and inability to transform the political, social, and cultural life of Spain. The nationalist nature of republican anticlericalism has been established in previous chapters, but the gendered quality of that discourse merits a detailed exploration, especially since its exclusivity was emblematic of the limits of republican anticlerical nationalism. The male republican machismo, sexism and, at times, misogynist understandings of women would persist deep into the twentieth century and inform very difficult debates on women's rights, suffrage, and divorce during the Second Spanish Republic.[15] I now turn to the most common themes of anxiety among Restoration radical republican men.

Anxieties Surrounding the Confessional

Republicans on both sides of the Pyrenees not only saw priests as threats to patriarchal authority but also identified the location where priests were most powerful. It was in the confessional where, according to republican journalists, novelists, and politicians, the waning influence of the husband over his wife met the growing influence of her confessor. Within the confessional, the priest won over the souls of women by listening to their innermost secrets and frustrations, usually concerning their sinful husbands. Having exposed their deepest worries to their priests, women were in a vulnerable position, as putty in their priests' hands.

One of the most prominent purveyors of this message in France was the eminent historian of the Revolution, Jules Michelet. In an extraordinarily successful book entitled *The Priest, the Woman, and the Family*, Michelet wrote about the rage and alienation that French men, especially bourgeois men, experience when they come home and try to discuss the world and their problems with their uncommunicative and indifferent wives.[16] According to Stephen Haliczer, Michelet's treatise was one of the most influential anticlerical works of the nineteenth century, going through eighteen editions between 1845 and 1918 in France, Spain, and beyond.[17] Drawn deeply into religious devotion by the influence of her confessor/spiritual advisor, the wife of the Frenchman "has become another person; she is present physically but her spirit is elsewhere."[18] Because women were more religious and fanatical about their Catholic faith than their rational and civic-minded husbands, Michelet believed that all family life was characterized by a profound lack of understanding and that the Church and its clergy were at fault. He blamed the destabilization of the family on the priests and their impressive influence:

> How can this family situation be explained? Our children, (and) our wives are taught and governed by *our enemies. Enemies of the modern spirit*, of liberty, of progress. It is not worth it to blame this preacher or that sermon. One voice can speak in favor of liberty, (but) one thousand voices can speak against it....There are so many locations, so much money, so many pulpits where they can raise their voices, so many confessionals in which they can speak in a whisper, the education of 200,000 children, of 600,000 young girls, the addresses of millions of women: this is their colossal machinery. The unity that (they) can generate is enough to alarm even the State.[19]

No household could be safe because the priest represented a foreign threat that invaded the family, undermining the husband's authority. Michelet bitterly laments:

> And it is because we are workers, because we come home tired every night that we more than anyone else need peace in our hearts. It is

necessary that the home is truly our home, that this table, is our table, and that we do not encounter a situation in which our wife or our son tells us a lesson that they learned from the words of another man.[20]

But even more frustrating for men—indeed for Michelet—was not that a priest could physically invade the household whenever he came to visit their spouses, but rather that the priest's influence reached the depths of women's souls. A man could keep a priest away from the home, but his wife's religiosity created a situation in which the priest, as minister of her faith, her confessor and counselor, was the most important man in her life.

Masculine values and patriarchal control over women and family were in serious jeopardy because the priest worked together with the women they enslaved to undermine the husband's authority. Michelet continues:

> Generally, it used to be believed that two persons were sufficient for a marriage. This changed. Here is the new system, as they (priests) have taught it. Three elements form the system: (1) *the man*, the strong and violent one; (2) *the woman*, fragile by nature; (3) *the priest*, born a man and strong, but who has preferred to make himself fragile, resemble women, and who in this way can participate as one or the other, and meddle between the two. But that's not all; one would expect of him an impartial intervention that alternately favored one or the other depending on reason. No. It is the woman to whom he directs himself, it is she whom he charges himself with protecting against her natural protector. What he offers is *to ally with her in order to transform the husband*.[21]

Michelet's understanding of the relationship between men, women, and their priests is central to the Spanish ethnographer Manuel Delgado's essays into the link between anticlericalism and misogyny. In his *Las palabras de otro hombre* (the title, *The Words of Another Man*, comes directly from Michelet), Delgado develops a complicated argument, which posits that religion is, or is perceived as, an essentially feminine sphere in which women and priests dominate because men grow out of their religiosity by their adolescence; that the Church and clergy promulgate a discourse that elevates feminine values while depreciating masculinity; and that male anxieties of being literally or figuratively castrated by the feminine result in the varied forms of anticlerical misogyny in the nineteenth and twentieth centuries.[22] In other words, the Church and clergy are at odds with men. If men seek to protect a situation in which they are the patriarchs over the family and household, the Church and clergy ally with women in order to privilege the opposite state of affairs: women as the moral heads of the family and household. Now Rousseau and republicans would, in theory, actually agree with this situation because women are potentially more virtuous than men. Ideally, women promote virtue/morality in their husbands and children, but anathema to anticlerical republicans was promoting Catholic virtue and morality rather than civic and liberal values. Everything men had won through the fraternal social contract established in the French Revolution was under attack, and if the clergy could destabilize the family—the very cell on which patriarchal authority and right to sex was based—the clergy could destabilize society.

The essentialist beliefs about the nature of the sexes for many republican males equated sexual difference with political difference. Because women could not be counted on to know very much, let alone understand, their husbands' ways of thinking, precisely because they were educated in Catholic schools and were under the thumb of their priests, it conditioned republican males to believe women should be excluded from public life. European republicanism was theoretically an articulation of egalitarian Liberalism, but it had to grapple with integrating women into its utopian vision when it held stereotypical and misogynist beliefs about women.

In Restoration Spain, Gil Blas de Santillán's anticlerical diatribes made frequent appearances in the pages of *El Motín*, asserting that the Jesuits were especially talented at taking a simple and free sacrament and turning it into a revenue stream for the "Company" (the Society of Jesus). In a curious way, republicans connected the danger posed by priests dominating women to the financial threat posed by the clergy. Financial ruin of men and families by the clergy was accomplished with the help of women who

> are dying to go confess themselves; the spiritual fathers (padres) have to shoo them away from that tribunal of penitence as if (women) were sticky flies. And as for the confessors, if they get to perform what they call confession, even if they have no other charge or source of revenue, they live splendiferously; they fill their home with valuable objects that are also gifts, and they believe it is feasible to ascend to the highest posts and secure the most coveted prebends that the Church has to offer.[23]

The implication in this passage is not only that the Jesuits are by nature ambitious and turned their backs on their poverty vow, but that they had also discovered that the financial generosity of their penitents was intrinsically tied to their well-being. The author concludes that female penitents:

> are the soul of clericalism, the life of the priests, the strength of the Church, the secret behind all of its influence, its prosperity, and the power of the Jesuits.
>
> The moment when you take away their female penitents, they will become agitated, they will scream to the tops of their lungs, they will not rest, and they will end up emigrating. Without penitents they cannot live.[24]

Similarly, Ramón Chíes (longtime coeditor of the Masonic organ *Las Dominicales de Libre Pensamiento*) in one of the most celebrated articles in the compendium of Spanish anticlericalism cynically argued that auricular confession lacked any Christian essence. Instead, confession was invented by the "Church in order to dominate consciences and exploit the faith for the benefit of Papal power."[25] The link between the confession of women and the loss of patriarchal authority was frequently replayed in the pages of *El Motín* and *Las Dominicales*. In October of 1889, *El Motín* warned husbands about the financial dangers of the confessional when it related the story of the wife of Mariano Porta of Zaragoza. While he was on a business trip, she allegedly handed over her family's possessions and some 10,000 *reales* to the Jesuits because her confessor had instructed her to do so.[26]

The confessional was also a special place for the priest or friar because there he could gather all sorts of information about his parishioners and their activities and desires.[27] The preoccupation with what a woman said to her confessor was central to Chíes' impassioned appeal to Spanish women about the dangers of the confessional. In the ideal form of matrimony, there were to be no secrets between husband and wife. However, Chíes assumed that a female penitent disclosed everything to her confessor that she did not want her husband to know, including, but not limited to, her sexual indiscretions or affairs.[28] By confiding in her priest, she violated the sanctity of marriage and created a dangerous situation because she gave the priest damaging and potentially humiliating information about her husband. Because not all priests were "unnaturally" celibate (see below), the priest could either use that information against the husband, or use it against her as he blackmailed her for sexual favors.[29]

One of the biggest concerns that anticlericals had with the confessional was not only how a husband could lose control of a spouse but also how a father could lose parental authority over a daughter. In 1924, the defrocked priest Segismundo Pey Ordeix published "Sor Sicalipsis," a serialized novel that had appeared in the pages of *El Motín* in the second decade of the twentieth century. The novel tells the story of a young girl who falls in love with her confessor as he insinuates himself into her home and carries out a "moral kidnapping" by robbing her parents of authority over her.[30] The novel also details how the priest, Fr. Sical, subtly turns the girl toward the cloister where he can dominate her completely.[31] In a society in which men built up dowries for their female offspring, anticlericals argued that priests greedily tried to convince young women to enter convents in order for the Church to reap the benefits of those dowries.[32] This was the explanation for the illustration in a February 1888 issue of *El Motín*, which depicted a couple of armed friars bringing a young wealthy woman *and her dowry* of 500,000 pesetas to a convent while members of the Civil Guard looked on (figure 5.1). The cartoon's caption read: "Kidnappings that go unpunished."[33] The *Mónita Secreta*, a Jesuit manual that the progressive press delighted in republishing on occasion, included details of the Jesuits' complicated long-term recruitment strategies. Little children were to be given gifts and allowed free reign around convent or monastery gardens so they would become accustomed to that environment, and would naturally enlist in the orders when they came of age.[34] Images and articles of young women being kidnapped or "mystically kidnapped" by their confessors against their fathers' wishes were so common that we can better understand the popularity of Benito Pérez Galdós' *Electra* in 1901 and the enormous uproar over the impeccably coincidental caso Ubao. *Electra* was a play about a young orphan teenager who is torn between obeying her foster parents, who were convinced by a Jesuit to put young Electra in a convent, and Máximo, her progressive modern-thinking champion. The Ubao legal case of 1901 reached the Spanish Supreme Court and pitted the Jesuits against parental rights when an aristocratic mother sued her daughter's confessor for convincing her to become a nun against her mother's wishes (see chapter six).

Besides the confessors' violation of their minds and usurping family fortunes, both wives and daughters were potentially subject to sexual attacks by their confessors. Whether the sexual misconduct resulted from the innate sensuality of women or the perverse nature of the priest—or a combination of both—the confessional was a place

Figure 5.1   "Kidnappings that go unpunished," September 22, 1910 *El Motín* cover

in which the priest could sexually seduce a vulnerable woman and undermine patriarchy.[35] This idea was, of course, informed by republican conceptions about celibacy, which they considered an unnatural state. Republicans, again steeped in the teachings of men such as Michelet, believed that sexual attraction is the first thing that pulls men into a relationship. As they understood the sexual drive to be natural, it made sense that priests would likely pursue their natural calling and prey on women. Radical republicans in their obsession with virility and masculinity often reduced women to sexual resources that belonged to them and not the clergy. It was imperative for the republican male to keep the women under his control away from the confessional so that sexually depraved priests would not make unwelcome advances on them or plant lewd ideas in their heads.

Of particular interest to many anticlericals were confession manuals. These how-to books for the benefit of confessors had proliferated during the Counter-Reformation, especially as confession began to be understood as a medium of instruction. Haliczer writes that "an entire ancillary literature aimed at instructing and informing confessors was created by the Catholic press" in the late sixteenth and the seventeenth centuries.[36] Fray Jayme de Corella's *Práctica del confesionario*, published in 1717, called on confessors to be instructors, teaching penitents how to live better lives; to be doctors, administering suitable spiritual medicine that would inoculate against future sinfulness; and to be Inquisitors, responsible for testing the religious knowledge of their penitents.[37] Because these manuals were used throughout the era of the Inquisition, many passages instructed priests to ask a number of probing questions about the sexual practices of penitents to expose transgressions against Scripture or dogma. Although the Church weeded out sexual lines of questioning, the older manuals still remained fresh in the imagination of anticlericals throughout Europe. In Italy, for example, the *Theologia Moralis of St. Alfonsus Liguoir*, a widely used text for the preparation of confessors, "was presented as an obscene book through ample quotations of the minute descriptions of lawful and unlawful sexual acts which it contained."[38] In Spain, Nakens used these historical texts to besmirch the Catholic Church's past, create deep grievances with the Church in the present, and justify the coming of a future Republic.

Anti-confession works in Spain's anticlerical industry, such as the ex-priest Constancio Miralta's *Secretos de la confesión* (1886), confirmed that the sexual questions asked by the priests could severely disrupt the family.[39] Young women were needlessly exposed to a whole new world of sexual possibilities—of lawful and unlawful sexual positions and practices including masturbation and oral copulation—by these inappropriate lines of questioning. The result of the confession of young girls, according to Chíes, was their tragic loss of purity or innocence: they were mentally and/or morally deflowered.[40] Mature women at the very least emerged feeling dirty or psychologically scarred by having to respond to a plethora of objectionable questions from their priests.[41]

More awful in the republican imagination was for the sexual inter-
rogation of the confession to lead to sexual acts.[42] The confessor's
job was to undress the soul to get at the most intimate secrets of the
woman, and in the republican mind-set, the priest's undressing of
his female penitent's body naturally followed.[43] If priests could make
their female penitents turn over family wealth through the confession,
or make women leave their liberal husbands, it was equally plausible that the sneaky priest could convince his penitents to surrender
themselves sexually to him. Anticlericals such as Nakens, Fernando
Lozano, and Pey de Ordeix happily kept alive the clergy's history of
confessional transgressions and presented them as everyday occurrences in order to besmirch the Church and clergy.

Anxieties about the Sexuality of the Clergy and Women's Sexuality

Male anxieties about the relationship between women and priests
were rooted in the sexual fantasies republican males held about
priests. To republican men, clergymen were not normal. They were
not strong, virile, violent men, nor were they delicate and passive
women.[44] Republican determinism or naturalism led them to prefig-
ure Freud in believing that the natural male has a sex drive, and he
must indulge it. Priests were hypocrites because they were foolish to
believe their faith and celibacy vows would supersede nature. Imagery
and discourses of sexuality and material excess were certainly not
new to the nineteenth century; new in the Restoration anticlerical
industry was the mass-production of these images for popular con-
sumption with the aim of uniting Spanish men against the clergy for
the sake of the Spanish nation.

Both *El Motín*'s and *Las Dominicales*'s content reproduced stories, jokes, poems, or illustrations of priests carrying on a domestic
life and fathering children with their "housekeepers" or "nieces," las-
civiously fondling women in the confessional, or engaging in sexual
and/or epicurean orgies with nuns.[45] For instance, a 1911 cartoon in
El Motín depicted a blissful clergyman's home life: the priest and a
nun (presumably his lover) hold a child who looks conspicuously like
the priest.[46] Another cartoon depicted a number of beautiful women
attending to a priest's every need; while one woman kisses his hand,
two others cushion his feet and bring him wine, and still another fans
him as if he were a sultan and she a member of his harem.[47]

At times this discourse of a sexual clergy overlapped with other
anticlerical discourses such as those designed to make people feel

aggrieved about the clergy's wealth. For example, in successive weeks in July of 1888, *El Motín* juxtaposed the interior of the home of "he who never works" (the priest) with that of the home of "he who always works" (the Spanish laborer).[48] In the second cartoon, a man comes home to his one-room apartment; his somber-looking children are barefoot; the laundry hangs on a clothesline across the room; the plaster is coming off the walls; and they eat roots, beets, radishes, and a small ration of what may be meat or fish. However, in the first cartoon, a priest sits on his rocking chair frolicking with his little girl—one of at least four children—while yet another child suckles at the breast of the priest's lover. The priest and his family do not lack anything; their table is set with fine china, golden flatware, and attractive goblets. They even have a maid who serves up roasted hens, fresh fish, lobster, and sausages.

Clerical sexuality also manifested itself in sexual perversions from which nobody was safe. In August of 1895, *El Motín* reported that a thirteen-year-old girl died of hypothermia when a lascivious priest spotted her bathing in a river. Because she was naked, the young girl refused to exit the river while the priest remained for hours before he was chased off by the girl's female relatives.[49] *El Motín* paid particular attention to scandals involving priests and young children.[50] Despite the fact that local authorities had asked the press not to sensationalize a 1910 rape of a six-year-old girl by a priest in Barcelona province, the best *El Motín* was willing to do was bury the enormous headlines and exposé toward the back of its weekly.[51]

In the republican imagination, clerical sexuality and materialist excess were also at the root of many of Spain's ills and even accounted for national disasters. For example, *El Motín* reported many accusations of clerical abuse in the Philippine Islands and ran a number of columns tying colonial problems in the archipelago to Spanish friars demanding tributes from the natives in the form of women and livestock.[52]

Keeping in mind the currents of naturalism that ran through republican anticlericalism and derived from a *fin-de-siècle* fascination with sexology, it should not be a surprise that the celibate clergy, who of course represented the vast majority of the priesthood, were not immune from attacks in anticlerical propaganda. Another recurring theme in the anticlerical industry was that true heterosexual love is privileged over a life of celibacy. To deny the urges within all men meant the priest was metaphorically torn apart by the profound tension created between what he was told to do by his Church and religion and what nature forced him to do.[53] The cassocks that priests wore were actually dresses to anticlericals. That these men ran around in skirts spoke to a perversion of their sex roles.[54] In a 1905 editorial, Alfredo Calderón, a widely read intellectual who frequently contributed to *El Motín*, demanded that priests get married and maintain normal sex-lives so that their sexual energies were no longer directed toward their female penitents.[55]

Nakens himself was particularly concerned with this aspect of the clergy's life and some of his most popular and reproduced essays dealt with priests trying to process their sexual cravings. In 1883, when Nakens received word that a priest had left the order after falling in love with one of his female parishioners, he wrote a long open letter counseling the priest about the "Law of life."[56] Nakens acknowledged that the priest must have grappled long and hard with the decision to follow his sexual and masculine nature, and he directly advised the ex-priest:

> The hungry eagerness with which your lips lock with hers, a nest of germinating possibilities, and the longing to take in her breath: are these nothing more than the brutal desires of squelched pleasure not fully enjoyed?
>
> Sacrilege! Falsehood! How have they deceived you, poor clergymen! The flesh that you were taught to hate is sovereign; and the soul that you thought was in charge, is a slave. (…)
>
> The chain of duty fuses itself with the fire of desire, the will withers, and reason collapses before the just rebellions of the flesh. What vows? What intentions? What fear of punishment or fear of the wrath of God.
>
> There is no other cure. One must abhor the dogmas that mutilate, and proudly and valiantly enter the concert of life; (you must) become a man and comply with the law that demands the *"abandonment of the father and mother, in order to unite with a woman, and become one in the flesh with her."*[57]

This priest who did cave in to his sexual urges was honorable in Nakens's eyes because he no longer enslaved himself to religious checks that were against nature.

According to one of Restoration Madrid's most respected literary critics, Nakens's office staff included one such priest, José Ferrándiz, a defrocked priest who was teased as much for his weight as he was for having an obese lover.[58] Ferrándiz was lauded and paraded around because many writers in the Madrid anticlerical industry wished that priests would simply leave the order, take *one* woman as a wife, build a family with her, and enter the republican family and natural order. Francisco Pi y Margall, the former president of the First Republic, wrote in a very natalist vein that "children serve to sustain and fortify ties that tend to weaken," and thus a marriage resulting in a family is whole. He goes on: "What would a marriage be without children? It was instituted for procreation; to reduce it to sterility is to destroy it. Marriage destroyed, family destroyed: family destroyed, society destroyed..."[59] Only after Ferrándiz eschewed the unmanliness of celibacy and the priesthood and only after taking on a lover was he able to enter the public world of *El Motín* and republican politics. To Nakens, and indeed to many anticlerical republicans, sexual relations socialized men for public life.

Of course, the sexual dysfunction rhetoric that attacked the clergy is only one part of the gendered language of anticlericalism. Like their French coreligionists, Spanish republicans saw women as sensual, irrational, and immature beings incapable of civic participation. The late sociologist Julio Caro Baroja wrote that all nineteenth-century Spanish boys were initially influenced by the fanaticism of their female relatives' religious beliefs. However, as they grew up, their older male family members, indeed all older secular men, expected boys to outgrow the religious superstitions of their mothers, sisters, and grandmothers.[60] The Catholic identity of the majority of Spanish women was the main reason some Spanish republicans felt strongly about secular education for *both* sexes. In 1899, Pi y Margall spoke the following words:

> For education to produce more results, it is indispensable, in my judg-
> ment, that general instruction, what today we understand as primary
> and secondary schooling, be common for both sexes. The woman, as
> you know, is the one that instructs and educates children in the first
> four years of life: the husband is generally busy, be that with his busi-
> ness affairs, in the service of his clients, in the field, the workshop or
> factory. If the woman lacks education, she will transmit to her children
> all her preoccupations and all her errors...[61]

It follows in the anticlericals' minds that women were perpetually locked in a realm of immaturity and irrationality, which made them particularly vulnerable to Church propaganda. Anticlericals argued that the Catholic Church and its clergy capitalized on the intellectu-ally deficient and sensual condition of women by constructing forms of religiosity and dogma in a way that appealed to the female sex.

Another example of sexual images and immorality republican anti-clericals used to impugn the Church was to argue that Catholicism and priests struck an emotive chord with women through its pornocracy. Pierre-Joseph Proudhon's thought on pornocracy, the antifeminist idea that political equality and economic independence of women undermined traditional marriage and bourgeois masculinity, were widely read in Spain, especially after his work was translated into Spanish in 1892.[62] Left to their own devices, anticlerical republicans believed priests would instill a pornocracy by teaching women that their devoutness and Catholicism elevated them to a higher plane of virtue and prominence. If a pornocracy is a rule by harlots or whores, it is certainly understandable how anticlericals believed the clergy represented one. Priests were a gang of prostitutes working to financially support the ultimate panderer, the Pope. Anticlericals argued that the Church and its pornocrats (the clergy) were particularly successful with women because the religious realm indulged women's sexual curiosities and cravings.

According to republican anticlericals, the clergy traded in pornography that was offensive to the self-respecting man. Catholic dogma, rites, rituals, and histories of saints and martyrs were meant to evoke emotional, even sexual, excitement in women.[63] Religious icons and images that were supposed to be offensive to women because they were offensive to republican men were actually part and parcel of the churches' altars and shrines. For example, an anonymous author writing under the name "An Antiquated Catholic" (*Un Rancio* Católico) complained about the increase of pornography and pornographic imagery in the churches, convents, congregations, and confraternities. Specifically, the author was offended that the Church approved the display of icons of *Virgen de la O*, a representation of the Virgin Mary that accentuated her role as the mother of Christ by leaving a hollow oval in her midsection. By putting fresh flowers in the Virgin of the O's void, the faithful were supposed to be celebrating the special nature and fruitfulness of her womb, from which the Son of God emerged. However, to "An Antiquated Catholic," it was an affront to common decency to bring any attention to the reproductive organs of any woman.[64] Anticlericals such as Nakens and "An Antiquated Catholic" read pornography into the Church's iconography and rituals as another means of tarnishing the images and challenging the sacred claims of the Church and clergy.

Other articles took on the relatively new and highly popular cults of the Sacred Heart of Christ or the Immaculate Conception of Mary that were instrumental in the clerical revival of the late nineteenth century.[65] In an August 1895 article in which he cites large portions of "An Antiquated Catholic's" work, Nakens laments that men cannot compete with the intense feelings women experienced from worshiping the Sacred Heart of Christ.[66] The Sacred Heart of Christ offered women a vessel through which they could find true expression for the erotic feelings of love that swirl within them. "An Antiquated Catholic" heard that women shuddered in orgasmic delight simply by contemplating and empathizing with the pain and suffering of the image of Christ—whose bloodied heart is crowned with thorns as it explodes out of his chest—and by anticipating a union with him in heaven.[67] More than implied in this message was that women go to church or participate in religious rites for base catharsis, a desire to become enraptured and to connect with their Christ in such a way that a woman could not connect with any mortal man. For anticlericals, the fact that bliss for women came in the pews, not in the bedroom with their husbands, was an unacceptable consequence of the Church and clergy's influence over women.

Anxieties about "Emancipating" Women

Having delved into the terrible things republican males believed could happen to girls and women in the confessional as well as in the realm or influence of their local priests, I now move on to the line of discourse that sought to save women from their priests and a society dominated by the Catholic Church. Timothy Mitchell in his exploration of sexual abuse by the clergy in Spain focuses his attention on Felipe Trigo (1864–1916), a military doctor who worked in the Philippines before returning to Spain after the war with the United States. Though not a republican, Trigo reached celebrity status in republican circles by suggesting that the Jesuits' influence in the archipelago accounted for Spain's overseas disaster. Upon returning from the Philippines, Trigo was a general practitioner in Extremadura. He became convinced many of his patients' ailments were often connected to repressive sexual norms. He argued that while young girls ached out of sexual frustration, society looked the other way as their boyfriends could enlist the services of a prostitute.[68] After Trigo quit medicine, he began writing hot-selling novels aimed at young bourgeois women, encouraging them to have lots of wholesome hygienic sex and to talk openly about it. Many young women still believed what the priests had told them from their earliest years in school; a woman could not be erotically free if she believed she would become pregnant from a single passionate kiss.[69] Thus, plugged into the major trends in sexology at the turn of the century, Felipe Trigo's major contribution to the anticlerical industry of the Restoration was a body of work arguing that women had to be freed from their Catholic sexual programming.

In Republican views and ideology regarding women's emancipation, their concern for the undue influence of priests was again evident throughout much of the anticlerical discourse. For this reason, what anticlericals had in mind was not so much the emancipation that John Stuart Mill had in mind (i.e., including them in the civil and political life), but rather the liberation of women from their priests, from their convents, and from their religious upbringing and fanaticism. Both French and Spanish republicans had a tortured history with the issue of granting women their suffrage because often republicans saw women as unable to break free from the influence of their illiberal, conservative priests, and therefore unable to participate civically in the nation.[70]

Republican Freemasons such as Francisco Pi y Margall and Odón de Buen had begun to speculate about a greater and more positive role for women in the coming Republic. No doubt this was due to the fact that often well-educated bourgeois women were seen alongside republican men in the circles of the press, as in the case of the Fourierists María Josefa Zapata and Margarita Pérez de Celis, in Freemasonry as in the case of the poet Rosario Acuña, and in political mobilization as in the case of Guillermina Rojas during the revolutionary "Sexenium" (1868–1874) or the federalist Belén Sárraga.[71] In 1899, Pi y Margall acknowledged that the Spanish Federalist Republicans lacked any platform for women and that they would be wise to consider the political reforms feminists talk about.[72] However, within the very same editorial in which the Masonic pedagogue Odón el Buen called for granting women certain well-deserved political rights (such as suffrage) with the coming of a Republic, he also argued that women were the primary enemy of the Republic and that their confessors would instruct them to fight the Republic.[73] Indeed, though she outlines the very active and political lives of leading republican women, María del Pilar Salomón Chéliz concedes that their demands often went beyond what republican men were comfortable with and these were pushed to the back burner until the Second Republic.[74] In the anticlerical-republican male's imagination, and despite evidence to the contrary, men clung to a belief that women were intellectually inferior to men and that women would have to go through a long process of reeducation in order to participate in a democratic polity.

The damage caused by women's religiosity and Catholic education was evident in repression of sexuality, and to men such as Nakens this was best illustrated in nuns. The anticlericals at *El Motín* were particularly concerned because the essence of woman was to become a mother and carry on the life cycle. In 1910, Pey Ordeix, who had by that time become *El Motín*'s main editor, began a column called "Sicalipsis Monástica" written primarily for men. Pey Ordeix hoped that after having read his column men would be left with no other choice but to forbid their daughters from ever entering convents.[75] In the "Sicalipsis Monástica" column, Pey Ordeix detailed the relationship between nuns and their priests, and how, for example, from the very beginning nuns were taught that their decision to marry Christ and live a chaste life made them more worthy than mothers and wives of men.[76] Because their vocation allegedly ran counter to nature, Pey Ordeix also argued that priests necessarily had to squelch any maternal instinct in the nuns by haranguing them with the dangers of the flesh.[77] Again, republicans believed that unnatural priests were perverting that which was natural: motherhood. Because even nuns were incomplete without a husband, Pey Ordeix argued that priests encouraged nuns to see them as the representations of the groom they had married, Jesus Christ.[78] In Pey Ordeix's mind, this mystical bride/groom relationship meant the priest and nun would eventually develop sexual feelings for each other, if they had not already done so from the start.

Nuns were to be pitied, according to the *El Motín* staff; they were useless women who had become slaves to their priests and faith. In 1893, when an allegedly deranged mother superior killed herself by jumping out of a convent window, *El Motín* took the opportunity not only to wonder how many convents and monasteries were being run by insane nuns and priests but also to suggest that the nun's mental illness was tied to a life of sexual repression.[79] All nuns were sick in some way because they denied the laws of nature. This sets the background through which we can understand Alejandro Lerroux calling for the young virile barbarians to "sack the decadent and miserable civilization of this unfortunate country, destroy its temples, finish off its gods, tear the veils from its nuns and turn them into mothers to invigorate the species."[80] It is this context of an anticlerical understanding of nuns that explains the ensuing childish acts and morbid curiosity of the 1909 Barcelona Tragic Week, mobs looting convents searching for underwear, perfumes, and marital aids in the nuns' armoires or searching for fetuses in cloistered convent crypts. The mobs sought evidence of the secret, depraved, and intense sexual life of priests and their vestal virgins, of which they had heard so much about in Lerroux's newspapers and through the anticlerical industry.[81]

Clearly just about every political party in the Restoration Republican movement was a men's club, with very few republican women alongside men agitating for the transformation of Spanish politics. But there were also anticlerical women in the movement, and even they echoed many of these assumptions. Belén Sárraga, a captivating federalist orator, raised a storm of controversy in Gijón in 1899 when she spoke of women going to confession and partaking in a conspiracy that undermined their men.[82] An anticlerical woman calling herself "Miryam" and writing in *El Pueblo* of Valencia argued:

> The Church, which with its unmarried priests brings unrest to families and societies; the Church, which places celibates in the confessional introduces spurious ideas into the family; the Church, which in its own homeland has given the shameful spectacle of an increase of illegitimate births reaching unprecedented levels; that Church should not speak at all about wives and households, because it neither knows nor understands them....
>
> We anticlerical women...., convinced that our greatest enemy is the Catholic Church, given that it is the cause of disrespect for us and of the backwardness in which we live, have taken on the honorable task of using clear proof to convince other women that, being ignorant and fanatically religious, they have allowed the priest to be the owner of their minds, making them beings lacking awareness, slaves without any will, attentive only to the commands of the papacy...[83]

In her essay on the state of women originally prepared in 1884, the polymathic Concepción Arenal (not a republican herself, but widely read and excerpted in the republican press) noted that Spanish women were imperfect, deficient, lacking in almost all things compared to the women of other nationalities, and suggested they are such because they confuse their religiosity with culture.[84]

Both learned men and women harbored a deep-seated concern with the backward state of women, especially Catholic women, and echoed the republicans' message that women needed to be emancipated from their own ignorance. In 1906, Demófilo (pseudo. Fernando Lozano y Montes) focused on the constructed and implausible quality of the

Gospels, which talk about Christ magically curing the sick and raising the dead. He wrote that miracles and resurrections were larks designed to amaze women's simple minds and get them to attribute superhuman powers to their priests.[85] Arenal editorialized in *El Motín* in1897 that the Church and clergy's hold over women was a "dictatorship" and that the clergy actively worked to keep women ignorant and old-fashioned because they would be preferable in this condition rather than as well-educated modern women.[86] In 1906, *Las Dominicales* eagerly reported on the successful whistle-stop tour by Belén Sárraga who traveled throughout Southern Spain to help poorly educated and devout women break the yoke of Catholicism.[87] In that same year, Sárraga wrote that Spanish women who are subjects of the clergy and educated in the uselessness of the religion are not good mothers because they are not accustomed to think for themselves, understand their bodies, or prepared to usher in a generation of good citizens.[88]

Anxieties about Spanish Virility

One final group of messages found within the gendered discourse of anticlericalism centered on the general lack of honorable men in Spain. Most often this concern for the honor or manliness of Spanish men manifested itself in whether Spanish men had the sexual vigor to be creative and politically engaged.[89] The international context that saw most of Spain's European neighbors expand their colonial empires while Spain struggled unsuccessfully to pacify Cuba, Puerto Rico, and later the Philippines is the backdrop for a general feeling among republicans that the nation's honor was compromised. In republican cultural production, this Spanish honor problem was illustrated, either in written word or visual media, by a reversal of gender roles. For example, in a very self-deprecating 1892 cartoon, *El Motín* depicts women putting on pants as they instruct their husbands— shown clad in their underwear—to wash the dishes, do the laundry, and dust while attending to their children. The cartoon's caption read: "Women putting on the pants that we men don't know how to wear."[90] Similarly, an 1895 cartoon depicted a woman about to leave her home dressed in a *traje de luces* (the matador's garb), while her meek husband kneels and prays for her safety.[91] Although republicans were fundamentally opposed to bullfighting, the message of the cartoon was clear: Spanish men had not only lost their honor, they lacked the virility to get it back.

That the modern republican populists such as Vicente Blasco Ibáñez and Alejandro Lerroux and journalists such as Nakens and Lozano frequently employed a language of virility to expose the honor problem in Spain is not surprising, as this was consistent with their understandings of the natural male and the natural female. On this understanding, even anticlerical women were on the same page as they looked to men to stand up and be men, especially vis-à-vis the Church. Miryam, that fascinating Valencian activist, writing in 1910 asserts:

> Radical men of all kinds should keep in mind that we anticlerical women place our confidence in them....All of them should understand that by separating their wives from the Church, they are watching out for the fate of their children...Here is one of the primary duties of any liberal man: to share with his wife the sacrosanct ideals of his creed. Only in this way can a man fulfill his duties as a republican, as a free-thinker, as a radical. To preach liberty outside the house, to combat clericalism in the streets, while taking a young lady, one's daughter, to take her first communion in church is not to be a republican, is not to be a liberal, is not to de-Catholicize Spain; it is to send commissions in the name of the Vatican, which asks governments for the destruction of radical men and even their disappearance from Spain.[92]

Sexual metaphors and a fascination with virility were not exclusive to republicans, but it was the republicans who actually employed those values to attain modern goals: uniting the nation, achieving social equality, and modernizing and democratizing the political system.[93] Because political creativity came with men's power to create, republican demagogues attributed their modest political gains not to their strategies but to the fact that republicans were simply behaving as men should. When the republican movement won a few local elections in April of 1886, Nakens proudly attributed those victories to the "virility of the party."[94] Likewise, for republicans, the popular uproar to Prussia's claim to the Caroline Islands—which were uninhabited Spanish possessions since 1526—was a testament to the nation's virility, not that of Prime Minister Cánovas who sat idly.[95]

However, republicans also dwelt upon a general malaise they claimed had enveloped Spanish society by the time of the Restoration. This talk of national decadence and degeneration that appeared in virtually every issue put out by Restoration republicans attributed these problems to the illegitimacy of the political system and the hegemonic values of Catholicism. A big component of the honor problem for republican males was that women, and their sacerdotal coconspirators, were working to emasculate men. Hanging in the balance was Spain's national honor. Nakens once wrote:

> Women think of nothing else but running to the Churches to listen to nonsense and immoralities, when they are not practicing them...Men, some out of hypocrisy, others for being foolish, allow the black serpent to introduce itself to their families even when this brings on bad luck or (injury) to their honor. In this way, come the scandalous donations, the dishonored young ladies, the forced incarceration in the convents, and those crimes against nature that hardly ever surprise what had always been a nation of virile men.[96]

Anticlerical males were convinced that priests and women in society were ganging up on them and winning. Other symptoms of this honor problem in Spain appeared in the growing number of men cross-dressing at the carnival,[97] and the continued popularity of Emilio Cástelar, who Nakens considered a "womanly man."[98]

Women had also noticed the lack of honor and virility among Spanish men. In 1906, the activist Belén Sárraga challenged men when she wrote:

> We wish all types of calamities to befall on the Spaniards if in the present year of 1906 they continue not to know how to attain the bravery and dignity necessary in order to comply with their duty as men (varonilmente): saving Spain through the Revolution.[99]

While Nakens very much agreed with Belén Sárraga's "virile language" and messages about lost honor, he also saw her as a symptom of the Spanish honor problem. In an 1899 article Nakens praised Sárraga for her ideas, then he criticized all Spanish men when he remarked that they should be ashamed that a woman is performing the virile work of men.[100] As frustrating as it may have been for Nakens and other anticlericals, it seemed men had simply given up and allowed the clerical-feminine conspirators to rule their lives and households.

Because gendered understandings of masculinity, femininity, family, and state were such fundamental components of modern Spanish anticlericalism, scholars have been uniquely fascinated over the last four decades with understanding the origin of anticlerical sexual attacks. In 1971, Pierre Conard studied the content of the Spanish anticlerical press and employed demographic techniques and social psychology to argue that sexual anticlericalism was more than just propaganda. Conard maintains that the acute sexual anticlerical attacks in *fin-de-siècle* Spain were motivated by a rebellion against the Church's containment of the erotic and its condemnation of various forms of contraception. A newer, freer sexual life for a new modern urban Spaniard, which included the right to put off marriage and the right to employ forms of birth control, clashed with the Church and its clergy's teachings on sexual norms.[101] From this fundamental conflict emerged the anticlericals' campaign to present the clergy as hypocrites and as promoters of crimes against nature, and the suggestion that Spaniards, especially Spanish women, needed some form of sexual, if not erotic, emancipation.

More recently, Timothy Mitchell, who neglected to consult Conard's thought-provoking article, develops the argument that Spain financed the Catholic Church's Counter-Reformation, hunted down its own Lutherans, and became a haven for the celibate/sexual power system that produced generations of psychosexually impaired Spaniards.[102] In a scathing attack on the Church and clergy, Mitchell suggests that little did Spaniards know that they allowed the Church to "betray the innocents," especially women and children, when it imposed a sexual authoritarianism over the clergy and the faithful. Mitchell's rather reductionist—he calls it a post-Freudian view of Marian masochism—argument posits that because seminarians at the beginning of their training were punished or instructed to punish themselves for masturbating, many priests grew up with psychological disorders or sexual perversions. Catholic authoritarianism not only can account for the terrible occurrences of sexual molestation and abuse but also a general religious and political belief that Spaniards could not be trusted or left to their own devices. He argues that only since the democratic transition has Spain been able to heal itself and find its own way free from Catholic sexual authoritarianism.

There is an element of truth to both Mitchell's and Conard's assertions. Like other forms of anticlericalism that are direct responses to forms of clericalism, sexualized anticlericalism was a nineteenth-century response to the sexual authoritarianism of the Church. Anticlericals such as Nakens, Lerroux, and Lozano turned up the heat of their sexual anticlericalism precisely because they perceived that the Church and clergy were either maintaining or increasing their hold over Spanish women and threatening the family. Because priests instructed their female penitents and parishioners to resist Liberalism, Catholicism was incompatible with the republicans' quest for a truly liberal-democratic polity. And because Spanish republicanism filtered misogynist assumptions through the blueprint to their society, anti-clerical republicans mobilized to end a situation in which the home and family were being polluted by the "words of another man."

However, sexual anticlericalism was more than a knee-jerk reaction to the Church's teachings on sexuality. While sexual anticlericalism tapped into assumptions of cultural patriarchy and the tradition of misogyny, this form of attack against the clergy was more complicated. Here I agree with José Alvarez Junco who argues that an acute sense of jealousy lay beneath the complicated threads of sexual and misogynist anticlericalism.[103] Beyond wanting to safeguard their sexual access to women, anticlerical men in nineteenth-century Spain may have resented the profound connection that women had with their faith and the administrators of that faith. In the case of republican men, perhaps they wanted so badly to connect with women that they not only resented the close relationship between priests and women but also recast it in such a spiteful way that it was made filthy and sinful. From either disregard or an unfulfilled desire to attract women to republicanism came the plethora of anti-confessional messages within the anticlerical industry, because the confessional was where priests were establishing deep connections with women and driving them away from republicanism. Within the rantings of anticlerical men—be it Jules Michelet, Alejandro Lerroux, or José Nakens—there is a tone that craved for women to love them and the idea of their Republic as much as they perceived women loved their priests and Catholicism. However, their inability to explore and do away with their sexism stood in the way of making republicanism anything but divisive during this period.

As much as the republicans hated the Church, they envied it at the same time. According to republicans, the power of the Church extended beyond finances; it enjoyed hegemony over the political, social, and cultural aspects of the lives of most Spaniards. The Church enjoyed everything the republicans aspired for their Republic. As a relatively new political tradition, republicanism lacked the cultural resources to compete with Catholicism, and it had to borrow those from whom it sought to destroy. The anticlerical nationalism of republicanism was an exercise in the transplanting of values: an attempt to transform Spanish values by denigrating and replacing Catholicism with new republican markers.

This exploration of sexual anticlericalism and anticlerical misogyny reveals that gender was central to the construction of republican national identity. Republicans were in the business of denigrating the clergy and its sexual norms (or lack thereof) in order to replace them with sexual and interpersonal norms of their own. The problem that I have illustrated over the course of this book is that while anticlericals, especially within the radical republican movement, were talented demolishers of Catholic morality, they were not particularly adept at putting anything in its place, especially for Spanish women. Thus, the anticlerical nationalism of republicans was a powerful but confusing discourse that could mean any number of things to any number of different people. It was also an incomplete discourse on nationalism. The presence of misogyny and sexual attacks that appear central to republican anticlericalism and nationalism illustrates that their vision of the future nation was defined by the victory of one segment of the Spanish nation, republican men, over the vast majority of the rest of the Spanish nation—women, priests, and all Spaniards who identified with Catholicism. While a vision of every Spaniard marrying, having children, and men and women playing their appropriate roles in the social order may be described as a communitarian vision, the limits of republican anticlerical nationalism are rooted in the insistence on a convulsive and divisive path to that end.

Spanish Anticlericalism's
Long Decade, 1898–1910

The antagonism between clericals and anticlericals over the course of the first decade of the twentieth century was heightened more so than at any other time during the Restoration. These years saw numerous examples of popular anticlerical mobilization, such as the demonstrations after the Madrid premiere of Benito Pérez Galdós' *Electra* in 1901 and the "Tragic Week" of the summer 1909, which resulted in the destruction or vandalism of eighty churches, convents, and clerical residences in Barcelona.[1] After the defeat in the Spanish-American War, radical republican discourse emphasized "the [M]anicheist division between the good people and the wicked representatives of clericalism."[2] Republicans, especially, were characterized by "the obsession with blaming all the evils of the country on a clerical conspiracy aimed at controlling Spain by means of its previous moral and material ruin; and the orientation of the people's wrath toward clericalism as the only, or main, enemy."[3] By 1900 and throughout the first decade of the twentieth century, republican anticlericalism had made deep inroads into the revolutionary left, which was now often willing to work or plot with radical republicans such as Lerroux, and which had been exposed to a steady flow of anticlerical paraphernalia designed to make them feel aggrieved with the regime.

In the aftermath of the Spanish-American War, the governments led by the Liberal Party found themselves in an increasingly difficult position. On one hand the regime itself faced tremendous pressure from republicans, intellectuals, workers, socialists, anarchists, and Catalan nationalists who had turned on Madrid. On the other hand, Liberal party officials continuously searched for ways in which the regime could attract moderate elements, including anticlerical republicans, in order to short-circuit the potentially disruptive revolutionary left.[4] The result, according José Andrés Gallego, was that the dynastic parties, especially the Liberals, were forced to alter relatively peaceful Church/state relations and pursue anticlerical politics to remain in power.[5]

Although it had always been clear in Nakens's mind before the *fin-de-siècle* crisis, the religious problem had been transformed into a national problem for more than just radical republicans. Studies have established that the geographical distribution of anticlerical demonstrations changed significantly in the first decade of the twentieth century. The older pattern of anticlerical flare-ups in Catalonia, Valencia, and pockets of Andalusia and the Ebro Valley, Madrid, Badajoz, Valladolid, León, and Oviedo spread out as a national phenomenon.[6] With popular anticlerical eruptions throughout Spain, the first decade of the twentieth century saw the state pursue anticlerical initiatives as some liberal oligarchs realized the need to alter the *modus vivendi* between the Spanish government and the Vatican, even if not for the good of the nation, for the good of the regime.

As a result, it was clear that anticlericalism's time had come: it was no longer solely a battle cry for radical republicans and hotheaded republican journalists, but an important tool through which the Liberal Party could promise national regeneration after the humiliating defeat to the Americans in 1898. It was the republicans who first recast anticlericalism as a nationalist tool and employed it as a weapon in their discursive arsenal prior to 1898, and the fact that anticlericalism was picked up by the Liberals demonstrates that radical republicans had established an interclass base of support for their antichurch stance. However, given the remarkable power of anticlericalism to elicit strong feelings, opinions, and even violence against the Spanish Church and clergy, the Liberals of the first decade of the twentieth century were keen on controlling anticlericalism primarily to disarm resurging republicanism and the revolutionary left.[7] This chapter, then, is concerned not only with the general anticlerical *événements* of this "long decade" (1898—1910), but also with the political football anticlericalism became in the early twentieth century.

The reason anticlericalism reached such a level of primacy in Spain during the first decade of the twentieth century was that the new nationalisms, or at least new needs and desires to nationalize the Spanish, were born from the rubble of the Spanish military defeat. Among both the elites and the republicans, this new nationalism urgency, according to Alvarez Junco, was "devoid of the confidence in past glory especially imperial fantasies, aside from Morocco, and concentrated on the modernization of the country."[8] Not only would the years between 1898 and 1910 see some forms of state-initiated anticlericalism, but they would also see any number of attempts to remedy the fact that Spanish patriotism appeared to be at an all-time low, necessitating the creation of the nation and the civic education of the Spaniards.[9] With the Spanish-American War and José Canalejas' "Padlock Law" of 1910 as important bookends for the decade, this final chapter briefly sets up the historical context of the Restoration's anticlerical decade and analyzes the transformation of anticlericalism from a discourse of opposition to the state to an important resource for the state's politicians.

The Disaster of 1898, Its Aftermath, and Responses and Challenges to the Restoration System

In order to understand how and why anticlericalism seemingly reached an apex as a pressing issue during the Restoration and became a topic on many Spaniards' minds, it would be helpful to recall the context of Spain's anticlerical "decade" beginning with the devastating defeat to the United States in 1898. It has been my assertion that anticlericalism was a crucial discourse of nationalism and opposition to the regime, but as demonstrated in this book, anticlericalism, especially that found in the mindsets and writing of Spanish republicans, was present and indeed picking up steam *before* the 1898 Disaster. Anticlericalism's time may have come with 1898 and the *fin-de-siècle* crisis as I describe below, but the anticlerical explosion of the early twentieth century was one of a number of alternatives or responses presented by groups in Spain that, like the republicans, pressed the regime into a politics of anticlericalism.

Although the Spanish military quelled a Cuban Independence movement and military charge in a vicious and deadly Ten Year War (1868–1878), Spain found itself embroiled anew in a war against Cuban independence fighters in 1895, only this time the Cubans had learned a number of important tactical lessons from the Ten Year War and were able to generate greater popular support for their movement.[10] The Spanish military, on the other hand, was saddled with myriad structural difficulties, including being poorly equipped and top-heavy, severely underpaid and, after the army in Cuba was augmented with conscripts, "composed almost exclusively of the most impoverished youth of all of Spain."[11] Perhaps most troublesome to the Spanish military effort was the disconnect between its commander, General Martínez Campos, who favored granting numerous concessions to Cuban nationalists so as to avoid a devastating war, and Prime Minister Cánovas and hardliners not willing to negotiate a settlement.[12]

Valeriano Weyler's arrival as Martínez Campos's replacement in January 1896 marked a bloody turn of policy in Cuba as Weyler lived up to his reputation for decisive, brutal action, which included concentrating the Cuban people in camps to isolate the insurgents and bring together dispersed Spanish forces that could destroy the main Cuban armies.[13] Hundreds of thousands Cubans were concentrated in overcrowded villages where thousands were left to die of starvation and disease while Weyler destroyed small holdings throughout the island.[14] As John Tone's recent unsuccessful attempt to determine the exact number of Cuban concentration camp deaths has shown, that number is elusive but most likely between 200,000 and 400,000 from the camps alone.[15] Nicknamed "The Butcher," Weyler was on a state-sponsored race against time as Cánovas believed suppressing the revolt and restoring stability would appease American public and business interests growing ever more sympathetic to the Cubans. But obviously, accounts of Spanish atrocities—often colored by sectors of America eager to drive out the Spanish and commandeer Cuba for American business interests, and built upon suspect Cuban sources— informed the press coverage that delivered Americans a "consistent and relentless tale of Genocide in Cuba."[16]

The situation grew worse for Spain beginning in the summer of 1897 when Prime Minister Cánovas was assassinated by the Italian anarchist Michele Angiolillo—who had spent part of the summer in Madrid befriending José Nakens.[17] Spain's war with the Cubans became a morass as American interest in intervening in the war increased to the point in which President William McKinley was compelled to declare war after the USS Maine was allegedly sunk off Havana Harbor by underwater Spanish mines killing 266 Americans.[18]

The outcome of the Spanish-American War confirmed what most people on both sides of the Atlantic knew: it was a mismatch between an emerging new world power and a decaying old world kingdom. Indeed, nineteenth-century American historians such as William H. Prescott and Henry Charles Lea focused on Spain's Catholicism and monarchical traditions and promulgated these as the causes for Spain's intellectual deficiency, moral decay, and economic decline, contrasted, of course, by the liberty and political stability of the United States.[19] Of course such racialist and religious stereotypes do not explain the rout, but these did permeate the American military leadership who must have been surprised by how poorly nourished, armed, and organized their Spanish opponents were during the brief conflict.[20] By the end of war in August 1898, official statistics revealed that 58,939 Spanish soldiers had lost their lives to illness (including bacterial infections and gangrene), hunger, or fatigue, while only 4,128 actually died in battle.[21]

With the centennial anniversary of the Spanish-American War came a number of important studies and debates that deepened our understanding of Spanish politics and society in 1898 and the aftermath of war.[22] It was inevitable that such a humiliating, rapid, and decisive defeat sent shockwaves across Spain's political, social, and economic circles, and yet the defeat was a "military disaster without political commotion."[23] The defeat did not change the government or the makeup of the Parliament; it did not lead to changes in the Constitution or significantly shake the power of the Liberals and Conservatives. Nonetheless, the aftermath of the war resulted in a flurry of collective soul searching, political antagonisms, and social mobilization and disturbances.

Many scholars begin their descriptions of post-1898 Spain by analyzing the intelligentsia's revolt against the Restoration regime, spearheaded by the Aragonese lawyer, polymath, and activist Joaquín Costa. As the main figure of the so-called Generation of 1898, Costa dissected the ills of the Restoration regime in order to find and suggest paths to Spain's modernization, Europeanization, and regeneration.[24] Reminiscent of the *arbitristas* (that is, lawyers, bureaucrats, politicians, and others who spent their days preparing proposals and solutions to Spanish decay in the seventeenth and eighteenth centuries), the Disaster and Costa stimulated anguished enquiries into the history and the soul of the nation with an end toward finding practical proposals for Spain's redemption.[25]

The Disaster also drew huge numbers of people living in Catalonia into political life under movements that had been brewing responses to the political system before the war, and many Catalans acquired a new sense of collective identity that was often predicated on being at odds with Madrid and the Spanish state. Because Catalan business and industrial interests were intrinsically tied to the remaining imperial markets, numerous Catalanist movements turned up the heat on Madrid and called for significant modifications of the relationship between Catalans and the state. During the era of the Disaster the language and strident pro-Catalanist tones of social conservatives such as Enric Prat de la Riba and Francesc Cambó made it increasingly difficult for Spaniards to believe Catalan claims could be reconciled with the continued existence of Spain as a unitary nation state.[26] This is ironic because Prat de la Riba's constant cries for "Catalan imperialism" or "Catalonia's imperial mission" were poorly understood at the turn of the century and continued to be so in our times, and his message was shorn of the Europe-wide held notion that imperialism was the inevitable and legitimate activity of a superior culture. Also missing was Prat's, Cambó's, and the *Lliga's* dream that "Imperial" Catalonia was destined to bring the other nations of Spain to self-realization within an Iberian federation.[27] It is important to remember that not all post-1989 agitation was elitist and spurred by pro-Catalan nationalism, as this was also the period in which anarchists, socialists, and republicans, led by Lerroux, were growing their political following and were often in opposition to the Catalanist movements.[28]

Of course no one emerged more traumatized in the aftermath of the war than the Spanish military, whose humiliated officers desperately searched for meaning in the time of sweeping social discontent. Cánovas's system was partially predicated on blocking the military from political participation given the destabilizing effects of dozens of coups and *pronunciamientos* between 1820 and 1874.[29] With the defeat, not only military officers but also rank-and-file grunts found themselves alienated from the liberal state, and once again when faced with what they saw as a nation breaking apart under the corrupt Restoration system their identity as defenders of Spanish nationhood surged.[30] Catalanist rumblings only fueled the military's perception that Spain was being torn apart and that their sacrifices in the Spanish-American War were in vain. As a result of their humiliation, Spanish officers increasingly turned toward antidemocratic political alternatives, especially with the rise of antimilitary sentiment after 1898. The military retaliated against the Press in 1905 by securing a new Law of Jurisdiction, which allowed it to try all offenses against both the armed forces and the nation in military tribunals, and thereby destroyed Cánovas's efforts to keep the military neutral in civil affairs.[31] Thus the rise of worker unrest and the strength of Catalan nationalism helped consolidate the rightward drift of military officers as they grew closer to the young Alfonso XIII, himself growing ever frustrated with the Restoration system. Their shift to the right took form in an aggressive, imperial, and intolerant nationalism.[32] This military nationalism found expression in Morocco where the Spanish military attempted to realize their imperialist dreams and regain their lost prestige after 1898, only to be frustrated and humiliated there as well.[33]

Finally, 1898 and the Disaster ushered in a period of violent riots throughout Spain, most often as a result of food shortages and/or price increases. Historians such as the late Carlos Serrano and Demetrio Castro Alfín have suggested that these were traditional forms of protest that were employed before the war and thus were connected to the Cuban Wars to the extent that shortages were due to war conditions.[34] Like other European countries of the time, Spain was undergoing a structural transformation marked by agrarian decline in the central and southern provinces, urbanization in the periphery, and the rise of labor organizations. Sensitive to these changes, the popular masses found themselves in a situation in which an already fragile social consensus was often undermined.

Still, the constant repatriation of ill and dying soldiers produced sorrow, dismay, anger, and disillusionment with the state, and even with the nationalistic republicans among lower-class families.[35] This was especially the case in light of the extraordinary mobilization of the Spanish people in jingoistic defense of the nation and empire prior to the war. The Disaster helped to delegitimate the national values, used by the regime's elites, among the workers and popular masses who bore the brunt of military service, and though it would take time for the revolutionary workers to reconcile themselves with republicans and their nationalism, anticlericalism became the common terrain on which republicans and the left shared their grievances against the state. Resentment toward the regime was at the root of the Tragic Week riots in Barcelona during the summer of 1909, and though religious buildings and institutions were attacked by the mobs, the increased conscription of young men to fight in the unpopular Moroccan War touched off those disturbances.

Differences within each of the challengers to the regime as well as Spanish structural problems account for why the regime avoided collapse. The general reluctance of the individualistic Generation of 1898 to engage in the politics of popular democracy and fear of mass rebellion limited their criticisms' impact.[36] Though the *Lliga* was able to pull off stunning electoral victories in 1901, unseating established oligarchs, its conservative elitist nature pushed together republicans, Catalanists, Carlists, and Catholics on one hand, and sizeable sections of the middle class and petty bourgeoisie, on the other, into *Solidaritat*

Catalana (Catalan Solidarity) in early 1906.[37] However, radical republicans such as Lerroux and revolutionary worker organizations such as the CNT (National Confederation of Workers, or the anarcho-syndicalist trade union) maligned *Solidaritat Catalana* as a bourgeois-clerical movement, which meant Catalonia's very active workers were not a base of significant support for the *Lliga* or *Solidaritat Catalana*. Though the revolutionary left was also picking up momentum and strength, it was many years before anarchists and socialists were able to cooperate and use collective mobilization against their employers and the state. So while Balfour has the unfortunate tendency of presenting 1898 as the moment when the Restoration regime entered into crisis despite its continuation for some twenty-five years, he is most certainly correct when he maintains that the persistence of traditional and corrupt networks of social and ideological control over an unevenly modernized society with a poor communication network and very high illiteracy short-circuited the coalescence of these new forces into viable alternatives to the *Turno Pacífico*.[38]

Still, Cuba, especially, was an important part not only of Spain's empire but also its psyche, and when Cuba was lost, not only were Catalan businessmen with connections to the island left holding the bag of goods of imperial greatness, but so too were the governing elites who could no longer hide the dysfunction of their state. Cuba, Puerto Rico, and the Philippines were an extension of Spanish territory before 1898, and as late as the period from 1890 to1894 Cuba not only produced 25 percent of the world's sugarcane, it also absorbed almost 15 percent of all Spanish exports, most of which came from Catalonia.[39] In spite of the intertwined economic relationship between Spain and the remnants of its empire, scholars reflecting on the differences between Spain's 1898 territorial losses and the loss of the majority of its American empire in the 1820s argue that more than Cuba was lost in Cuba: without an empire, Spain had lost its place among the community of modern, racially superior, imperial powers.[40] After tracing the historically constructed identity shaped and held by Spanish elites over the nineteenth century—an identity that deluded them into thinking Spaniards were a uniquely powerful and successful military people—Alvarez Junco argues that the Disaster left the Spanish nation itself completely in doubt. He adds, " 'What was lost in Cuba' was not, in all certainty, something of great material value, but rather an illusion, an imperial daydream, the fiction of still being one of the great colonial powers."[41] The elites might have been the only group in Spain to have had the rug truly pulled from under them by equating the colonial debacle with the collapse of the nation. By tying their class and power interests with those of the nation, the Disaster left them with an immediate crisis of legitimacy.

It was precisely that issue of the state's legitimacy that made the republicans particularly dangerous to the oligarchy. In the studies on republican politicians acting in *fin-de-siècle*, urban environments like Lerroux's Barcelona, or Blasco Ibáñez's Valencia, it is clear that life in the bourgeoning cities made putting *caciquismo* into practice more difficult. The depoliticized, highly illiterate populace so relatively easy to manipulate in the countryside contrasted with the urban masses who took an active interest in local politics because they felt change *was* possible. Sources of opposition came from many more places in the cities, be it from heterogeneous lower-middle-class workers and artisans, to revolutionary leftist workers, who had been swelling their ranks since the early 1870s. Thus, given the structural transformation of Spain in the *fin-de-siècle* and coupled with a discredited regime after 1898, increasing members of the popular masses centered especially in Spain's large cities gravitated toward alternative challengers to the system; these included anarchism and socialism, but also republicanism, especially the radical republican traditions that originated with Ruiz Zorrilla, coursed through Nakens, and were best exemplified by Lerroux and Blasco.

Republican agitation, as this book has shown, predated 1898 but also increased after the Disaster. Radical republicans, especially, amplified their anticlerical-nationalist discourse that had been Nakens's *raison d'être*, and that too attracted members of the petty bourgeoisie and Spaniards with revolutionary leftist leanings. As I have shown, the local or federalist orientations and political schisms that developed within republicanism meant that they too could threaten, but not overthrow, the regime without rehabilitating links to the military and the masses. Anticlericalism was imperative for republicanism in building that following. Between 1898 and 1910, anticlericalism, long the currency of radical republicans, was diffused and recast into a discourse employed not only by republicans but also by virtually all political actors.

The Disaster and Its Anticlerical Aftermath

The eruption of such a remarkable wave of anticlericalism and anticlerical demonstrations after 1900 is puzzling because the nineteenth-century conflicts that put the Church and the Liberal governments at loggerheads were, in general, resolved at the outset of the twentieth century. As far as the state was concerned, gone were the days that Carlism could count on unfailing support of Catholics in its antiliberal, antidemocratic project.[42] The tensions precipitated by the disentailment of Church property in the 1830s and 1840s were largely smoothed over by the 1851 Concordat, in which the Church accepted the land expropriation in exchange for an annual budget from the state, fiscal exemptions, and major concessions on education. Though the Church of the nineteenth century was powerful anew, it was not at all the behemoth of the ancien régime. For instance, regulations of rights of press censorship during the Restoration were in the hands of the government, not the Church, after the Press Law of June 26, 1883.[43] Still, José Nakens and radical republicans such as Lerroux spoke of the Church and clergy as if it remained all powerful, and over the course of the first decade of the twentieth century many Spaniards identified with that idea.

The profound shock that gripped middle-class journalists and politicians after the war suggests that many informed people, knowing the hopelessness of a war with the United States, had suspended their disbelief and allowed themselves to be carried away by the prevailing mood of jingoism prior to the war.[44] Even republicans, who initially opposed the war because it was foolhardy, vigorously rallied around the Spanish military as it prepared to defend national honor against the "Yankee Pigs." Just prior to the war, a republican daily forecast that

If the war lasts a long time
the price of ham will fall
because of the many Yankees
that the Spaniards will kill.[45]

But the "Disaster" proved that the Spanish nation was no longer a ranking power in the international age of empire; the defeat was proof of Spain's terminal decline and decay. In the search for a scapegoat, fingers were pointed in all directions. For example, the clergy, who had contributed to the frenzied jingoism before the war by declaring the Americans Protestant as enemies seeking to strip Spain of her cultural empire, immediately blamed Spain's defeat on a shady international Masonic conspiracy.[46] In June of 1899, ultramontane factions launched a spirited albeit unsuccessful campaign to keep the Grand Master of the Spanish Orient, Miguel Morayta, from assuming a seat in the *Cortes*.[47] The Catholic "Masonic psychosis" was clearly exaggerated because though the 64,900 Spanish Freemasons scattered in 531 lodges included highly influential men and women, their power was perceived as greater than it actually was.[48]

But it was not simply the conservative clergy digging in. Both *turno* parties were moving toward breaking the Restoration's religious settlement in one way or another, setting the stage for religion as a central issue of political polarization. During the war, Francisco Silvela and the ruling conservatives gravitated toward neo-Catholicism with the appointment of conservative General Camilo Polavieja—who almost launched a coup d'état that would have toppled the regime after the Spanish-American War—and Alejandro Pidal y Mon to the cabinet. Belief in Masonic conspiracies gave way to the belief in a conservative, if not clerical, conspiracy to regain control of Spain. As a result, an increasing number of the intelligentsia, male and female members of both the bourgeoisie and working classes, and even soldiers gravitated toward anticlerical explanations for the disaster.

In the process, the new segments of the population drawn to anticlericalism offered republican haranguers such as Blasco Ibáñez, Lerroux, and Nakens a wider constituency for political protests. Part of the message of anticlerical republicans and populists was that the clergy was not only responsible for the war but also for the defeat. While republican reviews such as *El Motín*, *Las Dominicales*, and *El Resumen* had long histories promulgating the idea that the costs necessary to support the Church and clergy crippled the nation, they were now joined by the mainstream liberal press, which also began to print stories about the clergy's accumulation of wealth and economic power.[49] In particular, it was argued that the clerical opulence and abuse of their power in the Philippines led to the independence movement in that colony.[50] Indeed, Andrés Gallego has shown that the clerical administration of the Philippines in 1898 had not changed since the sixteenth century. Spanish Jesuits, Franciscans, and Augustinians—who were in charge of administrating the colony in lieu of secular government officials—lived in luxurious haciendas and administered merely 2 percent of the territory's population.[51] The native Tagalog clergy was undermanned, treated poorly, and became important mouthpieces of the Filipino grievances against the Spanish administration. While stopping short of endorsing the Philippine insurrection, anticlericals highlighted the mistreatment of indigenous islanders by the clergy, and could thereby portray the regular clergy as traitors against the nation.[52]

The anticlerical agitation after the collapse of the empire was exacerbated by the repatriation to the mother country of thousands of members of the religious orders and the reorganization of the Church hierarchy. For instance, in 1904 Blasco Ibáñez led an ultimately successful campaign against the appointment of the Dominican friar Bernardino Nozaleda, formally the archbishop of Manila, as archbishop of Valencia.[53] Though the conservative Antonio Maura was briefly at the helm of the government, republicans understood the appointment as provocation and were particularly adept at using anticlericalism's popularity to lock horns with the Church and state. Simultaneously, Spain saw several thousand French monks, friars, and nuns cross her borders seeking shelter from the French Third Republic's anticlerical legislation. The republican and liberal press maintained Spain was overrun by non-Spanish clergymen and nuns, thereby fulfilling anticlerical prophecies. The increased presence of the religious orders not only made it appear as if Spain was being colonized, but also that the new clergy posed an economic threat to everyday Spaniards. Members of the religious orders enjoyed economic advantages not afforded to all Spaniards: the goods (shoes, garden produce, wine, and pastries) they produced were tax-exempt, and the regular clergy constituted "scab laborers" who undercut workers. Ullman suggests that these economic grievances explain why the anticlerical mobs of the Barcelona Tragic Week assaulted religious properties, where the clergy not only lived but also worked, rather than attacking clergymen themselves. However, she ultimately blames the radical republicans, Lerroux especially, for the Tragic Week because it was they that deftly and persistently hammered home the message that the clergy fleeced the Barcelona working class.[54] Alvarez Junco, on the other hand, denies that the Tragic Week bore the modern traits of a Lerroux-led movement and instead argue that the Tragic Week thwarted Lerroux's goal of transitioning Spain from an oligarchic political system to a mass electoral one.[55]

The Jesuits especially took the brunt of the almost everyday anticlerical demonstrations in June of 1899. Bread riots and tax demonstrations during this period were directed at the clergy rather than the local *cacique* or state administrator. One priest in Manresa informed his bishop that a crowd protesting increased taxes shouted out: "Down with the Jesuits!" The priest expressed bewilderment when he wrote: "As if we have anything to do with the budgets."[56] Both these issues— the loss of Spain's colonies because of clerical abuse and the invasion by the French clergy—were tailor-made for a fusion of anticlericalism and nationalism.

Adding to the building of anticlerical pressure since the loss of the empire was the proposed marriage of Princess María Mercedes to the son of the Carlist Pretender. While the move was a pragmatic attempt at reconciling Carlists with the regime, such a union provoked the republicans who were opposed to any peaceful overtures to the traitorous Carlists. Although Nakens had been mass-producing histories of Carlist atrocities and other forms of anti-Carlist propaganda since before the Spanish-American War to keep Spain vigilant against a possible fourth Carlist War, clearly the Carlists were not any more powerful than any of the other opposition groups. Once again, anticlericals perceived the power of clericals to be greater than it actually was.[57]

One politician who refused to ignore the wave of anticlericalism that swept across Spain in the 1900s was José Canalejas. There may be no other Restoration politician who continues to be as acclaimed as this bright forward-looking democrat.[58] Unlike any other politician within the oligarchy, Canalejas realized the need to reform the monarchical parties and integrate rather than suppress the popular classes into the regime. Like Giovanni Giolitti who perfected the mechanisms of Italy's version of a *turno pacífico* (called *trasformismo*), Canalejas was concerned with Spain's social and religious questions and favored the state moving toward a degree of quasi-socialism to restabilize the monarchy after 1898.[59] In what is perhaps his most famous series of speeches, Canalejas brought anticlericalism and the need to alter Church/state relations to the floor of the *Cortes* in December 1900. He warned that the Conservatives were deceiving themselves if they thought they were dealing with a genuine religious revival; they were dealing instead with the "dominating and tentacle-like spirit of neo-Catholicism."[60]

Although ultramontane factions painted Canalejas as a godless persecutor of the faith and the religious orders, nothing could be further from the truth. Unlike many anticlerical republicans who had no tolerance for religion, Canalejas was a devout Catholic who admired the political sophistication and modernity of nations farther along in the secularizing process. Canalejas urged the *Cortes* to see the difference between religion and clericalism, which was a movement seeking to undo the gains of liberalism.[61] Echoing the misgivings of pessimistic republicans, Canalejas warned the Parliament that Spain would split between conflicting loyalties to the Church and the nation, leading to yet another civil war. In a statement reminiscent of the one given by Leon Gambetta to the Third Republic's Assembly, Canalejas shouted: "We must make war with clericalism!"[62]

If the Liberals were to be champions of individual and associational rights in Spain, Canalejas understood the importance of remaking the party so that it was both traditional and modern at the same time: traditional in the sense that it stressed the independent rights of the monarchy, and modern and socialist in the sense of including programs designed to mitigate forms of inequality.[63] When Spain seemed "moribund," the verve with which people from across the political and social spectra engaged in anticlerical protestation suggested that anticlericalism was linked to national regeneration.

Republicans, socialists, and anarchists all shared in a belief that anticlerical attacks, both verbal and physical, were tied to the transformation of society. Curtailing (or in some cases obliterating) the role of the clergy in Spain was but one important step in addressing the injustices perpetrated by the clergy. It was the clergy who were considered to be behind Spain's degeneration, and it was the Church and clergy who were portrayed as the malefactors of the nation's prosperity. On the flip side, anticlericalism could also offer Liberals a vehicle through which they could connect with the masses on the regime's own terms, or at least, on terms with which the regime was most comfortable.

Such was the message in Benito Pérez Galdós' favorite play, *Electra*,[64] whose Madrid premiere week beginning on January 30, 1901 touched off furious disturbances. The play is about Electra, a bright young orphan teenager raised by her aristocratic relatives. When the family priest, the nefarious Jesuit Pantoja, convinces her guardians to enter Electra into a convent, Máximo, the guardians' anticlerical scientist son, angrily challenges Electra's "enslavement." Stories or essays about clergymen kidnapping young rich women and either deflowering them or entering them in a convent to secure their dowries for the Church were quite common in the republican anticlerical press long before the turn of the century (see chapter five). However, *Electra* was written by Pérez Galdós, Spain's greatest contemporary writer and literary champion of Liberalism. Moreover, it was written at a time of heightened anticlerical sentiment throughout the world.[65] And while *Electra* may have meant a great deal more to Galdós—the play was about the eternal quest for truth revealed through the battle between science and religion—it offered anticlericals another opportunity to showcase their antipathies toward clericalism.[66] At the Madrid premiere, Ramiro de Maeztu, a pillar of the Generation of 1898, stood up and shouted: "Down with the Jesuits!" The crowd grew frenzied as it joined Maeztu in turning the Teatro

Español into a "revolutionary club."[67] At the moment in the play in which Máximo thinks of burning down the convent, a box of matches was thrown from the galleries and someone yelled: "Do it now! What are we waiting for?"[68]

On *Electra*'s third night in Madrid, civil disorder continued. This time it was fueled by a rumor that the civil governor was going to suspend the play, and by two *agents-provocateurs*, Pedro Vallina, an anarchist who would later be implicated in the attempted regicide of Alfonso XIII in Paris in 1905, and Rosendo Castell. Vallina and Castell bribed newsboys to shout out: "Down with Liberty! Death to Galdós!" They hoped, and succeeded, to precipitate a riot.[69] Castell had a contingent of federal republicans and anarchists ready to meet the theatergoers with their own chants of "Long Live Galdós," and "Death to the Jesuits." Pushing and shoving ensued, and when the police showed up to restore order, a riot broke out.[70]

Adding fuel to the fire was the impeccably coincidental Caso Ubao, a court case that pitted the Jesuits against parental rights, and which had reached the Supreme Tribunal in February 1901. A Jesuit priest named Fr. Cermeño secretly convinced a young heiress named Adelaida Ubao to become a nun without her mother's consent. The mother retained Nicolás Salmerón to represent her against the Church, which had retained the conservative statesman, Antonio Maura y Montaner. Salmerón may have won the case when he produced two letters in which Adelaida expressed her love for a young man and her severe doubts about her religious vocation.[71] The republican statesman accused Cermeño of a "moral kidnapping"; the tribunal agreed and by a vote of 5 to 2 returned the young girl to her mother. During and after the court hearing there were anticlerical demonstrations throughout the city of Madrid and in over a dozen Spanish cities.

Not only were the popular masses mobilized in an anticlerical frenzy, but Spain's intellectual community was abuzz with anticlerical fever. Galdós' *Electra* inspired the short-lived anticlerical literary magazine, *Electra*. The magazine boasted anticlerical poetry, essays, and stories from the titans of the Spanish literary world, including Galdós, Valle Inclán, Pío Baroja, and Maeztu. *Electra*'s (the magazine) anticlerical tone was elaborate and erudite. Its contributors blamed the Holy See for Spain's cultural deficiencies, religious fanaticism, and its decay.[72] A similar antireligious search for the origins of Spain's cultural backwardness came from Dr. José María Escuder when he argued that a religious (read Catholic) falsehood, which governs how

Spaniards see the world and dictates their behavior, has become part of the Spanish blood, thereby preventing the forward progress of the nation. Like a virus or a nonlethal dose of poison that corrodes the human body, this "religious falsehood" corrodes the nation.[73]

At other times, in keeping with the anti-Jesuitism of that moment, Jesuits were the targets of the anticlerical diatribes.[74] José Martínez Ruiz, an avid reader of Nietzsche, began an article claiming that Christianity was dead, and he called on Spaniards to engage in the "religion of life," which entailed the exaltation of work, health, and pleasure.[75] While these types of articles had been appearing in *El Motín* and *Las Dominicales* for almost twenty years, the aftermath of the Spanish-American War created the conditions of a general sense of national malaise and a deep-seated concern for regeneration. The Disaster and its aftermath created the conditions for the expansion of the anticlerical message into all levels of Spanish society and for the solidification of the link between anticlericalism and nationalism.

The breakdown of public order was enough to convince the governing conservatives to hand over the reigns of power to Práxedes Sagasta and the Liberals. On March 19, 1902, Sagasta returned to power with his so-called "Electra Cabinet," which included the token appointment of Canalejas to the Ministry of Agriculture. Canalejas' presence in the cabinet was Sagasta's only concession to the anticlericals.[76] Unlike Canalejas, Sagasta was an opportunist: while Canalejas truly believed anticlericalism offered a path toward the democratization of Spain, Sagasta grudgingly accepted a degree of anticlericalism only as a way to make the Liberal Party appear as a source of regeneration. Canalejas, however, proved much more radical in his commitment to anticlericalism than Sagasta had hoped.

Canalejas wove his anticlericalism into the larger context of the need for political innovation, which he considered a matter of life or death for the nation. If the population was now enfranchised, at least in theory, then it was imperative that they be enfranchised in practice. Canalejas pointed to the "neutral mass" of the Spaniards who had grown apathetic toward the major parties, and he warned the *Cortes* that if these parties could not offer revitalization, the country would be drawn "either to the narrowly materialistic goals of the extreme left or to the religious fanaticism and superstition of the extreme right."[77] Thus while Canalejas agitated for a groundbreaking modification of Church/state relations that would give the state complete authority over religious orders and curb the influx of new members, Sagasta and Segismundo Moret, then the minister of the interior, secretly negotiated a deal with the Vatican that precluded the state from denying admission or restricting the activities of the religious orders in exchange for receiving reports on activities prepared by the religious orders themselves.

From the very beginning of the "Electra" Cabinet, Sagasta sought to remind Canalejas that the Liberal Party was a liberal-democratic party and not a radical one. Sagasta put him in charge of Agriculture, something Canalejas knew nothing about, to minimize his threat. Aware that he was only a token anticlerical in Sagasta's government and that Sagasta was not prepared to move toward either the democratization of Spain or a significant modification to the religious settlement, Canalejas resigned in May 1902. Thereafter, Canalejas and his democrats began their own anticlerical campaign and sought active support from the socialists and the republicans.[78]

Because the tide of members from various religious orders entering Spain continued to be a problem after the Liberals handed back power to the Conservatives in late 1902, anticlerical demonstrations flashed throughout Spain's urban settings. This was especially true after anticlerical legislation in Portugal and France's separation of Church and state in 1905 forced more members of religious orders to flee to Spain.[79] The success of the Conservatives' hold on power between 1902 and 1905 and then again between early 1907 and late 1909 could not mask the fact that anticlerical and clerical agitation continued to boil throughout Spain. In late 1903, Maura's appointment of Bernardino Nozaleda (the former archbishop of Manila who was rumored to have collaborated with the Americans during the war) to the archbishopric of Valencia sparked off a year of conflict between anticlericals and clericals.[80] Perhaps as talented as Canalejas, Antonio Maura realized the importance of broadening the base of support for the Conservative Party, and he publicly defended clerical interests after allying with powerful Catholic laymen such as Pidal y Mon and the Marquis of Comillas, as well as with Catholic trade unions.[81] Maura hoped his pro-clerical stance would encourage apathetic Catholics to participate in politics as did the anticlericals within the middle class.

The Barcelona Tragic Week of July 26–August 1, 1909 offers a concrete example of the magnitude of the anticlerical/clerical conflict despite the regime's efforts to maintain social order. When Maura called up troops from Barcelona to help the Spanish army suppress an Arab insurrection in Northern Morocco, a massive riot erupted in Barcelona in which eighty religious buildings, including schools and residences, were sacked or burned down.[82] Military intervention was necessary to put down the rioters, and the army was brutal in imposing order. Although only three priests died that week, over one hundred Barcelona citizens died in the suppression, and over 1,700 rioters and insubordinate military men were arrested.[83] In the aftermath, the military set up a kangaroo court that tried, convicted, and executed the anarchist pedagogue Francisco Ferrer, despite scanty evidence that he instigated the Tragic Week. Ferrer's trial and death became a *cause célèbre*, provoking Europe-wide demonstrations against Inquisitorial Spain, and Maura was forced to resign within three months of the riots.

The behavior of the mobs that rioted in Barcelona's Tragic Week has drawn a great deal of attention from scholars. The mobs, made up primarily of workers, directed their rage against religious property rather than at the clergy itself, the army or police, the upper classes, or the economic system. Ullman makes the provocative suggestion that anticlericalism in Spain, particularly during the Tragic Week, did not serve to further any political ideology nor did it have any political meaning. It often functioned as radical republicanism's safety valve through which the masses' aggression could be channeled away from institutions of political power.[84] However, Romero Maura believes the primary movers in the Tragic Week were the anarchists, symbolized, although not led, by Ferrer.[85] But anticlericalism did serve as an essential pillar in the republicans' political ideology, and it had remained so long before these flashes of spontaneous manifestations. Whether it was Lerroux imploring the crowd to sack religious buildings or Nakens imploring Spaniards to think nationally by internalizing the messages of the anticlerical industry, anticlericalism served to win over and expand a constituency for the Spanish republican movement.

Lerroux was the dominant political force at the local level in Barcelona prior to the Tragic Week. Republican activity and support surged in 1901 with Lerroux's arrival. He actively campaigned not only in republican centers but also among workers' associations, and by 1905–1906 a network of clubs, fraternities, working-class centers, and youth and women's organizations were coordinated by the republicans.[86] A master of histrionics and a superb orator, Lerroux won over large segments of the working class by equating the nation or the people (*el pueblo*) with the working class and promising to that *pueblo* a better Spain through a republic. Lerroux surely must be blamed in part for the Tragic Week mobs' thirst for anticlerical violence and iconoclasm. After all, it was an impetuous Lerroux who addressed his young cronies in the following way in September of 1906:

> Young barbarians of today, enter and sack the decadent and miserable civilization of this unfortunate land: destroy its temples; throw over its gods; tear off the veil of its novices, and elevate them to the category of mothers in order to invigorate the species, penetrate property registrar offices and make a bonfire of the papers so that the flame will purify the infamous social organization; enter the homes of the humble and raise legions of proletariat so that the world will tremble before its awakened youth.[87]

Radical republicanism's stock-in-trade was an unusually virulent form of anticlericalism that eventually found full expression in the Tragic Week.[88] After arsonists attacked the residence of the Camillians, which included a public school installed on the second floor, it was discovered that rioters had scribbled on a wall: "Down with the Camillians. Long live Lerroux!"[89]

However, there is no evidence that the anticlerical and iconoclastic violence and manifestations were understood to be nationalist by the revolutionary mobs. Although the Tragic Week was precipitated by a popular refusal to accept a state order of conscription, Church property was burned by Barcelona's workers as a protest against the failings of the clergy in their religious and social roles. Church property was attacked because the message that the clergy was wealthy, corrupt, and representative of economic competition went from the mouths of radical republicans to the hearts and minds of those in the mobs. Church property was also sacked as a popular manifestation of the anger that the (republican-)mobilized masses harbored for the clergy siding with elites over the course of the Restoration.[90] Once again the dissonance between the nationalist messages put forward by the republicans and what the revolutionary masses heard is exposed: though anticlericalism was wholly nationalist to republicans, it was not necessarily understood as such by much of their audience.

Maura's resignation brings us back to Canalejas and the other bookend to the Restoration's anticlerical decade: the "Padlock Law" of 1910. Although post-1898 Liberal leaders such as Sagasta sought to stem the tide of members of foreign religious orders entering Spain, reduce dioceses and parishes, and create a modern public education system, it was only the devout Canalejas—prime minister from 1910 to 1912—who was willing to push for reform despite the whirlwind of criticism and agitation. William Callahan notes that Canalejas was moved by a firm belief that the "liberal State's evolution toward a more democratic and pluralistic direction depended on its ability to resolve the contradiction of a parliamentary, constitutional form of government with the existence of an established Church determined to impose its rigid and vaguely theocratic ideas on a rapidly changing and increasingly secular society."[91] When Canalejas's diplomatic relations with the papal nuncio on a plan to draw up a new Law of Associations broke down, the mobilization of Catholics against Canalejas ensured that his efforts to pass any such legislation would be hotly contested at best and impossible at worst.[92] Canalejas responded with the "Padlock Law" of 1910, which put a moratorium on state/Vatican negotiations and stopped the entry of new religious orders into Spain for two years, while a new law of associations was debated and passed in Parliament. It was the best he could have hoped for, given the circumstances; but as I have demonstrated in this book, the Restoration period was one that was rife for anticlerical/clerical disturbances to erupt at the drop of a hat.

There was very little for Catholics to fear from the "Padlock Law," because there already were some 3,800 communities of clergymen and nuns totaling nearly 55,000 *religiosos*,[93] and because the permanent measures necessary for the law to take any real effect were never codified. Canalejas was also not closing the door to the future founding of religious orders, or even the future immigration of foreign members of the religious orders into Spain. He was simply closing Spain's borders to the religious orders for two years while his government formed a plan that would reinstate the founding of convents and monasteries and immigration on the state's terms, not the Vatican's.

Nonetheless, the "Padlock Law" was imbued with significantly different meanings for the regime's opposition. For anticlericals, especially the republicans, the "Padlock Law" proved that the state realized the need to control the Church, even by employing the very same restrictions on freedom of association the regime used on them. On the other hand, religious elements saw the "Padlock Law" as evidence that the state had betrayed the Church, which in turn, called the regime's legitimacy into question. While anticlerical agitators celebrated the "Padlock Law" as the first legal victory in Church/state relations during the Restoration, Catholic elites, workers, and clergymen mobilized in organized protests of unprecedented numbers. In Cantabria, for example, Julio de la Cueva notes that new forms of Catholic mobilization helped Catholics coalesce into a united front against Canalejas' "Padlock Law." On October 2, 1910, a total of 70,000 priests, nuns, members of lay Catholic groups, leagues, and parishes engaged in anti-Padlock Law demonstrations, 16,000 in Santander alone.[94]

Reunited with traditional Liberal elites with whom he had broken up earlier, Canalejas put forward a program that emphasized freedom of conscience and education, civil marriages and burials for those who wanted them, and control over the religious orders. All of these were benchmarks of the various republican parties, politicians, and other movements, who suddenly saw their anticlericalism hijacked or co-opted by the Liberal oligarchs. However, the Liberals did not get very far with their program. Because the Liberals, as per the concessions of the *turno pacífico*, gave up the parliamentary majority, Canalejas was effectively gridlocked in his attempts to address the problem regarding the religious orders. He could not change the religious settlement without the support of Maura's conservatives, who had been moving toward neo-Catholicism and a "hands-off" stance toward the religious agreement. Alas, Canalejas was gunned down in Madrid's Puerta del Sol by an anarchist assassin late in 1912, and with him went the hope of controlling the religious orders and any serious effort to secure major clerical reforms through legislation.

Clerical mobilization and dynamism would intensify throughout the second decade of the twentieth century, culminating with the privately funded building of large monuments to the Sacred Heart of Christ outside of Madrid and with King Alfonso XIII consecrating the Spanish nation to Christ in 1919.[95] Anticlericalism as a tool of the state's nation-building project fizzled out after Canalejas' death and the outbreak of World War I, but the table was set for an apocalyptic battle between clericals and anticlericals some twenty years down the line.

Nakens and Republican Anticlericalism Beyond 1912

The anti-Carlist almanacs produced in 1913 and 1914 would be among the last of Nakens's anticlerical propaganda forms. They provoked a new round of threats from Carlists, the most serious being the detonation of a small explosive in the offices of *El Motín*'s administration.[96] Nakens was slowed down not by the threats of bodily harm and threats of litigation but by the marked decline in his readership compared to *El Motín*'s heydays in the anticlerical decade of

1898–1910. Pérez Ledesma estimates that the newspaper may have lost some six thousand readers between 1911 and 1914, and El Motín's malaise was compounded by Nakens's health problems, which compromised his hearing and sight.[97] By the end of World War I, the weekly was made up of copied columns from other newspapers and reprinted diatribes from its old issues, which explains the newspaper's monotonous quality and its insignificant circulation in the 1920s.[98]

It seems fitting that Nakens went to his grave while fighting one of the many legal cases brought up against him. Nakens faced a three-year, six-month, and twenty-one day prison term; a two hundred and fifty peseta fine; and court and attorney fees for allegedly challenging the religious doctrines of the nation's faith. At issue was an article that appeared in El Motín on April 9, 1921 in which he teased Catholics for the absurd mathematical concept of the Trinity. Always quick to poke fun at Catholicism's traditional antipathy to science and mathematics, Nakens claimed he failed to wrap his mind around the idea that three deities equaled one.[99] His failing health and his lawyer's repeated motions to delay or dismiss the proceedings ensured that Nakens never set foot in the courtroom for this particular case, which was thrown out five years after legal action was initiated.

His November 1926 funeral was organized and paid for by colleagues in the Press Association (Asociación de la Prensa), and the ceremony and procession leading to Madrid's Civil Cemetery was attended by many important journalists, Freemasons, and dignitaries, including Lerroux. Tributes and life retrospectives appeared in the liberal press, which was answered by antipathetic reflections in the conservative, Catholic, and Carlist press. Nakens's daughter, Isabel, continued the spirit of El Motín in 1926 with the short-lived literary magazine Reflejos de "El Motín" (Reflexions of "El Motín"), which included old anticlerical and republican articles from El Motín but also pieces on feminism, naturalism and phonetic orthography.[100] Isabel Nakens and friends supportive of "the Nakens" (los Nakens) formed the "Nakens Group" soon after his death and tried to unify disparate anticlericals and even financially assist those who eschewed religious sacraments in favor of civil ceremonies.[101]

As Nakens's star fell meteorically after 1907, Lerroux's popularity took off, until he eventually rose to head the Second Republic between 1933 and 1935. After the attempted regicide of 1906, Lerroux faced a two-year, four-month prison sentence for writing and taking credit for a pro-Nakens article. Rather than go to prison, Lerroux exiled himself in France and Argentina from 1908 to 1909, but he returned a vastly different man.[102] Gone was Lerroux's revolutionary and hotheaded edge, gone was the demagogic nationalist appeals to members of the working classes regardless of what political creed they had embraced, and gone was the political creativity and verve with which he became the everyman's political hero.[103] While in exile Lerroux invested wisely, so by 1910–1911 he could boast a modest fortune, but it was a fortune larger than he had ever enjoyed in his life. Perhaps the desire to protect his newfound wealth softened his rhetoric and made him amenable to working with the same elites that the "young Lerroux" had delighted in maligning and undermining. Even worse for the few republicans with an active nineteenth-century record, Lerroux and his associates instituted a system of political clientage and corruption that made them virtually no different than the regime's oligarchs.

When Lerroux decided that if he could not beat them he should join them, he betrayed so much of the republican message that had served him so well and that was present in virtually every page of his journalistic endeavors and those put out every week by José Nakens. For decades the criticism of the Restoration regime was that it was responsible for the decay and malaise of the nation. In orchestrating and manipulating elections, the monarchist elites and their network of *caciques* sapped the vigor of the Spanish nation embodied by the mobilized masses. Added to this discourse was the argument, especially in *El Motín*, that by allowing the clergy to insinuate into the state and regain the wealth and influence enjoyed before 1840, the Restoration regime itself was unpatriotic. At a time when Spanish national identity was in flux, given the rise of peripheral nationalisms in Catalonia and the Basque Country, the mobilization of the revolutionary left and ultramontanes, and the Restoration regime's inability or unwillingness to nationalize the Spaniards, Nakens, Lerroux, and other radical republicans were obsessed with rescuing the nation from its incongruent antimodern government. In order to rescue or redeem the nation, new civic republican values had to penetrate into the masses to tear down their traditional identification with Catholicism. This message was abandoned by Lerroux during his second coming.

It is also only fitting that Lerroux was nicknamed "El León" (The Lion) because he has rightfully drawn the lion's share of scholarly attention on *fin-de-siècle* republicanism. However, this book has focused much attention on José Nakens, the godfather of modern Spanish anticlericalism, and his fundamental belief that the emancipation, modernization, and democratization of Spain would come only through severely altering the relationship between the Catholic Church, state, and society. That, of course, would not come to Spain before his death, but from his very early beginnings, through the years as an annoying watchdog of the republican movement and his years as the cranky, semi-blind, semi-deaf, honorable delinquent, Nakens never stopped shouting the message that the Catholic Church stood as the ultimate source of oppression and the biggest impediment to the consolidation of a Spanish nation for Spaniards. Like the leaders of the Second Republic of 1931–1936 who suddenly found themselves in control of a populace, much of which was rural, illiterate, and ignorant of what liberal democracy promised them,[104] republicans such as Lerroux, Blasco Ibáñez, and Nakens did not assume that the Spanish nation existed. Nakens, perhaps more so than any other Restoration Spaniard, was engaged in the everyday exercise of taking such traditional attitudes and approaches as popular anticlericalism and recasting them anew through the mass production of his newspapers, cartoons, posters, postcards, plays, almanacs, and other media. He and his republican coreligionists were among the modern Spanish nationalists and nationalizers who were neglected in the important studies of comparative nationalism of our time. The establishment of an anticlerical tradition replete with the rhetorical, visual, and symbolic artifacts that hammered home the message that nationalism and political freedom came through anticlericalism was how Nakens sought to create Spaniards. As the campaign to issue a commemorative Nakens postage stamp in 1936 suggests, his efforts were anything but forgotten when a Second Spanish Republic became a reality.

Conclusion

The aftermath of the Spanish-American War did indeed constitute an opportunity for the regime's opponents to precipitate a dramatic trans-formation of the political system. At a time when the size and number of colonies were benchmarks of national vigor, Spain had lost all her colonies and had to be content with partition in Northern Morocco. British Prime Minister Lord Salisbury's assessment of a "moribund" Spain resonated among many Spaniards.[1] However, although it seemed that the collapse of the regime was imminent, no political changes disrupted the regime, which went on to govern for twenty-five more years. The military—discredited and factionalized—was left to their own devices in Morocco. The Carlists were a shadow of the once powerful movement that warred thrice with the Spanish state. The republicans too were divided between an older generation that worked within the political system and a generation of revolutionary populists agitating at the local urban level. Finally, the working class was much more concerned about problems of employment and prices than about lending support to groups planning political conspiracies. The Restoration regime survived the scare of the Spanish-American War largely because of a profound lack of consensus over how to regenerate Spain.

One force that permeated the boundary between the liberal and revolutionary-left oppositions was anticlericalism, which took cen-ter stage early in the twentieth century. A degree of commitment to curbing the Church and clergy's influence in society was perhaps the only factor that could unite some intellectuals, Liberals, republicans, anarchists, and socialists. Nakens therefore persisted with his pro-duction of an anticlerical review read by the learned and the lowest of peasants alike. Though his political credibility was shattered after aiding Morral, he was dearly admired by many and not forgotten when Spain experimented with liberal democracy in 1931.

Anticlericalism's potential was not lost on some of the Liberal Party's politicians, especially Canalejas. The aftermath of the Spanish-American War also presented the Liberal Party with an opportunity to rebuild support, incorporate the masses, and revive the dying nation. For the purposes of regenerating Spain, the Liberal Party's leadership adopted anticlericalism from the start of 1901. However, just as there was a lack of consensus over what should have been done politically after the Spanish-American War, an even more profound lack of consensus became manifest over what anticlericalism meant and what was to be done with its mobilizing power.

This book has presented the argument that anticlericalism was a crucial discourse of opposition to the regime and of republican nationalism. Anticlericalism, however, was too powerful a discourse for fragmented Liberals and republicans to control on their own terms. The central problem with anticlericalism was that it was multivocal: anticlericalism had too many messages and meanings, and it meant different things to different groups. Those republicans who emerged from *zorrillismo* were the best at incorporating anticlericalism as part of their nationalist culture. In other words, republicans convinced many when they preached that the answers to Spain's problems lay in politics, culture, and education rather than in economic reform or socialist revolution. Anticlericalism was a weapon used by the republicans to jar people into breaking out of the hegemonic Catholic mind-set. On the other hand, socialists and anarchists, especially those who engaged in the Tragic Week riots, saw in anticlericalism an expression of their dissatisfaction with social and economic failings of the Church, clergy, and Restoration state. That the state defended the property of the Church convinced them that the Church and state were collaborators in their oppression, and by the time the Second Republic was proclaimed in 1931, anticlericalism had become part and parcel of the social revolution for them.

Anticlericalism for Canalejas and the Liberal Democrats offered a path toward the modernization of the political system as well as a way to battle resurgent republican and leftist challenges. Canalejas genuinely hoped to reinvent the political system by accommodating nonelites and addressing their grievances so as to head off politicization from either the left or the right. He discovered that anticlericalism was wholly democratic because it meant obliterating the barriers to the liberation of the individual, but he could not control its power. Liberals such as Sagasta and successors, on the other hand, saw in anticlericalism an important way to differentiate themselves from the conservatives and also stay afloat while the united conservatives coalesced under Maura. This lack of consensus, or crisis of hegemony, explains why anticlericalism had the potential to, but ultimately could not, transform the regime. No one was in agreement over what to do with the anticlerical energy that had been built up since the end of the Spanish-American War.

The renewed anticlerical campaign that began as the Liberal Party's defensive action gradually became a full-scale assault aimed at modernizing liberal doctrine and reshaping the party's following. However, the Tragic Week convinced many intellectuals and politicians that ordinary Spaniards were not ready for a modern polity, and many military officers quickly shifted allegiances toward the right because they feared the working classes.[2] The events of the Barcelona Tragic Week were frightening to oligarchic and traditionalist Spain, and Maura's brutal repression of the rioters, which resulted in over one hundred deaths, including five executions, and about two thousand arrests, reflected the regime's keenness to put things right again.[3] The ferocity of this anticlerical episode provoked an even more ferocious response from a state that genuinely felt challenged by radical republicans and revolutionaries. If the rioters were actively seeking to disrupt the political order, to exercise their liberty by going against even the common respect traditionally afforded nuns and to the dead, then the regime felt impelled to exorcize the revolutionary threat and impose public order.[4] Anticlericalism became too out of hand for most people's taste, and when Canalejas was assassinated no one in formal position of power had the intestinal fortitude to carry on an anticlerical project.

The republicans, of course, never stopped. They were the first to link anticlericalism with nationalist aspirations. And while the state chose not to manufacture nationalism because it was too afraid of politicization, republicans such as Nakens had mass-produced the artifacts of an anticlerical nationalism through his journal, its cartoons, and other propaganda. But in linking anticlericalism with nationalism, radical republicans were putting forward a vision of Spain that was divisive rather unifying. They envisioned one Spain winning over and punishing the traditionalist/Catholic other. Anticlericalism's wholly liberal qualities were lost on republicans such as Nakens, Lerroux, and Blasco because their anticlericalism emphasized demolishing traditional Catholic morality over building a new imagined community. By advocating that rebels transform nuns into mothers, or asserting that Catholicism and republicanism were irreconcilable, they failed to realize that they were trying to destroy an entire way of life without putting something back in its place. Rather than accepting anticlericalism's liberal messages, the divisiveness of radical-republican anticlericalism is what the revolutionary classes took from them. And thus, the anticlerical nationalism of radical republicans helped polarize rather than unify Spanish identity, setting the stage for the religious/national antagonism of the Second Republic and the Spanish civil war.

*   *   *

Ironically, contemporary post-Franco Spain appears troubled by a national identity crisis given the reemergence of micro-nationalist ideas beyond those from industrialized Catalonia and the Basque Country.[5] The strength of these regional nationalisms can be explained by the Spanish state's poor showing during the age of nationalism when nationalizing the masses was needed not only by newly formed nation-states such as Germany and Italy but also by old monarchies reinvented in order to survive the modern world. While the Restoration regime's leaders seemed to understand the need for a nationalization project that could modernize the state, integrate or democratize the mobilized masses, and generate deep-seated love of the idea of a unified Spain, they were left seemingly helpless watching what remained of Spain's great empire get snatched away precisely when other European powers divided up the world.

The strength of contemporary regional nationalism can also be explained by the experience of the Franco Regime. Immediately after winning the Spanish Civil War, Franco and his sympathizers spent years eliminating anarchist, republican, and socialist ideologies, as well as the germinating regional identities. Extreme Catholicism and markedly conservative nationalism permeated every sphere of Spanish life and was symbolized by General Franco himself, portrayed as a neo El Cid who "re-conquered" Spain from atheists and communists.[6]

Yet Spanish national identity somehow continued to exist within the storm of competing and conflicting identities in the Iberian peninsula just as a nineteenth-century Spanish nationalist identity withstood the challenges of competing regional and religious identities during the Restoration. This book has shed light on one of the many articulations of how the Spanish nation was imagined during the Restoration: a secular, modern, and democratic Spain achieved through the internalization of anticlericalism and curbing clerical influence in society. While much of that nationalist idea of Nakens and the radical republicans was noble and positive, it was simultaneously vacuous in content and punitive toward Spaniards trying to reconcile their Catholic faith with the modern world. But the godless-republican-anticlerical-nationalist conception of Spain was no more intolerant of other Spaniards than was Carlism, racialist Basquism, or the National-Catholic ideas and movements of the Restoration. Spanish national identity has survived the challenges of Spain losing its empire, regional nationalisms after 1898 and after the end of the Franco Regime, radical republican efforts to make Spain similar to France (or at least recreate Spain in Republican France's image), and decades of living under the thumb of Franco's National-Catholicism, and this survival of the Spanish national identity bodes very well for the idea of Spain. When seen from this perspective, writes Alvarez Junco, Spanish identity "has been the political identity of greatest success to emerge in the Iberian peninsula during…the last millenium."[7]

Today what Spanishness means is to associate oneself with a "constitutional patriotism," a civic nationalism that celebrates multiculturalism and distances itself from Francoism.[8] That Spanishness now shines through in the spontaneous peaceful demonstrations against ETA's Terrorism, the record voter turn out after the Madrid train bombings in 2004, and taking pride in the fact that Spain's transition to democracy is considered practically paradigmatic to nations governed by nondemocratic polities.[9] Rooted in the 1978 Constitution is the enshrinement of a symbiotic relationship between Madrid and the periphery that at once makes Spain one of the most decentralized nation-states in the world and civically sanctifies the idea and history of one *España*. Given the experience and memory of the Franco Regime, I would add that today's Spanish identity is suspicious of the Catholic Church and unwilling to let it or any other institution undo the secularized modern nation that Spain has become. Though the Catholic Church, clergy, and lay activists currently grumble in opposition to very liberal and secular state legislations, these institutions face a prohibitive uphill climb if they share in Pope John Paul II's or Pope Benedict XVI's persistent unease with the modern world. For this reason the Spanishness of today will continue to be a pioneer in safeguarding the rights, freedoms, and identities of all its citizens, Basque or Castilian, gay or straight, female or male, religious or godless.

Notes

Introduction

1. AHN-GCE (Salamanca) P.S. Madrid, Leg. 4001, caja 455, exp. 44.
2. According to the *Diario de las sesiones de las Cortes Constituyentes de la República Española*, III, no. 54 (October 10, 1931): 1610–1611, Isabel Nakens was awarded 4,000 pesetas annually by the Republic.
3. AHN-GCE (Salamanca) P.S. Madrid, Leg. 4001, caja 455, exp. 44.
4. Standard works on nation-building projects in the late nineteenth- and early twentieth centuries include Eugen Weber, *Peasants into Frenchmen: The Modernization of Rural France, 1870–1914*; Linda Colley, *Britons: Forging the Nation, 1707–1837*; George Mosse, *The Nationalization of the Masses: Political Symbolism and Mass Movements in Germany from the Napoleonic Wars through the Third Reich*; Eric Hobsbawm and Terrence Ranger, eds. *The Invention of Tradition*, Canto edition; Eric Hobsbawm, *Nations and Nationalism since 1780*; and Norman Rich, *The Age of Nationalism and Reform, 1850–1890*.
5. To date, José Nakens has only been the subject of a book chapter: Manuel Pérez Ledesma, "José Nakens (1841–1926): pasión anticlerical y activismo republicano," in *Liberales, agitadores y conspiradores: biografías heterodoxas del siglo XIX*, ed. Isabel Burdiel and Manuel Pérez Ledesma, 301–330. I borrow the term "anticlerical industry" from Timothy Mitchell, *Betrayal of Innocents: Desire, Power, and the Catholic Church in Spain*, 37.
6. Joan Connelly Ullman, *The Tragic Week: A Study of Anticlericalism in Spain, 1875–1912*.
7. In addition to Ullman's *The Tragic Week*, see also Vicente Cárcel Ortí, *La persecución religiosa durante la Segunda República (1931–1939)*; Antonio Montero Moreno, *Historia de la persecución religiosa en España, 1936–1939*; Manuel Revuelta, S. J., *El anticlericalismo español en sus documentos*; Manuel Delgado Ruiz, *La ira sagrada. Anticlericalism, iconoclastia y antirritualismo en la España contemporánea*, c.f. Manuel Delgado Ruiz, "Anticlericalismo, espacio y poder. La destrucción de los rituals católicos, 1931–1939," in *El Anticlericalismo*; Demetrio Castro Alfín, "Cultura, política y cultura política en la violencia anticlericalismo," in *Movilización y cultura*

en la España contemporánea, 69–97; and the ethnographic study by Bruce Lincoln, "Revolutionary Exhumations in Spain, July 1936," *Comparative Studies in Society and History*, 27 (April 1985): 241–260.

8. Among these studies see especially, José Alvarez Junco, *El Emperador del Paralelo: Lerroux y la demagogia populista*, esp. 397–414; José Alvarez Junco, "El anticlericalismo en el movimiento obrero español," in *Octubre 1934. Cincuenta años para la reflexión*, 283–300; José Alvarez Junco, "Los intelectuales: anticlericalismo y republicanismo," in *Los orígenes culturales de la II República*, ed. José Luis García Delgado, 101–126; Julio de la Cueva Merino, *Clericales y anticlericales. El conflicto entre confesionalidad y sec-ulariazación en Cantabria. 1875–1923*; and Emilio La Parra and Manuel Súarez Cortina, *El anticlericalismo español*.

9. José Alvarez Junco's, *El Emperador* has been condensed and translated as *The Emergence of Mass Politics in Spain: Populist Demagoguery and Republican Culture, 1890–1910*. See also Alvarez Junco, "Los intelectu-ales: anticlericalismo y republicanismo," 101–126; and the essays in Nigel Townson, ed., *El Republicanismo en España (1830–1977)*. See also Julio de la Cueva Merino, "Movilización política e identidad anticlerical, 1898–1910," in *El Anticlericalismo*, ed. Rafael Cruz, 101–125, Ayer Series no. 27, and María del Pilar Salomón Chéliz, "El discurso anticlerical en la construc-ción de una identidad nacional española republicana (1989–1936)," *Historia Social* 54, 110 (2002): 485–498.

10. Mahadev L. Apte, *Humor and Laughter: An Anthropological Approach*, 30–31.

11. Ibid., 55–66.

12. Pérez Ledesma, "José Nakens," 303.

13. Víctor Manuel Arbeloa, *La Semana Trágica de la Iglesia en España (1931)*, 98; 210–211, n. 15. There is record of at least one man, a Freemason, taking the symbolic name of "Nakens" in the Barcelona KRONOS lodge at the time of the Spanish Civil War. See AHN-GCE (Salamanca)–Sección Masonería, Legajo 618, exp. 3.

14. At this the Spanish republicans were not alone. See for instance Michael B. Gross, *The War Against Catholicism: Liberalism and the Anti-Catholic Imagination in Nineteenth-Century Germany*; and more generally, René Rémond, *Religion and Society in Modern Europe*, esp. Parts II–III.

15. John A. Davis, "Italy," in *The War for the Public Mind: Political Censorship in the Nineteenth Century*, 113. See also Adrian Lyttelton, "An old Church and a New State: Italian Anticlericalism, 1876–1915," *European Studies Review* 13, 2 (1983): 225–245.

16. Gross, *The War against Catholicism*, 137.

17. Ibid., 136–184.

18. See Borja de Riquer, "La debil nacionalización española del siglo XIX," *Historia Social* 20 (1994): 97–114; Carlos Serrano, *El nacimiento de Carmen: símbolos, mitos, nación*; José Alvarez Junco, "The Nation-Building Process in Nineteenth-Century Spain," in *Nationalism and the Nation in the Iberian Peninsula: Competing and Conflicting Identities*, 89–106; and

Carolyn Boyd, *Historia Patria: Politics, History, and National Identity in Spain, 1875–1975*, esp. Chapters 1–5.

19. Among the "primordialist" school, see Carlton Hayes, *Nationalism: A Religion*; and Hans Kohn, *Nationalism, Its Meaning and History*, Revised edition; Adrian Hastings, *The Construction of Nationalism and Ethnicity: Religion and Nationalism*, 2–5; Anthony D. Smith, *The Ethnic Origins of Nations*, Second edition, c.f. Anthony D. Smith, "The Origins of Nations," in *Becoming National: A Reader*, ed. Geoff Eley and Ronald Grigor Suny, 106–130 (New York: Oxford University Press, 1996).

20. Benedict Anderson, *Imagined Communities: Reflections on the Origins and Spread of Nationalism*, revised edition, 4–8; Elie Kedourie, *Nationalism*, Fourth and expanded edition; Ernest Gellner, *Nations and Nationalism*; Eric Hobsbawm, *Nations and Nationalism since 1780*; and Eric Hobsbawm and Terence Ranger, ed. *The Invention of Tradition*.

21. Geoff Eley and Ronald Grigor Suny, "Introduction," in *Becoming National*, 7.

22. Albert Balcells and Geoffrey J. Walker, eds. *Catalan Nationalism: Past and Present*; Stanley G. Payne, *Basque Nationalism*; Daniele Conversi, *The Basques, the Catalans, and Spain: Alternative Routes to Nationalist Mobilization (Ethnonationalism in Comparative Perspective)*; Juan Díez Medrano, *Divided Nations: Class, Politics, and Nationalism in the Basque Country and Catalonia*, Wilder House Series in Politics, History, and Culture (Ithaca, NY: Cornell University Press, 1995); and Angel Smith and Clare Mar-Molinero, "The Myths and Realities of Nation-Building in the Iberian Peninsula," in *Nationalism and the Nation in the Iberian Peninsula*, 1–30.

23. José Alvarez Junco, *Mater dolorosa: la idea de España en el siglo XIX*; Carlos Serrano, *El nacimiento de Carmen. Símbolos, mitos y nación*; E. Inman Fox, *La invención de España. Nacionalismo liberal e identidad nacional*; Boyd, *Historia Patria*; and Sandie Holguín, *Creating Spaniards: Culture and National Identity in Republican Spain*.

24. Although Spain is one of the oldest political units in Europe, along with Britain and France, Liah Greenfeld, *Nationalism: Five Roads to Modernity*, chooses to completely ignore Spain's path to nationhood and, based on her index, Spain is not mentioned even once in this very important and influential study. One recent exception that devotes a great deal of space on Spain is Anthony W. Marx, *Faith in Nation: Exclusionary Origins of Nationalism*.

25. Prasenjit Duara, "Historicizing National Identity, or Who Imagines What and When," 153, cited in Holguín, *Creating Spaniards*, 8.

26. Holguín, *Creating Spaniards*, 6–7. See also Pamela Beth Radcliff, "La representación de la nación. El conflicto en torno a la identidad nacional y las prácticas simbólicas en la Segunda República." Holguín parts company with scholars who accuse the Second Republic leaders of not seeing the need to create new traditions or revive old ones. See for instance Helen Graham, "Community, Nation and State in Republican Spain, 1931–1938," 133–147.

27. Alvarez Junco, *Mater dolorosa*, 19.

28. Ibid., 20.

29. Ibid., 12–16. Hobsbawm, *Nations and Natonalism since 1870*, 163–192. See also José Alvarez Junco, "Hobsbawm sobre nacionalismo," *Historia Social* 25 (1996): 179–187, for additional critiques of Hobsbawm.

30. Alvarez Junco, "Nation-Building in Nineteenth-Century Spain," especially 102. See also Juan Sisinio Pérez Garzón, "Los mitos fundacionales y el tiempo de la unidad imaginada del nacionalismo español," *Historia Social* 40 (2001): 7–28.

31. Mary Vincent, *Spain, 1833–2002*, 51–78.

32. See Nigel Aston, *Religion and Revolution in France, 1780–1804*; Michael Burleigh, *Earthly Powers: The Clash of Religion and Politics in Europe from the French Revolution to the Great War*; Christopher Clark and Wolfram Kaiser, eds., *Culture Wars: Secular-Catholic Conflicts in Nineteenth-Century Europe*; Maurice Cowling, *Religion and Public Doctrine in Modern England*, 3 vols.; Marcel Gauchet, *The Disenchantment of the Modern World: A Political History of Religion*; Sudhir Hazareesingh, *Political Traditions in Modern France*; Arlie J. Hoover, *The Gospel of Nationalism: German Patriotic Preaching from Napoleon to Versailles*; Dale K. van Kley, *The Religious Origins of the French Revolution: From Calvin to the Civil Constitution, 1560–1791*; Anthony Marx, *Faith in Nation*; Richard John Neuhas, *The Naked Public Square: Religion and Democracy in America*; Anthony Rhodes, *The Power of Rome in the Twentieth-Century: The Vatican in the Age of Liberal Democracies, 1870–1922*; Roland Sarti, *Mazzini: A Life for the Religion of Politics*; Helmut Walser Smith, *German Nationalism and Religious Conflict: Culture, Ideology, and Politics, 1870–1914*; Michael Sutton, *Nationalism, Positivism and Catholicism: The Politics of Charles Maurras and French Catholics, 1890–1914*; and A. N. Wilson, *God's Funeral: A Biography of Faith and Doubt in Western Civilization*.

33. See Manuel Revuelta González, "Religión y formas de religiosidad," in *Historia de España, Ramón Menéndez Pidal*, Vol. XXXV, 221–237; Scott Eastman, "Constructing the Nation within a Catholic Tradition: Modernity and National Identities Across the Spanish Monarchy, 1793–1823," (Ph.D. diss, University of California, Irvine, 2006).

34. Manuel Suárez Cortina, *El Gorro Frigio: Liberalismo, Democracia y Republicanismo en la Restauración*, 192, n. 10.

35. José Sánchez, *Anticlericalism: A Brief History*, 7.

36. Rafael Cruz, "Introducción," in *El Anticlericalismo*, Ayer Series no. 27, 11.

37. See José Alvarez Junco, "Los intelectuales: anticlericalismo y republicanismo," in *Los orígenes culturales de la II República*, 101–126; José Alvarez Junco, *El Emperador*, 397–418; Julio de la Cueva Merino, *Clericales y anticlericales*.

38. J. Salwyn Schapiro, *Anticlericalism: Conflict between Church and State in France, Italy, and Spain*, 32.

39. Nigel Aston and Matthew Cragoe, eds., *Anticlericalism in Britain, 1500–1914*; and D. G. Paz, *Popular Anti-Catholicism in Mid-Victorian England*; and John Wolffe, *The Protestant Crusade in Britain, 1829–1860*.

40. Sánchez, *Anticlericalism,* 3–75; Peter A. Dykema and Heiko A. Obeman, *Anticlericalism in Late Medieval and Modern Europe.*

41. Julio Caro Baroja, *Introducción a una historia contemporánea del anti-clericalismo español,* 14, 44; Sánchez, *Anticlericalism.,* 79–93; and René Rémond, "Anticlericalism: Some Reflections by way of Introduction," *European Studies Review* 13, 2 (April 1983): 121–126. See also René Rémond, *L'Anticlericalisme en France de 1815 à nos jours,* new and updated version, 3–16.

42. Sánchez, *Anticlericalism,* 79.

43. William J. Callahan, *The Catholic Church in Spain, 1875–1998,* 51. See also Joan Connelly Ullman, "The Warp and Woof of Parliamentary Politics in Spain, 1808–1939: Anticlericalism versus 'Neo-Catholicism,'" *European Studies Review* 13, 2 (1983): 155–161.

44. David A. Martin, *A General Theory of Secularization;* Owen Chadwick, *The Secularization of the European Mind,* Canto edition; Richard Fenn, *Toward a Theory of Secularization;* and Karel Dobbelaere, *Secularization: A Multi-Dimensional Concept,* a special issue of *Current Sociology* 29, 2 (1981): 1–216.

45. Julio de la Cueva Merino, "The Stick and the Candle: Clericals and Anticlericals in Northern Spain, 1898–1913," *European History Quarterly* 26 (April 1996): 248–249.

46. *European Studies Review* 13 (1983). Two exceptional historiographic essays on Spanish anticlericalism are: Pilar Salomón Chéliz, "Poder y ética. Balance historiográfico sobre anticlericalismo," *Historia Social,* 19 (1994): 113–128; and Manuel Pérez Ledesma, "Studies on Anticlericalism in Contemporary Spain," *International Review of Social History* 46 (2001): 227–255.

47. Here the work of Pamela Beth Radcliff, *From Mobilization to Civil War: The Politics of Polarization in the Spanish City of Gijón, 1900–1937,* especially pages 3–8, is illustrative. Radcliff uses John Clarke, Stuart Hall, Tony Jefferson, and Brian Roberts, "Subcultures, Cultures and Class: A Theoretical Overview," in *Resistance Through Rituals: Youth Subcultures in Post-War Britain,* 9–74, in order to understand hegemony and counterhegemony as a contest over winning space, or over competing systems of power and legitimacy. On the application of Gramscian notions of hegemony to historical research, see T. J. Jackson Lears, "The Concept of Cultural Hegemony: Problems and Possibilities," *American Historical Review* 90 (June 1985): 567–593, c.f. Antonio Gramsci, *Selections from the Prison Notebooks.*

48. Jürgen Habermas, *The Structural Transformation of the Public Sphere: An Inquiry into a Category of Bourgeois Society,* originally published in German in 1962.

49. Exceptional histories of nineteenth-century Spain include Vincent, *Spain 1833–2002;* Raymond Carr, *Spain, 1808–1975,* Second edition; and Charles Esdaile, *Spain in the Liberal Age: From Constitution to Civil War, 1808–1936.* On Spain's Carlist Wars, see Josep Carles Clemente, *El Carlismo. Historia de una disidencia social (1833–1976);* Román Oyarzúra, *Historia del Carlismo,* Third edition; and John Coverdale, *The Basque Phase of Spain's First Carlist War.* For the military problems, see Manuel Balbé,

Orden público y militarismo en la España constitucional, 1812–1983; Julio Busquets, *Pensamiento y golpes de Estado en España*; Carolyn P. Boyd, *Praetorian Politics in Liberal Spain*; and Eric Christiansen, *The Origins of Military Power in Spain*. For Spain's nineteenth-century economy see David R. Ringrose, *Spain, Europe, and the "Spanish Miracle," 1700–1900*; Gabriel Tortella, *The Development of Modern Spain: An Economic History of the Nineteenth and Twentieth Centuries*; and Leandro Prados de la Escosura, *De imperio a nación. Crecimiento y atraso económico en España (1870–1930)*. On Spain's First Republic, see C. A. M. Hennessy, *The Federal Republic in Spain: Pi y Margall and the Federalist Republican Movement, 1868–1874*.

50. José Varela Ortega, *Los amigos políticos. Partidos, elecciones y caciquismo en la Restauración (1875–1900)* (Madrid, 1977); c.f. José Varela Ortega, "Los amigos políticos: funcionamiento del sistema caciquista," *Revista de Occidente* 127 (1973): 45–74. See also Javier Tusell, *Oligarquía y caciquismo en Andalucía (1890–1923)*; Miguel Martínez Cuadrado, *Elecciones y partidos en España (1868–1931)*; Miguel Artola, *Partidos y programas políticos, 1808–1936*; Robert Kern, *Liberals, Reformers and Caciques in Restoration Spain, 1875–1909*; Luis Sánchez Agesta, *Historia del constitucionalismo español*, Second edition; Juan J. Linz, "The Party System of Spain: Past and Future," in *Party Systems and Voter Alignments: Cross-National Perspectives*, 198–282; and Vincent, *Spain, 1833–2002*, 51–78.

51. Carolyn Boyd, *Historia Patria*, xviii, 3–40.

52. José Alvarez Junco, *Mater dolorosa*, 533 ff.

53. Pamela Beth Radcliff, "The Emerging Challenge of Mass Politics," 154.

54. See Hilda Sábato, "Citizenship, Political Participation, and the Formation of the Public Sphere in Buenos Aires, 1850s–1880s," *Past and Present* 136 (August 1992): 139–163 for a case study of informal means of political participation; and David Ortiz, Jr. *Paper Liberals: Press and Politics in Restoration Spain*.

55. Antonio Montero Moreno, *Historia de la persecución religiosa en España, 1936–1939*, 761–764, cited in Julio de la Cueva Merino, "Religious Persecution, Anticlerical Tradition, and Revolution: On Atrocities against the Clergy during the Spanish Civil War," *Journal of Contemporary History* 33, 3 (July 1998): 359. See also Bruce Lincoln, "Revolutionary Exhumations in Spain, July 1936," 241–260.

Chapter 1

1. On the immediate post-Napoleonic period, see Robin W. Winks and Joan Neuberger, *Europe and the Making of Modernity, 1815–1914*, especially 1–40 and 130–193; and Michael Rapport, *Nineteenth-Century Europe*, especially 31–52 and 271–322.

2. Burleigh, *Earthly Powers*, 23–66.

3. Nigel Aston, *Religion and Revolution in France*, 81–162; David Bell, *The Cult of the Nation in France. Inventing Nationalism, 1680–1800*; and Dale K. van Kley, *The Religious Origins of the French Revolution*.

4. Eastman, "Constructing the Nation Within a Catholic Tradition," vi, 10–11, 259–263.
5. Ibid., 261.
6. Calhoun, *Nationalism*, 125.
7. Ibid.
8. John N. Schumacher, "Integrism: A Study in Nineteenth Century Spanish Politico-Religious Thought," *Catholic Historical Review* 48 (1962): 343.
9. José María Díaz Mozaz, *Apuntes para una sociología del anticlericalismo*, 56.
10. Alvarez Junco, "The Nation-Building Process in Nineteenth-Century Spain," 89–91.
11. Peter Sahlins, *Boundaries: The Making of France and Spain in the Pyrenees*, esp. 110–132.
12. Francisco Martí Gilabert, *La Iglesia en España durante la revolución francesa.*
13. Castro Alfín, "Cultura, política y cultura política," 86.
14. Manuel Revuelta González, S. J., *Política Religiosa de los Liberales en el Siglo XIX*, 2; Stanley G. Payne, *Spanish Catholicism: An Historical Overview*, 72; and Raymond Carr, *Spain, 1808–1975*, 81–92, 105–106.
15. Payne, *Spanish Catholicism*, 72.
16. William J. Callahan, *Church, Politics, and Society, 1750–1874*, 81; and José Antonio Portero Molina, *Púlpito e ideologia en la España del siglo XIX.*
17. Eastman, "Constructing the Nation Within a Catholic Tradition," 78–79.
18. Charles J. Esdaile, *Fighting Napoleon: Guerrillas, Bandits and Adventurers in Spain, 1808–1814.*
19. José Alvarez Junco, "La invención de la Guerra de la Independencia," *Studia Historica* 12 (1994): 75–99. See also Alvarez Junco, *Mater dolorosa*, 119–184; and Joan Mercader Riba, "La feria tradicional de San Narciso y las autoridades napoleónicas," *Anales del Instituto de Estudios Gerundenses* 3 (1984): 222–225.
20. William J. Callahan, "Two Spains and Two Churches, 1760–1835," *Historical Reflections* 2 (1975): 158–181; Manuel Revuelta González, "Clero viejo y clero nuevo en el siglo XIX," in *Estudios históricos sobre la Iglesia española contemporanea*, 153–197.
21. Francisco Xavier Tapia, "Las relaciones Iglesia-Estado durante el primer experimento liberal en España (1820–1823)," *Revista de Estudios Políticos* 173 (1970): 69–89.
22. Manuel Revuelta González, S. J. "La supresión de la Compañía de Jesús en España en 1820," *Razón y Fe*, 170–171 (1970): 103–120.
23. Revuelta González, *Política Religiosa*, 378; Callahan, *Church, Politics, and Society*, 122.
24. Miñano Bedoya's *Lamentos políticos de un pobrecito holgazán que estaba acostumbrado a vivir a costa agena*, is analyzed in Revuelta González, *Política Religiosa*, 60–74.
25. The heated passions over forcing the clergy to accept the liberal constitution mirrored a similar battle in Revolutionary France. See for instance Timothy Tackett, *Religion, Revolution, and Regional Culture in Eighteenth-Century*

France: The Ecclesiastical Oath of 1791; Kley, The Religious Origins of the French Revolution; and John McManners, The French Revolution and the Church.

26. Viscount de Martignac, Essai historique sur la révolution d'Espagne et sur l'intervention de 1823 (Paris, 1823), I: 161, cited in Francisco Rodríguez de Coro, "Anticlericalismo y sociedad madrileña en el siglo XIX," Anales del Instituto de Estudios Madrileños 28 (1990): 362.

27. Memorias de Don Alcalá-Galiano, publicadas por su hijo (Madrid, 1886), II: 118–119, cited in Francisco Rodríguez de Coro, "Anticlericalismo y sociedad madrileña en el siglo XIX," 363.

28. Callahan, Church, Politics, and Society, 134. For the creation and rise of Madrid as the political capital see Vincent, Spain, 1833–2002, 58–64 and Santos Juliá et al., Madrid: Historia de una capital.

29. Ibid., 124.

30. Pío Baroja cited in Edouard Barry, ed., España y españoles: paisaje, monumentos, tipos de la corte y de provincias, usos y costumbres, leyendas y tradiciones (Paris, 1913), 235.

31. William Callahan, "The Origins of the Conservative Church in Spain, 1793–1823," European Studies Review 10 (April 1980): 217.

32. See Portero Molina, Púlpito e ideología.

33. See Juan Mercader Riba, "Orígenes del anticlericalismo español," Hispania 33, 123 (1973): 100–123; and Emilio La Parra López, "Los inicios del anticlericalismo español contemporáneo (1750–1833)," 45–61.

34. Juan Sisinio Pérez Garzón, "Curas y liberales en la revolución burguesa," in Rafale Cruz, ed., El Anticlericalismo, 77–78; Juame Torras, Liberalismo y rebeldía campesina, 1820–1823; and Esteban Carro Celada, Curas guerrilleros en España (Madrid, 1970).

35. Callahan, Church, Politics, and Society, 128.

36. Payne, Spanish Catholicism, 78; Callahan, Church, Politics, and Society, 141–142.

37. Vicente Cárcel Ortí, Política eclesial de los gobiernos liberales españoles, 1830–1840; and Manuel Revuelta González, La exclaustración, 1833–1840.

38. Coverdale, The Basque Phase, 263–283.

39. Javier Puerto and Carlos San Juan, "La epidemia de cólera de 1834 en Madrid," Estudios de Historia Social, 15 (1980): 9–61.

40. Payne, Spanish Catholicism, 82; and Salvador Camacho Pérez, "Violencia anticlerical en Madrid en julio de 1834," Almotacín. Revista de la E.U. del Profesorado de EGB de Almería, 9 (Jan–June 1987): 68–101. See also Anna M. García Rovira, La revolució liberal a Espanya i les classes populars (1832–1835).

41. Pérez Garzón, "Curas y liberales," 82.

42. Ibid., 84.

43. Caro Baroja, Introducción a una historia contemporanea del anticlericalismo español, 155.

44. Ibid., 87–88.

45. Angel Bahamonde Magro and Jesús A. Martínez-Martín, "La desamortización y el mercado inmobilario madrileño (1836–1868)," in *Urbanismo e historia urbana en el mundo hispano*, 2 vols, II: 939–956; Simón Segura, *La desamortización española del siglo XIX*; and Germán Rueda Hernanz, ed., *La desamortización en la península ibérica*, Ayer Series 9.
46. David Ringrose, *Spain, Europe, and the "Spanish Miracle,"* 180.
47. Callahan, *Church, Politics, and Society*, 183. See also Riquer i Permanyer, "La débil nacionalización española," 111–112.
48. Callahan, *Church, Politics, and Society*, 181–182.
49. Ibid., 199–201; Payne, *Spanish Catholicism*, 90; Segura, *La desamortización*, 175.
50. Riquer i Permanyer, "La débil nacionalización española," 112.
51. Callahan, *Church, Politics, and Society*, 236–237.
52. Gómez Aparicio, *Historia del periodismo*, I: 449–452.
53. Caro Baroja, *Introducción a una historia contemporanea del anticlericalismo español*, 203. See also Gómez Aparicio, *Historia del Periodismo*, I: 559–565.
54. Gómez Aparicio, *Historia del Periodismo*, II: 109.
55. Callahan, *Church, Politics, and Society*, 250–251; Payne, *Spanish Catholicism*, 93; and Vicente Cárcel Orti, *Iglesia y revolución en España (1868–1874): estudio histórico-jurídico desde la documentación vaticana inedita*, 134–139.
56. Callahan, *Church, Politics, and Society*, 265.
57. Cárcel Ortí, *Iglesia y revolución*, 135.
58. Payne, *Spanish Catholicism*, 93; see also Francisco Pérez Gutiérrez, *El problema religioso de la generación de 1868: la leyenda de Dios*, and Paul Drochon, "Juan Valera et la liberté religieuse," *Mélanges de la Casa de Velázquez* 8 (1972): 407–444.
59. Vincent, *Spain 1833–2002*, 38–44; José A. Piqueras Arenas, "Detrás de la política: República y federación en el proceso revolucionario español," in *Republicanos y repúblicas en España*, 1–44; and C. A. M. Hennessy, *The Federal Republic in Spain*.
60. Julio de la Cueva Merino, *Clericales y anticlericales*, c.f. Julio de la Cueva Merino, "The Stick and the Candle," 241–265. For Málaga, see Elías de Mateo Avilés, *El anticlericalismo en Málaga (1875–1923)*; and Mateo Avilés, *Paternalismo burgués y beneficiencia religiosa en la Málaga desde la segunda mitad del siglo XIX*. On Valencia, see Ramiro Reig, *Blasquistas y clericales. La lucha por la ciudad en la Valencia de 1900* (Valencia, 1986).
61. José Alvarez Junco, *La ideología política del anarquismo español (1868–1910)*, esp. 204–214, and 217–220; and José Alvarez Junco, "El anticlericalismo en el movimiento obrero español."
62. José María Palomares Ibáñez, "La recuperación económica de la iglesia española (1845–1931)," and Juan Carlos Frías Fernández, "Imágenes y explicaciones de la recuperación económica de la iglesia: los anticlericales entre 1876–1899," in *Iglesia, Sociedad y Estado en España, Francia e Italia (ss. XVII al XX)*, 153–172 and 173–183, respectively (Alicante, 1991); Manuel

Revuelta González, "La recuperación eclesiástica y el rechazo anticlerical en el cambio del siglo"; William Callahan, "The Spanish Parish Clergy, 1874–1930," *Catholic Historical Review* LXXV (1989): 405–422; and Callahan, "An Organization and Pastoral Failure," *European Religion in the Age of the Great Cities, 1830–1930*, 43–60.

63. Manuel de Puelles Benítez, "Secularización y enseñanza en España (1874–1917)," in *España entre dos siglos*, 191–212, VII Coloquio de Historia Contemporánea de España; Manuel de Puelles Benítez, *Educación e ideología en la España contemporanea*, Second edition (Barcelona, 1991); Yvonne Turin, *La educación y la escuela en España de 1874 a 1902. Liberalismo y tradición*; Angel Smith, *Anarchism, Revolution and Reaction: Catalan Labour and the Crisis of the Spanish State, 1898–1923*, 146–148; and Carolyn Boyd, *Historia Patria*.

64. Ullman, *The Tragic Week*; Alvarez Junco, *El Emperador*, 375–378; Xavier Cuadrat, "La Setmana Tràgica i el moviment obrer a Catalunya," *L'Avenç* 2 (1977): 44–48; and Joan B. Culla i Clará, *El republicanisme lerrouxista a Catalunya (1901–1923)*, 205–217.

65. Joaquín Romero Maura, *La rosa del fuego. Republicanos y anarquistas: la política de los obreros barceloneses entre el desastre colonial y la semana trágica, 1899–1909*, especially 509–540.

66. The link between nationalism and *ressentiment* (defined as a psychological state resulting from suppressed feelings of envy and hatred [or existential envy] and the impossibility of satisfying these feelings) is central to the work of Liah Greenfeld, *Nationalism: Five Roads to Modernity*, 15–17. Though she applies the concept to how one nation (say France) feels about another's national model (say England), I suggest the Catholic Church was both resented and admired as a model of cultural hegemony and authority.

67. For French anticlericalism see Sánchez, *Anticlericalism*, 95–122; Philip Spencer, *The Politics of Belief in Nineteenth-Century France*; Rémond, *L'anticlericalisme en France*; Geoffrey Cubitt, *The Jesuit Myth: Conspiracy Theory and Politics in Nineteenth Century France*; Theodore Zeldin, *Conflicts in French Society: Anticlericalism, Education, and Morals in the Nineteenth Century*; Pamela M. Pilbeam, *Republicanism in Nineteenth-Century France, 1814–1871*, 87-ff; Sanford Elwitt, *The Making of the 3rd Republic: Class and Politics in France, 1868–1884*, 135-ff; Philip A. Bertocci, *Jules Simon: Republican Anticlericalism and Cultural Politics in France. 1848–1886*; Malcolm O. Partin, *Waldeck-Rousseau, Combes, and the Church: The Politics of Anticlericalism, 1899–1905*; and Jacqueline Lalouette, "El anticlericalismo en Francia, 1877–1914," in *El Anticlericalismo*, 15–38, Ayer Series 27.

68. Jean-Denis Bredin, *The Affair: The Case of Alfred Dreyfus*, 522.

69. See Partin, *Waldeck-Rousseau, Combes, and the Church*.

70. See Ford, *Creating the Nation in Provincial France: Religion and Political Identity*, 320. Herman Lebovics, *True France: The Wars over Cultural Identity, 1900–1945*.

71. Philip Nord, *The Republican Moment*.

72. Ralph Gibson, *A Social History of French Catholicism, 1789–1914*, ix, 241–247; see also Ralph Gibson, "Hellfire and Damnation in Nineteenth-Century France," *Catholic Historical Review* LXXIV (July 1988): 383–402.
73. Jacques Gadille, "On French Anticlericalism: Some Reflections," *European Studies Review* 13 (April 1983): 131.
74. Jean Faury, *Cléricalisme et anticléricalisme dans le Tarn (1848–1900)*, Series A, no. 41.
75. Joseph N. Moody, *The Church as Enemy: Anticlericalism in Nineteenth Century French Literature*, 115–121; see also Bertocci, *Jules Simón*, 18–19.
76. Lebovics, *True France*, 189. Of course, this does not mean that the Third Republic did not undertake the challenge of mass-producing a nationalist tradition. See Eugen Weber, *Peasants into Frenchmen*, and Eric Hobsbawm, "Mass-Producing Traditions: Europe, 1870–1914," 269–273.
77. See Johnathan Sperber, *Popular Catholicism in Nineteenth-Century Germany*. On the German Center Party, see Ronald J. Ross, *Beleaguered Tower: The Dilemma of Political Catholicism in Wilhelmine Germany*; and David Blackbourn, *Class, Religion, and Local Politics in Wilhelmine Germany: The Center Party in Württemberg before 1914*.
78. Ian Farr, "From Anti-Catholicism to Anticlericalism: Catholic Politics and the Peasantry in Bavaria, 1860–1900," *European Studies Review* 13 (1983): 250.
79. Studies in English of the *Kulturkampf* include Sperber, *Popular Catholicism*, 207–276; Helmut W. Smith, *German Nationalism and Religious Conflict*, esp. 19–49; Margaret Lavinia Anderson, "The *Kulturkampf* and the Course of German History," *Journal of Modern History* 19 (1986): 82–115; and Gross, *The War Against Catholicism*.
80. Sperber, *Popular Catholicism*, 219.
81. Helmut W. Smith, *German Nationalism and Religious Conflict*, 233.
82. Ibid., 238.
83. Giovanni Spadolini, *I repubblicani dopo l'unità* (Florence, 1960); and Giovanni Spadolini, *L'Italia repubblicana: attraverso i simboli, i dipinti, le foto d'epoca, e i documenti revive una straordinaria storia per immagini dell'idea repubblicana*.
84. Sánchez, *Anticlericalism*, 143–157; Schapiro, *Anticlericalism*, 72–85; Adrian Lyttleton, "An Old Church and a New State: Italian Anticlericalism 1876–1915," *European Studies Review* 13 (1983): 225–245; and S. William Halperin, "Italian Anticlericalism, 1871–1914," *Journal of Modern History* 19, 1 (March 1947): 17–34.
85. Donald Howard Bell, *Sesto San Giovanni: Workers, Culture, and Politics in an Italian Town, 1880–1922*; c.f. Bell, "Worker Culture and Worker Politics: The Experience of an Italian Town, 1880–1915," *Social History* 3 (1978): 1–21.
86. Lyttelton, "An Old Church and a New State," 225.
87. Burleigh, *Earthly Powers*, 185–198, and Roland Sarti, *Mazzini*.
88. Sánchez, *Anticlericalism*, 144.
89. Gregory L. Freeze, "A Case of Stunted Anticlericalism: Clergy and Society in Imperial Russia," *European Studies Review* 13 (1983): 177–200; c.f.

Gregory L. Freeze, *The Parish Clergy in Nineteenth-Century Russia: Crisis, Reform, Counter-Reform*.

90. Freeze, "A Case of Stunted Anticlericalism," 183–185, 193.

Chapter 2

1. *El Debate*, November 16, 1926, cited in María Cruz Seoane and María Dolores Saíz, *Historia del Periodismo en España. Vol. III: El Siglo XX: 1898–1936*, 114.
2. Arturo Mori, "El martiro de Nakens," *El País*, February 22, 1913.
3. Ledesma, "José Nakens (1841–1926)," 301–330.
4. Callahan, *The Catholic Church in Spain*,173. According to *Enciclopedia Universal Ilustrada Europea Americana*, Vol. XXXVII (Madrid, 1987), s.v. "Nakens, José," 954–955, over fifty legal proceedings, including libel lawsuits by angry priests or parishioners were filled against Nakens.
5. Alvarez Junco, *El Emperador*, 53–90.
6. See especially Ramiro Reig, *Blasquistas y clericales*.
7. Rafael Cansinos-Asséns, *La novela de un literario*, 3 vols., I: 39.
8. Cansinos-Asséns, *La novela de un literario*, I: 41.
9. On Ferrándiz see José Luis Molina Martínez, *Anticlericalismo y literatura en el siglo XIX* (Murcia, 1998), 293–345.
10. See "Un nuevo Panamá," *El Motín*, December 11, 1897; and "Panamá Clerical," *El Motín*, December 25, 1897.
11. Cansinos Asséns, *La novela de un literario*, I: 45.
12. See Alvarez Junco, *El Emperador*, 213–214, n. 121.
13. The work of Nietzsche appeared to have been widely read by the *El Motín* circle of friends. See for example, Viriato Díaz Pérez, "El irreverente Nietzsche," *El Motín*, October 10, 1903.
14. José Nakens, "Apuntes Biográficos," *El Motín*, September 12, 1889. This article also appears in Nakens, *Trozos de mi vida* (Madrid, 1914? or 1915?), 7–16.
15. José Nakens, "Por qué soy anticlérico," *El Motin*, December 9, 1894.
16. "Apuntes Biográficos," *El Motín*, September 12, 1889. Alcolea, a small town on the Guadalquivir River near Córdoba, was the site of the decisive battle between military factions led by Generals Prim and Serrano and Royalist troops whose defeat led to Queen Isabel II's abdication and exile.
17. Ibid.
18. This early version of *El Resumen* should not be confused with the radical-liberal Madrid daily founded in 1885 under the same name. According to Pedro Gómez Aparicio, *Historia del Periodismo Español*, II, 143 and 265, Moja y Bolívar's federal-republican newspaper only produced eighteen weeks of issues. Moja moved on to write for the mouthpiece of the republican movement in the 1880s, *El Solfeo*.
19. For a history of the First Republic generally sympathetic to the Federalists see Hennessy, *The Federal Republic in Spain*.

20. Nakens, "Carta a un amigo," *El Globo*, November 30, 1885: 241. See also Nakens's other articles on this subject in *El Globo*, December 23, 1885: 333–334, and December 24, 1885: 337–338. On the plagiarism incident see Emilia Pardo Bazán, *Campoamor. Estudio biográfico* (Madrid, 1893?): 47–49.

21. José Alvarez Junco, "Los 'Amantes de la Libertad,'" in El republicanismo español (1830–1977), 275; and José Alvarez Junco, "Racionalismo, romanticismo y moralismo en la cultura política republicana de comienzos de siglo," in *Clases populares, cultura, educación. Siglos XIX–XX*, Jean-Louis Guereña and Alejandro Tiana, eds., 355–375 (Madrid, 1989), esp. 358–361.

22. Gómez Aparicio, *Historia del periodismo español*, II: 445–447.

23. Pérez Ledesma, "José Nakens," 309, 313.

24. In 1883, Nakens took full author credit for the book *Espejo Moral de Clérigos* (Madrid, 1883), a compilation of anecdotes from *El Motín's* "Manojo de Flores Místicas" section.

25. Jesús Timoteo Alvarez, *Restauración y prensa de masas*, 302.

26. Ortiz, Jr., *Paper Liberals: Press and Politics in Restoration Spain*, 13, 108–113.

27. "Ley de Imprenta de 26 de junio de 1883," in *Colección Legislativa de España*, Second Semester of 1883, Volume CXXXI (Madrid, 1884), 221–225.

28. *El Motín*, April 10, 1881.

29. José María López Ruiz, *La Vida Alegre: Historia de las revistas humorísticas, festivas y satíricas publicadas en la Villa y Corte de Madrid*, 28.

30. See Carmen Llorca, *Emilio Castelar. Precursor de la democracia cristiana*.

31. "Hasta las mujeres," *El Motín*, January 15, 1888.

32. *El Motín*, April 11, 1896.

33. Nakens, "Apuntes Biográficos," *El Motín*, September 12, 1889.

34. "Lealtad a Pi," *El Motín*, September 29, 1889.

35. *El Motín*, October 13, 1889.

36. "Lo de siempre," *El Motín*, December 15, 1889.

37. Carlos Dardé, "Biografía política de Nicolás Salmerón (c. 1860–1890)," in *Republicanismo y República en España*, 135–161 (Madrid, 2000).

38. "Actos y palabras," *El Motín*, February 16, 1890.

39. "Lealtad Filosófica," *El Motín*, February 30, 1890.

40. Prior to his death in June of 1895, Ruiz Zorrilla formally withdrew from politics in an open letter to his coreligionists reprinted in "Despedida," *El Motín*, February 23, 1895.

41. Mosse, *The Nationalization of the Masses*, 2.

42. Eric J. Hobsbawm, "Introduction: Inventing Traditions," in *The Invention of Tradition*, 1–14. In addition to Mosse's *The Nationalization of the Masses*, see George L. Mosse, "Caesarism, Circuses, and Monuments," *Journal of Contemporary History* 6 (1971): 167–182, and Charles Rearick, "Festivals in Modern France: The Experience of the Third Republic," *Journal of Contemporary History* 12 (1977): 435–460.

43. See Jean-Jacques Rousseau, *On the Social Contract*, in *The Basic Political Writings*, edited and translated by Donald A. Cress (Indianapolis, 1987), 141–227.

44. Clifford Geertz, "Centers, Kings, and Charisma: Reflections on the Symbolics of Power," in *Culture and Its Creators: Essays in Honor of Edward Shils*, ed. Joseph Ben-David and Terry N. Clark, 151–170 (Chicago, 1977).

45. Lynn Hunt, *Politics, Culture, and Class in the French Revolution* (Berkeley, 1986), 53–58.

46. Mona Ozouf, *Festivals and the French Revolution*, translated by Alan Sheridan (Cambridge, MA, 1988), 9. See also Jonathan Sperber, "Festivals of National Unity in the German Revolution of 1848–1849," *Past and Present* 136 (1992): 114–138.

47. Hobsbawm, "Introduction: Inventing Traditions," 12.

48. David Kertzer, *Ritual, Politics, and Power*, 178.

49. David Cannadine, "The Context, Performance and Meaning of Ritual: The British Monarchy and the 'Invention of Tradition,' c. 1820–1977," in Hobsbawm and Ranger, eds., *The Invention of Tradition*, 101–164; and David Cannadine, "Splendor Out of Court: Royal Spectacle and Pageantry in Modern Britain, c. 1820–1977," in *Rites of Power*, ed. Sean Wilentz, 206–243 (Philadelphia, 1985).

50. Kertzer, *Ritual, Politics, and Power*, 2.

51. Ibid., 76.

52. Sperber, "Festivals of National Unity in Germany," 119–130, 137–138.

53. Rafael Cruz, "La cultura regresa al primer plano," 24.

54. Ibid.

55. Demetrio Casto Alfín, "Orígenes y primeras etapas del republicanismo en España," in Nigel Townson, ed., *El republicanismo español (1830–1977)*, 33–57.

56. For Spanish republicanism see Nigel Townson, ed., *El republicanismo en España (1830–1977)*; Alvarez Junco, *El Emperador;* José A. Piqueras and Manuel Chust, eds., *Republicanos y repúblicas en España*; Angel Duarte and Pere Gabriel, ed., *El republicanismo español*, Ayer Series 39 (Madrid, 2000); and Manuel Suárez Cortina, *El gorro frigio*.

57. Raymond Carr, *Spain, 1808–1975*, 326–27.

58. AHN—FC, Mº de Interior—Serie A, Leg. 63A, no. 15: Anonymous intelligence report titled "Informe sobre los partidos políticos," and dated November 12, 1887.

59. Alvarez Junco, *El Emperador*, 186.

60. Ibid., 91.

61. Ibid., 433.

62. Ibid., 453–454.

63. On the overlapping linkages between anarchists and republicans in Barcelona see Angel Smith, *Anarchism, Revolution, and Reaction*, esp. 163–173; and Alvarez Junco, *El Emperador*, 145, 170–171.

64. Alvarez Junco, *El Emperador*, 190–194.

65. Ibid., 195.

66. Ibid., 197.

67. Vincent, *Spain, 1833–2002*, 92–39; Smith, *Anarchism, Revolution, and Reaction*, 149–150; Alvarez Junco, *El Emperador*, 91–103.

68. Duarte, "La esperanza republicana," 172.

69. Gómez Chaix, *Ruiz Zorrilla*, 89.

70. Jordi Canal, "Manuel Ruiz Zorrilla (1833–1895): De hombre de Estado a conspirador compulsivo," in *Liberales, agitadores y conspiradores*, 267–299.

71. Alvarez Junco, *El Emperador*, 407–409.

72. Gómez Chaix, *Ruiz Zorrilla*; and Emilio Prieto y Villarreal, *Don Ruiz Zorrilla (1875–1895)* (Madrid, 1903).

73. Andrés de Blas Guerrero, *Tradición republicana y nacionalismo español*, 33.

74. Carlos Seco Serrano, *Militarismo y civilismo en la España contemporánea*, 200–202, claims Cánovas never exiled Ruiz Zorrilla: he fled to Paris of his free will.

75. Carlos Dardé Morales, "Los republicanos," in *Historia general de España y América*, ed. José Andrés Gallego, Vol. XVI-2, 144; see also Alvarez Junco, *El Emperador*, 96–97; Blas de Guerrero, *Tradición republicana...*, 37. On nineteenth-century Spanish military coups and *pronunciamientos*, see Busquets, *Pronunciamiento y golpes de Estado en España*. On the ARM, see Miguel Pérez (pseud. *Siffler*), *Don Manuel Ruiz Zorrilla ante la ARM. Noticias sobre la formación y desarrollo de la misma. Historia de la conspiración militar que produjo la sublevación de Badajoz y de la Seo de Urgel y detalles interesantes del ejercito. Escrito por* Siffler-725 (Madrid, 1883).

76. Alvarez Junco, *El Emperador*, 93. See also Miguel Artola, *Partidos y programas políticos, 1808–1936* (Madrid, 1991), 184–187.

77. Xosé M. Núñez Seixas, "Historia e actualidade dos nacionalismos na España contemporánea: unha perspectiva de conxunto," *Giral*, 128 (1995), 503–504, cited in Alvarez Junco, *Mater dolorosa*, 552.

78. Andrés de Blas Guerrero, *La tradición republicana y nacionalismo español*, 34.

79. Dardé Morales, "Los republicanos," 145–146; The manifesto/pact is transcribed in Artola, *Partidos y programas políticos*, II: 185–187.

80. Manuel Ruiz Zorrilla, *Tres negaciones y una afirmación. Cuatro folletos* (Madrid, 1864), 17, cited in Blas Guerrero, *Tradición republicana*, 88, n. 27.

81. Ruiz Zorrilla cited in the Introduction to V. Alvarez Villamil and Rodolfo Llopis, eds., *Cartas de conspiradores. La Revolución de Septiembre. De la emigración al poder* (Madrid, 1929), 12.

82. "Sueños y realidades," *El Motín*, January 24, 1886.

83. José Nakens, *La dictadura republicana* (Madrid, 1904? or 1905?). This pamphlet was also transcribed in its entirety in José Nakens, *Cosas que yo he dicho (Esbozo de ideas)* (Madrid, 1912?), 155–184.

84. Alvarez Junco, *El Emperador*, 125.

85. José Alvarez Junco, "El populismo como problema," in *El populismo en España y América*, ed. José Alvarez Junco and Ricardo González Leandri, (Madrid, 1994), 11–38; and Ramiro Reig, "Populismes," *Debats* 12 (June 1985): 6–21.

86. John R. Mosher, "The Birth of Mass Politics in Spain: Lerrouxismo in Barcelona," (Ph.D. diss, University of California, San Diego, 1977), 4.

87. On republican/*lerrouxismo* electoral support in Barcelona, see Mosher, "The Birth of Mass Politics in Spain: Lerrouxismo in Barcelona," 19–79, and José Alvarez Junco, *El Emperador*, 347–370.

88. Reig, *Blasquistas y clericales*, 23–62.

89. Mosher, "The Birth of Mass Politics in Spain: Lerrouxismo in Barcelona," 6.

90. Alvarez Junco, "El populismo como problema," 16.

91. Ramiro Reig, "Entre la realidad y la ilusión: el fenómeno blasquista en Valencia, 1898–1936," in *El republicanismo español (1830–1977)*, 402.

92. Alvarez Junco, "El populismo como problema," 17.

93. See Ruth Ann Willner, *The Spellbinders: Charismatic Political Leadership*. On the Spanish case see Raúl Martín Arranz, "El liderazgo carismático en el contexto del estudio del liderazgo," and José Alvarez Junco, "Magia y ética en la retórica política," in *Populismo, caudillaje y discurso demagógico*, 73–99 and 219–270, respectively.

94. Alvarez Junco, "El populismo como problema," 17.

95. Alvarez Junco, *El Emperador*, 408–412.

96. Ramiro Reig, "Entre la realidad y la ilusión: el fenomeno blasquista en Valencia, 1898–1936," in *El republicanismo español (1830–1977)*, 395–423.

97. "Banquetes," *El Motín*, February 7, 1886; "El 11 de Febrero," *El Motín*, February 6, 1892; Nakens, "¡Basta ya de fiestas!" *El Motín*, February 24, 1889; and José Nakens, "Los banquetes," *El Motín*, February 10, 1900.

98. José Nakens, "¡A Berlín! ¡A Berlín!," *El Motín*, April 12, 1902 (originally printed in *El Motín*, December 12, 1896).

99. Ibid.

100. For a report on the Assembly of February 14, 1903, see *El Motín*, February 21, 1903 or *El País*, February 15, 1903. See also Romero Maura's discussion of 1903 unity-fever in *La rosa del fuego*, 278–281.

101. José Nakens, "Mi candidatura," *El Motín*, February 21, 1903. The rejection was also transcribed in "La renuncia del Sr. Nakens," *El Imparcial*, February 21, 1903.

102. *La Epoca*, March 24, 1903. See also *El País*, March 26, 1903, and "La Asamblea republicana," *El Motín*, April 4, 1903.

103. Nakens and Salmerón quoted in *La Publicidad* (Barcelona), March 21, 1903, in Romero Maura, *La rosa del fuego*, 279–280 and n. 29.

104. Carlos Dardé Morales, "Los Republicanos," in *Historia General de España y América*, 150. Dardé Morales, "Biografía política de Nicolás Salmerón (ca. 1860–1890)," in *Republicanismo y repúblicas en España*, ed. José A. Piqueras and Manuel Chust, 135–161 (Madrid, 2000).

105. Alvarez Junco, *El Emperador*, 125–127; 293–309.

106. José Nakens, "Carta Abierta," *El Motín*, June 17, 1905.

107. "Nakens Edifica," *El Baluarte*, n.d., cited in *El Motín*, September 2, 1905.

108. Dardé Morales, "Los republicanos," 150.

109. José Nakens, *La dictadura republicana* (Madrid, 1904? or 1905?). This pamphlet was also transcribed in its entirety in José Nakens, *Cosas que yo he dicho (Esbozo de ideas)* (Madrid, 1912?), 155–184. In "Un dictador," *El Motín*, 7 October 1905, Nakens lauds Porfiriato Díaz as paradigmatic of the type of dictator he seeks because Díaz had "turned México around." The desire for an "Iron Surgeon" are central to Joaquín Costa, *Oligarquía y caciquismo como la forma actual de gobierno en España* (Madrid, 1902).

110. "Golpe Contundente," *El Motín*, December 16, 1905. See also *El Intransigente* (Barcelona), April 25, 1907 cited in Alvarez Junco, *El Emperador*, 359, n. 127, for Nakens's endorsement of Lerroux.

Chapter 3

1. See José Alvarez Junco, "Los 'Amantes de la Libertad' "; *El Emperador*, esp. 205–212 and 397–414; and *The Emergence of Mass Politics in Spain*, 70–84. To this date, only Manuel Pérez Ledesma has dedicated a biographer's attention to Nakens. See Pérez Ledesma, "José Nakens (1841–1926)."

2. Lamennais' popular effort to reconcile liberalism with Catholicism in Belgium and Northern France failed to take root in Spain. See Jesús Longares, "El pensamiento de Lamennais criticado por un católico español de la época isabelina," *Hispania sacra*, XXV (1972): 379–390. Additional studies on Spanish National-Catholicism include Alfonso Botti, *Cielo y dinero. El nacionalcatolicismo en España (1881–1975)* and Julio de la Cueva Merino, "Cultura y movilización en el movimiento católico de la Restauración (1899–1913)," in *La cultura española de la Restauración*, 169–192; and José Andrés Gallego, *La política religiosa en España, 1889–1913*.

3. Alvarez Junco, *El Emperador*, 407–408.

4. See for example, Andrés de Blas Guerrero, *Tradición republicana y nacionalismo español*; and Alvarez Junco, *El Emperador*, 205–212.

5. Pérez Ledesma, "Studies on Anticlericalism in Contemporary Spain," *International Review of Social History*, 46 (no. 2, 2001): 245.

6. María Cruz Seoane and María Dolores Saiz, *Historia del Periodismo en España*, III: 113–114, 113–114, cited in Pérez Ledesma, "José Nakens," 310.

7. Manuel Pérez Ledesma, "La sociedad española, la guerra y la derrota," in *Más se perdió en Cuba: España, 1898 y la crisis de fin de siglo*, (Madrid, 1998), 136. See also Lily Litvak, *Musa libertaria: arte, literatura y vida cultural del anarquismo español (1880–1913)*, 33, 67, and 89; and Alvarez Junco, *El Emperador*, 277 and 400.

8. *Vida Nueva* (HMM, 241/2).

9. On Azcárate's ideologies see Alfredo Marcos Oteruelo, *El pensamiento de Gumersindo de Azcárate* (Léon, 1985), esp. 307–338; and Pablo de Azcárate, *Gumersindo de Azcárate. Estudio biográfico documental*, 60–66.

10. Manuel Suárez Cortina, "Anticlericalismo, religion y politíca durante la Restauración," in *El anticlericalismo español contemporáneo*, eds. Emilio La Parra and Manuel Suárez Cortina, 127–210.

11. Manuel Suárez Cortina, "Anticlericalismo y republicanismo en la Restauración, 1874–1898," *Bulletin d'Histoire Contemporaine de l'Espagne* 23 (June 1996): 73.

12. *El Motín*, March 4, 1883. The cartoon caption reads: "What they think of the *EL MOTIN* editors in the sacristies."

13. See *La Publicidad* (Barcelona), July 7, 1904; and José Nakens, "¡Pero si no puede ser!" *El Motín*, August 12, 1899.

14. For the Church's financial recovery see José María Palomares Ibáñez, "La recuperación económica de la iglesia española (1845–1931)," and Juan Carlos Frías Fernández, "Percepciones, imágenes y explicaciones de la recuperación económica de la iglesia: los anticlericales entre 1876–1899," in *Iglesia, Sociedad y Estado*, ed. Emilio La Parra López and Jesús Pradells Nadal, 153–172 and 183, respectively. See also Manuel Revuelta González, "La recuperación eclesiástica y el rechazo anticlerical al cambio de siglo," in *España entre dos siglos (1875–1931)*, 213–234.

15. Clara Eugenia Núñez, *La fuente de la riqueza: educación y desarrollo económico en la España contemporánea*, 203, 308, cited in Vincent, *Spain, 1833–2002*, 55.

16. *El Motín*, May 19, 1910. A similar cartoon in the center of *El Motín*, May 3, 1885, depicts young students kneeling down to pray the rosary in math class.

17. Mitchell, *Betrayal of Innocents*, 38.

18. For scapulars see Antonio Machado, "El Escapulario," *El Motín*, April 28, 1887; and Brian J. Dendle, *The Spanish Novel of Religious Thesis, 1876–1936*, 47.

19. Maurice Agulhon, *Marianne into Battle: Republican Imagery and Symbolism in France, 1789–1880* (Cambridge, 1981); Maurice Agulhon and Pierre Bonte, *Marianne. Les visages de la République*. For comparison of Marianne, Germania and Britania see George Mosse, *Nationalism and Sexuality: Respectability and Abnormal Sexuality in Modern Europe*: 90-ff.

20. Mosse, *Nationalism and Sexuality*, 18.

21. Sarah White, "Liberty, Honor, Order: Gender and Poltical Discourse in Nineteenth-Century Spain," in *Constructing Spanish Womanhood: Female Identity in Modern Spain*, 227–232.

22. "España ante un coronel prusiano," *El Motín*, October 14, 1883.

23. *El Motín*, May 19, 1889.

24. Alvarez Junco, *El Emperador*, 407.

25. "El origen de todo," *El Motín*, July 15, 1888. On the Crime at Fuencarral Street, see María Cruz Seoane, *Oratoria y política en la España del siglo XIX*, 404–409.

26. See Daniel Pick, *Faces of Degeneration: A European Disorder, c. 1848–1918*; and Joshua Goode, "Corrupting a Good Mix: Race and Crime in

Late Nineteenth- and Early Twentieth-Century Spain," *European History Quarterly* 35, 2 (2005): 241–265.

27. Juan Meslier, *El Testimonio de Juan Meslier* (Madrid, 1887?). An English translation does exist: (Superstition in all ages by Jean Meslier, a Roman Catholic Priest, who, after a pastoral service of thirty years at Etrepigny and But in Champagne, France, wholly abjured religious dogma, and left his last will and testament to his parishioners, and to the world, to be published after his death, the following pages entitled *Common Sense*), edited and translated by Paul Henry Thiry and Baron d'Holbach (New York: Peter Eckler Company, 1920).

28. "Tarjetas Postales," *El Motín*, December 1, 1910.

29. "Proyecto de Reforma del Escudo Nacional," *El Motín*, June 8, 1911. For republican criticism of bullfighting and alcoholism see the cartoon for *El Motín*, December 18, 1913, which is captioned: "Projected crest of the Maurist-Carlist-Loyolaesque (Jesuit) Party, which is now incubating."

30. Sue, *Le Juif Errant*, 4 vols. (Paris, 1845), I: 406, cited in Cubitt, *The Jesuit Myth: Conspiracy Theory and Politics in Nineteenth-Century France*, 183.

31. R. W. Scribner, *For the Sake of Simple Folk: Popular Propaganda for the German Reformation*, 75.

32. See Ottavia Niccoli, *I sacerdoti, i guerrieri, i contadini. Storia di un'immagine della società*.

33. Cubitt, *The Jesuit Myth: Conspiracy Theory and Politics in Nineteenth-Century France*, 184.

34. *El Motín*, July 27, 1884. This cartoon was also reproduced on the front page of *El Motín*, April 21, 1910, with the caption: "What the clericals want education to be."

35. "Los reptiles hambrientes," *El Motín*, July 27, 1884.

36. Cubitt, *The Jesuit Myth: Conspiracy Theory and Politics in Nineteenth-Century France*, 185.

37. *El Motín*, December 25, 1887. A similar illustration appears on the front page of *El Motín*, February 3, 1910. In the January 22, 1882 issue of *El Motín*, a similar illustration was used to convey clerical dominion in Spain, but an octopus rather than a spider is used by the artist.

38. *El Motín*, July 20, 1884. The first set of years refer to victories for liberalism. The decade between 1823 and 1833 marked the absolutist Restoration of Ferdinand VII, who threw out the Constitution and reinstated the Inquisition.

39. Dendle, *The Spanish Novel of Religious Thesis*, 47–48.

40. "La serpiente negra," *El Motín*, August 17, 1884.

41. Hans Biedermann, *Dictionary of Symbolism*, 316.

42. Cubitt, *The Jesuit Myth: Conspiracy Theory and Politics in Nineteenth-Century France*, 184.

43. *El Motín*, August 3, 1884. The word *parrajaco* can mean raven or some other large and ugly bird. However, it is also a slang term for someone who is sly, underhanded, or untrustworthy.

44. *El Motín*, June 15, 1911.

45. Biederman, *Dictionary of Symbolism*, 84, 280–281.
46. Ibid., 280.
47. Scribner, *For the Sake of Simple Folk*, 229–230.
48. I thank Juan Hernández Andreu of the Universidad Complutense Madrid for passing along these proverbs.
49. Nadia Julien, *The Mammoth Dictionary of Symbols: Understanding the Hidden Language of Symbols*, 246.
50. Biederman, *Dictionary of Symbolism*, 281.
51. Ibid., 280–281.
52. Sánchez, *Anticlericalism*, 10.
53. Cubitt, *The Jesuit Myth: Conspiracy Theory and Politics in Nineteenth-Century France*,185–186.
54. Cited in José Nakens, *La Vuelta de Cristo*. Biblioteca del Apostolado de la Verdad #1 (Madrid, 190?): 15.
55. Ibid., 18–19.
56. José Nakens, *En Broma y en serio: artículos anticlericales* (Madrid, 1909?): 90–91. This article originally appeared in José Nakens, "Unica solución," *El Motín*, August 6, 1882.
57. *El Motín*, April 4, 1896, cited in Frías Fernández, "Percepciones, imágenes, y explicaciones," 178. The vast majority of the anticlerical evidence this author selects comes from *El Motín*. For other similar examples of *El Motín*'s numerical fetishism see *El Motín*, March 18, 1886; *El Motín*, September 6, 1888; and "¡Si no puede ser!" *El Motín*, August 12, 1899.
58. *El Motín*, March 25, 1896.
59. See for example, "Iniquidad Triunfante," *El Siglo Futuro*, January 29, 1901.
60. Nakens, "La guerra civil," *El Motín*, May 17, 1885; also reprinted in *El Motín*, April 28, 1889; and E*l Motín*, September 30, 1894.
61. "¡Viva la República francesa!" *La Dominicales (del Librepensamiento)*, December 15, 1905; "Christianismo y Humanismo," *Las Dominicales (del Librepensamiento)*, June 12, 1903; "La religión maldita," *Las Dominicales (del Librepensamiento)*, June 12, 1908. In *Las Dominicales*, May 10, 1907; José Ferrandiz, "Francia y la Iglesia," *El Motín*, April 29, 1905; "Los religiosos franceses," *El Motín*, October 17, 1903; and Mercurio (pseud.), "Francia y España," *El Motín*, March 24, 1906.
62. *El Motín*, January 26, 1890.
63. "A pies de Roma," *El Motín*, March 25, 1888.
64. See for example, "Frailes y clérigos," *El Motín*, July 8, 1893, and "Frailes y clérigos, II," *El Motín*, July 29, 1893.
65. Fernando Lozano, "Abrid los ojos, católicos," *Las Dominicales del Librepensamiento*, April 28, 1898.
66. *El Motín*, July 25, 1886.
67. Pick, *Faces of Degeneration*, 97–106.
68. "Si ocurriera ese milagro ¿veríamos esa escena?" *El Motín*, October 6, 1910.
69. *El Motín*, January 10, 1886.
70. "Los que predican la abstinencia y los que la practican," *El Motín*, April 14, 1910. Originally this cartoon appeared in *El Motín*, January 30, 1887.

71. *El Motín*, January 19, 1911. This illustration's caption reads: "Full belly, God he praises!" A similar cartoon appeared in *El Motín*, December 13, 1890. Here a fat priest is juxtaposed with a man afflicted with a humpback. The caption reads: "Those with a hump on their abdomen laughing at those with a hump on their back." This particular image dates back at least until the Counter-Reformation. An anti-Luther broadsheet from sixteenth-century Berlin portrays the drunkard Luther with a giant beer mug, his stomach so bloated that he must push it around in a wheelbarrow. On his back he carries a commode full of his followers, and in the barrow the books of his fellow "heretics"—Zwingli, Calvin, and others. Behind Luther is his wife, Katherina von Bora, clad as a nun, and carrying a Bible, a pannier, and their illegitimate child named "Faith Alone." See Scribner, *For the Sake of Simple Folk*, 235.

72. "Ejerciendo la caridad cristiana," *El Motín*, June 9, 1910.

73. *El Motín*, September 24, 1882.

74. *El Motín*, October 2, 1884. These were transcribed from a Puerto Rican newspaper called *El Deber* (the Duty). For the cases in La Coruña see AHN, FC—Mº de Interior, Serie General, leg. 2342, nos. 18–21 bis, and AHN, FC—Mº de Interior, Serie General, leg. 2342, no. 28.

75. *El Motín*, Issue 28, 1885 (most probably July 12, 1885). *El Motín* often omitted dates from its newspapers: a loophole in the press law helped the newspaper avoid censorship and confiscation if they never put the date on their paper.

76. "Suplica y consejo," *El Motín*, September 14, 1884.

77. See for example, "A propósito de higiene," *El Motín* May 11, 1899.

78. Joshua Seth Goode, "The Racial Alloy: The Science, Politics, and Culture of Race in Spain, 1875–1923," (Ph.D. diss., University of California, Los Angeles, 1999), 343.

79. Ibid., 348.

80. "Obispado del Sentido Común," *El Motín*, January 29, 1885.

81. The center illustration in the May 17, 1885 issue of *El Motín* depicts a man who resembles Nakens in the sky like a God-figure, excommunicating the clergy on earth.

82. Nakens, *Viaje al Infierno*, 10.

83. "Nuestra encíclical," *El Motín* (Supplement), July 25, 1889.

84. Víctor Hugo, *Cristo en el Vaticano* (Madrid, n.d.), 10. This collection of essays was not Hugo's, but rather those of Nakens and other authors who wrote about the corruption of Christ's teachings.

85. The column was called "El Evangelio cristiano y el Evangelio de la República" (The Christian gospel and the Gospel of the Republic).

86. See for example, "Manojo de Flores Místicas," *El Motín*, August 3, 1884.

87. "Amazonas religiosas," *El Motín*, January 7, 1886.

88. See for example, *El Motín*, Supplement, n.d. (between April 27 and May 3, 1884); *El Motín*, n.d. (between June 1 and 8, 1884); *El Motín*, n.d. (between June 31, and July 7, 1884); *El Motín*, Supplement, April 2, 1885; and *El Motín*, Supplement, April 16, 1885.

89. This advertisement for Nakens, *Espejo moral del clérigo*, which was released on March 19, 1883 appears in *El Motín*, April 1, 1883.

90. Sam Pryke, "Nationalism and Sexuality, What Are the Issues?," *Nations and Nationalisms* 4 (1998): 541.

91. "Libro Curioso," *El Motín*, n.d. (most probably May 20, 1885). Nakens most probably referred to Gaétan Delaunay, *Memoirs sur l'infériorité des civilizations précoces* (Paris, 1885).

92. "Los Frailes," *El Motín*, May 1, 1881.

93. *Mónita Secreta: Instrucciones reservados de los jesuítas*. Translated from the Latin by Anonymous. Biblioteca del Apostolado de la Verdad (Madrid, n.d.).

94. "Santos asilos de paz y castidad," *El Motín*, October 20, 1910.

95. Hobsbawm, "Introduction: Inventing Traditions," and "Mass-Producing Traditions," in *The Invention of Tradition*, 10–14 and 272–274, respectively; Weber, *Peasants into Frenchmen*, 303–338; and Gellner, *Nations and Nationalism*, 48–49.

96. Boyd, *Historia Patria*, xiii–xxi, and 3–40; Vincent, *Spain, 1833–2002*, 79–87.

97. Alvarez Junco, *Mater dolorosa*, 187–226; and Inman Fox, *La invención de España*, 35–54.

98. Segismundo Pey Ordeix, "El Carlismo (sin Dios, sin patria, sin rey)," *El Motín*, 3–4.

99. *Almanaque de la Inquisición por El Motín* (Madrid, 1912?); *Almanaque del Carlismo, para los años 1913 á 1999, por El Motín* (Madrid, 1912?); and *Almanaque cómico del Carlismo para los años 1914 á 1999* (Madrid, 1913?).

100. Nakens, "Casi prólogo," *Almanaque del Carlismo, para los años 1913 á 1999*, 7–9.

101. *Gil Blas* was founded in Madrid in 1864; *La Flaca*, which featured some illustrations by Demócrito, began publishing in Barcelona in 1869; and the hard to find and short-lived *Cañón Krupp* was a product of anti-Carlist sentiment in Barcelona in 1874. All were characterized by their anticlerical imagery.

102. All four of these illustrations filled the cover to *El Motín*, August 4, 1910. The caption read: "Recurring trends." The first appearance of these particular illustrations in Nakens' newspaper was *El Motín*, August 9, 1885.

103. *El Motín*, December 2, 1909, copied an illustration that appeared in Berlin's *Lustige Blatter*, which depicted a monkey-like/demon-like Jesuit priest sitting on Ferrer's bloodied casket.

104. "EL MOTIN en la Inquisición," *El Motín*, January 4, 1912.

105. *Almanaque de La Inquisición por El Motín*, 7. For a very favorable English review of this almanac, see William Heaford, "The Spanish Inquisition," *The Free Thinker* (London), January 28, 1912.

106. *Almanaque de la Inquisición*, 90–91.

107. Ibid., 96–98.

108. Ibid., 93.

109. These illustrations were available in 43 x 15(?)cm size for 25 *céntimos* (cents), and in 85cm size for 50 *céntimos*.

110. Mitchell, *Betrayal of Innocents*, 37.

Chapter 4

1. My recounting of the regicide is based on the official report of the event: Ministerio de Gracia y Justicia (Spain), *Causa por regicidio frustrado, 1906–1909. Atentado de 31 de mayo de 1906. Causa contra Mateo Morral, Francisco Ferrer, José Nakens, Pedro Mayoral, Aquilino Martínez, Isidro Ibarra, Bernardo Mata y Concepción Pérez Cuesta*, 5 vols., (Madrid, 1911). In addition, I have consulted numerous studies: Melchor Fernández Almagro, *Historia del Reinado de Alfonso XIII*, Second illustrated edition, 90–93; Alvarez Junco, *El Emperador*, 303–309; Ullman, *The Tragic Week*, 45, 98–100; José Montero Alonso, *Sucedió en Palacio*, Chapter Four entitled "Una bomba en un ramo de flores," Fifth edition; Joaquín Romero Maura, "Terrorism in Barcelona and Its Impact on Spanish Politics. 1904–1909," *Past and Present* 41 (XII): 130–183; and Ricardo de la Reguera and Susana March, *La boda de Alfonso XIII*. See also their "¿Fue culpable Ferrer Guardia?" *Historia y vida*, 8 (November 1968): 92–105, and "La muerte de Mateo Morral, el regicida frustrado," *Historia y vida*, 6 (September 1968): 90–103. Other accounts include: A. Aguilar, "Los motivos de Mateo Morral," *Historia y vida*, no. 56, extra (August 1973): 24–29; F. Hernández Girbal, "José Nakens ampara a Mateo Morral," *Historia y vida*, 126 (September 1978): 44–59, and newspaper accounts from *El Imparcial* and *La Epoca*.

2. Montero Alonso, *Sucedió en Palacio*, 372.

3. Ibid.; *Causa por regicidio frustrado*, Vol I, 20.

4. Conde de Romanones, *Notas de una vida (1868–1901)*, Volume I, 241. Alvarez Junco, *El Emperador*, 306, n. 103, does not believe Morral was sick, but Romero Maura, "Terrorism in Barcelona," 145–146, accepts the testimonies of people who knew or knew of Morral.

5. Joaquín Romero Maura, *La rosa del fuego*, especially 461–542; José Alvarez Junco, "El anticlericalismo en el movimiento obrero español," 283–300; Julio de la Cueva, *Clericales y anticlericales;* David Gilmore, "The Anticlericalism of the Andalusian Rural Proletarians," in *La religiosidad popular. Vol I: Antropología e historia*, 478–498; Elías de Mateo, *Anticlericalismo en Málaga, 1874–1923*; Víctor Manuel Arbeloa, *Socialismo y anticlericalismo*; Ullman, *The Tragic Week*; and Callahan, *Church, Politics, and Society*. For later periods see Bruce Lincoln, "Revolutionary Exhumations in Spain, July 1936"; Richard Maddox, "Revolutionary Anticlericalism and Hegemonic Processes in an Andalusian Town, August 1936," *American Ethnologist* 22, 1 (February 1995): 125–143; Manuel Delgado, *La ira sagrada*, 25–49; Julio de la Cueva, "El anticlericalismo en la Segunda República y la Guerra Civil," in *El anticlericalismo español*, Emilio La Parra López and Manuel Suárez Cortina, 211–301; and Julio de la Cueva, "Religious Persecution, Anticlerical Tradition, and Revolution: Atrocities against the Clergy in the Spanish Civil War," *Journal of Contemporary History* 33, 3 (July 1998): 359–369.

6. On Ferrer see Ullman, *The Tragic Week*; Sol Ferrer Sanmartí, *Le veritable Francisco Ferrer*, and Sol Ferrer Sanmartí, *La vie et l'oeuvre de Francisco*

Ferrer: Un Martyr au XXE siècle, Preface by Charles August Bontemps; and Maurice Dommanget, *Francisco Ferrer*, Grandes Educateurs Socialistes Socialistes Series. On his Modern School pedagogy see Francisco Ferrer, *La Escuela Moderna: Póstuma explicación y alcance de la esnseñanza racional*, edited and with a prologue by Lorenzo Portet.

7. *Causa por regicidio frustrado*, Vol. I: 492.

8. Ibid., I: 296–298.

9. Alvarez Junco, *El Emperador*, 303–307.

10. In *Causa por regicidio frustrado*, I: 319, Villafranca told the police that her relationship with Ferrer was strictly professional. However, Ullman and others take as given that they were lovers. See Ullman, *The Tragic Week*, 99 ff. See also Fernández Almagro, *Historia del Reinado de Alfonso XIII*, 90 ff.

11. Fernández de la Reguera and March, *La boda de Alfonso XIII, 348.*

12. Montero Alonso, *Sucedió en Palacio*, 378–379.

13. Esenwein, *Anarchist Ideology and the Working-Class Movement in Spain*, 166–188. See also Rafael Núñez Florencio, *El terrorismo anarquista (1888–1909).*

14. Cited in Alvarez Junco, *El Emperador*, 305 n. 99.

15. Romanones, *Notas de una vida*, 241.

16. Alvarez Junco, *El Emperador*, 306–307, On Nakens's meetings with Angiolillo, see Nakens, *Trozos de mi vida*, 113–130; and Esenwein, *Anarchist Ideology and the Working-Class Movement in Spain* 197–199.

17. Montero Alonso, *Sucedió en Palacio*, 384; Fernández de la Reguera and March, *La Boda de Alfonso XIII*: 435–436.

18. Ródenas' statement is transcribed in *Causa por regicidio frustrado*, I: 544.

19. Montero Alonso, *Sucedió en Palacio*, 385.

20. Alvarez Junco, *El Emperador*, 306.

21. See Federico Urales, *Mi vida*: III, 25–27. See also the letters that Ferrer wrote to his friend Charles Malato in Francisco Ferrer Collection-UCSD, MSS 0248, Series 1A; Box 1 folders 4 and 5.

22. "El atentado de jueves," *El Motín*, June 2, 1906.

23. *El País*, June 7, 1906.

24. Ibid.; *Causa por regicidio frustrado*, II: 99–100.

25. For the verdicts see *Causa por regicidio frustrado*, Vol. IV: 392–406.

26. *Causa por regicidio frustrado*, II: 12–16. Ullman, *The Tragic Week*, 93–96, discusses how anarchists in France and his contacts with Freemasonry played a major role in his own life as well as in the curriculum at the Modern School.

27. *Causa por regicidio frustrado*, IV: 399.

28. Ibid., I: 477.

29. Ibid., IV: 397.

30. Ibid.

31. Ibid., 397–398.

32. Nakens, *La celda número 7 (impresiones de la cárcel)* (Madrid, 1908), 9.

33. Nakens, "Lo que veo y lo que oigo," *El País*, October 27, 1906.

34. The *El País* column was re-transcribed and published in Nakens, *Mi paso por la cárcel* (Madrid, 1907?).

35. See for example, "Vigliantes," in *Mi paso por la cárcel.*, 20–21 (*El País*, October 29, 1906); and "Los dos sacerdotes," in *Mi paso por la cárcel*, 54–56 (*El País*, November 19, 1906).

36. The Lawyer Fernando Cadalso was one of the most vocal and cogent critics of the clerical presence in the penitentiaries, especially that of nuns in the female prisons. See Cadalso, "Religiosas en la cárcel," *Revista de las Prisones* 16 (June 1, 1897): 149–151; and "Religiosidad en la cárcel II," *Revista de las Prisones* 17 (July 10, 1897): 157–160.

37. Romanones, *Notas de una vida*, 242.

38. See for example the petitions of Francisco Martí Correa, Eduardo García Díaz, and Manuel Monroy in *Causa por regicidio frustrado*, IV: 515–516.

39. Nakens's own words in *El Motín*, October 1, 1908.

40. See for example, "La reacción clerical," and "Regla de conducta," *El Motín*, October 1, 1908.

41. Nakens, "Saludo," *El Motín*, October 1, 1908.

42. José Alvarez Junco, "El anticlericalismo en el movimiento obrero," in *Octubre del 34. Cincuenta años para reflexión*, 283–300 (Madrid, 1985). See also José Alvarez Junco, *La ideología política del anarquismo español (1868–1910)* (Madrid, 1976) and Esenwein, *Anarchist Ideology and the Working-Class Movement in Spain*, especially 134–154 and 205–216.

43. Vincent, *Spain, 1833–2002*, 68–72; Smith, *Anarchism, Revolution and Reaction*, 150–173.

44. Pamela Radcliff, "Política y cultura republicana en el Gijón del fin de siglo," 383. See also Radcliff, *From Mobilization to Civil War*. On Valencia, see Ramiro Reig, *Blasquistas y clericales;* on Barcelona, see Alvarez Junco, *El Emperado*; John R. Mosher, "The Birth of Mass Politics in Spain," and Pere Gabriel, "Insurreción y política. El republicanismo ochocentista en Cataluña," in *El republicanismo español (1830–1977)*, 341–371.

45. Radcliff, "Política y cultura republicana," 383–384.

46. Alvarez Junco, *La ideología política del anarquismo español (1868–1910)*, 596 ff.

47. For an analysis of the mobilizing power of anticlericalism in generating an alternative political culture in revolutionary Spain, see Castro Alfín, "Cultura, política y cultura política en la violencia anticlerical," 69–97. Radcliff, *From Mobilization to Civil War*; and Angeles Barrio Alonso, "Anarquistas, republicanos ysocialistas en Asturias (1890–1917)," in *El anarquismo español y sus tradiciones culturales*, 41–56, offer detailed analyses of the complex web of interaction between anarchists, republicans and socialists in Gijón. Demetrio Castro Alfín, "De la clandestinidad republicana a la clandestindad anarquista," in *El anarquismo español y sus tradiciones culturales*, 57–68, suggests that republicans, socialists, and anarchists were able to develop close ties primarily out of similarities in their histories of persecution and clandestine opposition to the Restoration state.

48. Alvarez Junco, *La ideología política del anarquismo español*.

49. Smith, *Anarchism, Revolution and Reaction*, 150–151.

50. Alvarez Junco, *La ideología política del anarquismo español*, 207.

51. This image appears in Litvak, *Musa libertaria*, 60.

52. "Función de desagravios," *La Flaca*, May 23, 1869.
53. *El Clarín*, July 5, 1883.
54. This drawing is reproduced in Litvak, *Musa libertaria*, 32.
55. *El Motín*, April 19, 1885. This cartoon was redone for the May 11, 1911 issue of *El Motín*, with Canalejas replacing Cánovas.
56. "Papel impreso," *La Voz del Cantero* 8, 140 (August 31, 1907): 7, cited in Litvak, *Musa libertaria*, 67. The citation for the collection is: José Nakens, *Cuadros de Miseria* (Madrid, 1907).
57. Ullman, *The Tragic Week*, 40.
58. Cited in Arbeloa, *Socialismo y anticlericalismo*, 159.
59. Ullman, *The Tragic Week*, 40. See also José Alvarez Junco, "El anticlericalismo en el movimiento obrero," in *Octubre del 34. Cincuenta años para la reflexión*, 283–300 (Madrid, 1985).
60. Determining the circulation of *El Motín* has proven to be a difficult feat. Because of missing or incomplete data in the press statistics for 1888 and 1913. AVM, Sección 7, leg., 97, no. 109: Ministerio de la Gobernación/ Dirección General de Seguridad, *Estadística de la Prensa Periódica* (Madrid, 1888), and Ministerio de Instrucción Pública y Bellas Artes, *Estadística de la Prensa periódica de España (Referida al 1.° de abril del año 1913)* (Madrid, 1914), I rely on the accounts of newspaper scholars who place the circulation figures at between 10,000 and 12,000. Pérez Ledesma, "Jose Nakens," 320, writes that *El Motín* reached a 20,000 copies per week apex after Nakens was pardoned and revived the weekly. See Valeriano Bozal Fernández, *La ilustración gráfica del XIX en España*, 183; Celso Almuñia, "Clericalismo y anticlericalismo a través de la prensa española decimonona," in *La cuestión social en la iglesia española contemporánea*, 123–175, and J. C. Frías Fernández, "Percepciones, imágenes y explicaciones de la recuperación económica de la Iglesia: los anticlericales entre 1876–1899," in *Iglesia, sociedad y estado*, 174.
61. Cansinos Asséns, *La novela de un literato*, Vol I: 18–19, 48.
62. According to Miguel Martínez Cuadrado, *La burguesía conservadora* (Madrid, 1986), 124, 55.8 percent of men, 71.5 per cent of women, for a total of 63.8 percent of the population was illiterate in 1900.
63. *El Imparcial*, November 28, 1901, cited in Rafael Pérez de la Dehesa, "El acercamiento de la literatura finisecular a la literatura popular," in *Creación y público en la literature española*, 156–157.
64. Roger Chartier, "Texts, Printings, Readings," in *The New Cultural History*, 161.
65. See Elizabeth L. Eisenstein, "Some Conjectures about the Impact of Printing on Western Society and Thought: A Preliminary Report," *Journal of Modern History* 40, 1 (March 1968): 1–56; and Benedict Anderson, *Imagined Communities*, 35–36.
66. Litvak, *Musa libertaria*, 157–158, and 174–175.
67. See for example, José Nakens, "Al oro," *Los Desheredados* 3, 110 (July 5, 1884): 4; and José Nakens, "El hambre y la honra," *Los Desheredados* 3, 111 (July 12, 1884): 2, cited in Litvak, *Musa Libertaria*, 33 and 89, respectively.

68. Clara Lida, "Literatura anarquista y anarquismo literario," *Nueva Revista de Filología Hispánica*, 19 (1970): 360–381.

69. This editorial of *El Motín*, January 25, 1902 is transcribed in *Causa por regicidio frustrado*, II: 126–132.

70. "Más sobre el obrerismo," *El Motín*, April 29, 1905.

71. Nakens, "O con los unos, ó con los otros," *El Motín*, July 14, 1905.

72. See *Causa por regicidio frustrado*, II: 146–150; and *El Motín*, July 22, 1905.

73. Moret's letter dated September 18, 1902, is transcribed in *Causa por regicidio frustrado*, II: 146–150. On June 16, 1905, Nakens solicited Moret for, and received, his permission to print these letters in *El Motín* and its publications.

74. Cansinos Asséns, *La novela de un literario*, 44.

75. See for example, José Nakens (?), "Basta de farsas," *El Motín*, November 27, 1887; and the illustration in the supplement to that issue of *El Motín*, December 1, 1887.

76. Manuel Delgado, *La ira sagrada*, 19–20.

77. See Romero Maura, *La Rosa del Fuego*, 177.

78. Pablo de Azcárate, ed., *Gumersindo de Azcárate*, 351–356.

79. Ibid., 353.

80. This nickname appears in Romero Maura, *La rosa del fuego*, 276.

81. José Nakens, "Carta abierta," *El Motín*, June 17, 1905: 1–2

82. Mosher, "The Birth of Mass Politics in Spain," 98.

83. On Nakens's call for a republican dictator or Iron Surgeon, see José Nakens, *La dictadura republicana* (Madrid, 1905?); reprinted in José Nakens, *Cosas que yo he dicho (Esbozo de ideas)* (Madrid, 1912), 155–184.

84. Manuel Suárez Cortina's "La quiebra del republicanismo histórico, 1898–1931," in *El republicanismo en España*, 139–163. On the break with Salmerón, see Romero Maura, *La rosa del fuego*, 319–353.

Chapter 5

1. On Spanish women in early republicanism, see Gloria Espigado Tocino, "Mujeres 'radicales': utópicas, republicanas e internacionalistas en España (1848–1874)," in *República y republicanas*, 15–43, *Ayer* Series 60. See also María Dolores Ramos, "La República de las librepensadoras (1890–1914): laicismo, emancipismo, anticlericalismo," in *República y republicanas*, 45–74. On the representation of Spanish women as victims of the Spanish clergy see María Pilar Salomón Chéliz, "Beatas sojuzgadas por el clero: la imagen de las mujeres en el discurso anticlerical en la España del primer tercio del siglo XX," *Feminismo/s: revista del Centro de Estudios sobre la mujer de la Universidad de Alicante*, Vol. 2 (2003): 41–58; and Enrique A. Sanabria, "Anticlerical Politics: Republicanism, Nationalism, and the Public Sphere in Restoration Madrid, 1875–1912," (Ph.D. diss., University of California, San Diego, 2001), 412–478.

2. Alvarez Junco, *El Emperador*, 250–252.

3. Ibid., 407.

4. Luz Sanfeliú, "Familias republicanas e identidades femeninas en el blasquismo: 1896–1910," in *República y republicanas*, 75–103.

5. Alvarez Junco, *El Emperador*, 207–210.

6. José Alvarez Junco, "'Los amantes de la libertad': la cultura republicana española a principios del siglo xx," in *El republicanismo español (1830–1977)*, 274; and José Alvarez Junco, "Racionalismo, romanticismo y moralismo en la cultura política republicana de comienzos del siglo," in *Clases populares, cultura, educación. Siglos XIX y XX*, 355–376.

7. Cited in Jean-Jacques Rousseau, *The Basic Political Writings*, 56.

8. Paul Thomas, "Jean-Jacques Rousseau, Sexist?" *Feminist Studies* 17, 2 (Summer 1991), 195–217. See also Jean Bethke Elshtain, *Public Man, Private Woman: Women in Social and Political Thought*, especially 147–197; Judith N. Shklar, *Men and Citizens: A Study of Rousseau's Social Theory*, especially 174–214; Joan Landes, *Women and the Public Sphere in the Age of the French Revolution* (Ithaca, NY, 1988), especially pp. 66–89; Christine Fauré, *Democracy without Women: Feminism and the Rise of Liberal Individualism in France*, especially 75–100; Lynda Lange, "Rousseau: Women and the General Will," in *The Sexism of Social and Political Theory: Women and Reproduction from Plato to Nietzsche*, 41–52 (Toronto, 1979); Joel Schwartz, *The Sexual Politics of Jean-Jacques Rousseau*; Nicole Fermon, *Domesticating Passions: Rousseau, Woman, and Nation*.

9. Fauré, *Democracy without Women: Feminism and the Rise of Liberal Individualism in France*, 101–135; Lynn Hunt, *The Family Romance of the French Revolution* (Berkeley, 1992), 97–99; Carol Blum, *Rousseau and the Republic of Virtue: The Language of Politics in the French Revolution*.

10. Carole Pateman, *The Sexual Contract* (Stanford, 1988), 2–38.

11. Bertocci, *Jules Simon*, 133–134; Peter McPhee, *A Social History of France, 1780–1880*, 249–256.

12. Mary Nash, *Defying Male Civilization: Women in the Spanish Civil War*, especially, 7–42.

13. Alvarez Junco, *El Emperador*, 185-ff.

14. Demófilo, "La Familia," *Las Dominicales del Libre Pensamiento*, May 27, 1883. See also Luz Sanfeliú, "El Blasquismo en Valencia (1898–1911): un proyecto político y la transformación de las identidades genéricas," in *Cultura Republicana: 70 años después*, 121.

15. Ana Aguado, "Entre lo público y lo privado: sufragio y divorcio en la Segunda República," in *República y republicanas*, 105–134; Rosa Capel, *El sufragio femenino en la Segunda República*; Mary Nash, "Género y ciudadanía," in *Política en la Segunda República*, 241–258, *Ayer* Series 20; and Judith Keene, "'Into the Clear Air of the Plaza': Spanish Women Achieve the Vote in 1931," in *Constructing Spanish Womanhood: Female Identity in Modern Spain*, 325–347. For examples of Lerroux's machismo, see Alvarez Junco, *El Emperador*, 249–265.

16. Jules Michelet, *Le prêtre, la femme et la famille* (Paris, 1912), II, cited in Delgado, *Las palabras de otro hombre. Misoginia y anticlericalismo*, 38.

17. Stephen Haliczer, *Sexuality in the Confessional: A Sacrament Profaned*, 194–195.
18. Michelet, *Le prêtre*, 211, cited in Haliczer, *Sexuality in the Confessional*, 194.
19. Michelet, *Le prêtre*, 4, cited in Delgado, *Las palabras de otro hombre*, 38. The emphases in the passage are Michelet's though the translation from the Spanish is mine.
20. Michelet, *Le prêtre*, 9, cited in Delgado, *Las palabras de otro hombre*, 39. The other man, of course, is the priest.
21. Michelet, *Le prêtre*, iv–v; cited in Delgado, *Las palabras de otro hombre*, 41–42.
22. Delgado, *Las palabras de otro hombre*.
23. Gil Blas de Santillán (pseud. Segismundo Pey de Ordeix), "Memorias de un jesuíta. Las confesadas," *El Motín*, June 2, 1910.
24. Ibid. See also "El jesuíta y la mujer," *Las Dominicales de Libre Pensamiento*, November 24, 1989, 4.
25. Ramón Chíes, "A una madre," *Las Dominicales del Libre Pensamiento*, February 23, 1888. On auricular confession, see Chapter One in Stephen Haliczer, *Sexuality in the Confessional*, 7–21.
26. "¡Ojo, maridos!" *El Motín*, October 9, 1889. See also "¡La iglesia se nos come!" *El Motín*, June 8, 1895.
27. Nakens, "¡Si you fuera fraile!" *El Motín*, June 1, 1895.
28. Chíes, "A una madre," *Las Dominicales del Libre Pensamiento*, February 23, 1888.
29. Ibid.
30. According to Haliczer, *Sexuality in the Confessional*, 169, the 1924 version of *Sor Sicalipsis* was censored and 3,000 copies were destroyed by the Primo de Rivera dictatorship. Another version was published in Barcelona during the Second Republic. See Segismundo Pey Ordeix, *Sor Sicalipsis*.
31. Pey Ordeix, *Sor Sicalipsis*, 88–95.
32. José Nakens, *La vuelta de Cristo*, Biblioteca del Apostolado de la Verdad, #1 (Madrid, 1910?), 18–19.
33. "Secuestros que no se castigan," *El Motín*, February 19, 1888, reprinted in El Motín, September 22, 1910.
34. Chapter Thirteen of *Mónita Secreta* in Folletos del Apostolado de la Verdad, first series (Madrid, 1910?), 25–26.
35. Jules Michelet excerpted in "La confesión," *El Motín*, February 3, 1910, 11.
36. Haliczer, *Sexuality in the Confessional*, 4.
37. Fray Jayme de Corella, *Práctica del confesionario y explicación de los sesenta y cinco proposiciones condenados por la santidad de N.S.P. Inocencio XI* (Madrid, 1717), 144–145, and 150, cited in Haliczer, *Sexuality in the Confessional*, 35.
38. See Adrian Lyttleton, "An Old Church and New State," *European Studies Review* 13 (1983): 243. A similar effort in France was Michel Morphy, *Les mystères de la pornographie cléricale; secrets honteaux de la confession, immoralités, obsenités, et guerre aux prêtres, corrupteurs de la jeunes* (Paris, 1884).

39. Constancio Miralta (pseud. José Ferrándiz), *Los secretos de la confesión...*, 303.
40. Chíes, "A una madre."
41. See Emilio López Domínguez, "En el confesionario," *Las Dominicales del Libre Pensamiento*, August 5, 1898.
42. Haliczer, *Sexuality in the Confessional*, 211, n. 1.
43. Chiés, "A una madre."
44. Michelet, *Le prêtre.*; Delgado, *Las Palabras de otro hombre*, 38.
45. For Medieval legends of the sexuality of the clergy see Harriet Goldberg, *Motif-Index of Medieval Spanish Folk Narratives* (Tempe, AZ, 1998).
46. The caption reads: "Holy Family!" *El Motín*, January 26, 1911.
47. *El Motín*, September 9, 1888.
48. "Interior de la casa del que nunca trabaja," *El Motín*, July 22, 1888; and "Interior de la casa del que siempre trabaja," *El Motín*, July 29, 1888.
49. "Hecho inconcebible," *El Motín*, May 31, 1895.
50. See for example, José Nakens, "La moral y los moralistas," *El Motín*, October 1, 1890.
51. "Crímen abominable. Violación y corrupción de una niña de seis años," *El Motín*, October 20, 1910, 13–14.
52. See for example, *El Motín*, November 1, 1890; and "La insurreción filipina," *El Motín*, September 26, 1896.
53. Mitchell, *Betrayal of Innocents*, 1–9. See also Richard Sipe, *Sex, Priests, and Power: Anatomy of Crisis*.
54. *El Motín*, July 31, 1887.
55. Alfredo Calderón, "¡Que se casen!" *El Motín*, April 29, 1905.
56. José Nakens, "Ley de vida," *El Motín*, July 5, 1883, reprinted in José Nakens, "Celibato eclesiástico: a un clérigo," *Muestras de mi estilo* (Madrid: Domingo Blanco, 1906?), 22–28; and José Nakens, *La Piqueta: Colección de artículos* (Madrid, n.d.), 26–30.
57. Nakens, "Ley de vida," *El Motín*, July 5, 1883 (Emphasis his).
58. Rafael Cansinos-Asséns, *La novela de un literario*, 3 vols. On Ferrándiz, see Molina Martínez, *Anticlericalismo y literatura*, 293–345.
59. Isidre Molas, ed., *Ideario de F. Pi y Margall*, 59.
60. Caro Baroja, *Introducción a una historia contemporánea del anticlericalismo español*, 120; and Stanley Brandes, *Metaphors of Masculinity: Sex and Status in Andalusian Folklore*, especially 172–182.
61. Molas, *Ideario de F. Pi y Margall*, 90.
62. Pierre-Joseph Proudhon, *La Pornocratié ou les femmes dans les temps modernes*. Paris, 1875. See Delgado, *Las Palabras de otro hombre*, 76.
63. Félix M. Samaniego, *Cuentos y poesías más que picantes* (Barcelona, 1899 [originally published in 1799]), cited in Delgado, *Las Palabras de otro hombre*, 77.
64. Un Católico Rancio, "La semana en la iglesia. Imágenes pornográficas," *El Resumen*, December 27, 1894.
65. See Julio de la Cueva, "Cultura y movilización en el movimiento católico," especially pp. 183–191.
66. "Devoción Voluptuosa," *El Motín*, August 10, 1895.

67. Ibid.
68. Mitchell, *Betrayal of Innocents*, 64.
69. Ibid., 65–66.
70. Michelle Perrot, "El elogio del ama de casa en siglo XIX," in *Historia y género: mujeres en la España moderna y contemporánea*, 255. See also James F. McMillian, "Clericals, Anticlericals and the Women's Movement in France under the Third Republic," *The Historical Journal*, 24 (1981): 361–376; Caroline Ford, *Divided Houses: Religion and Gender in Modern France* (Ithaca, NY, 2005); and Steven C. Hause and Anne R. Kenney, *Women's Suffrage and Social Politics in the French Third Republic* (Princeton, 1984).
71. See Gloria Espigado Tocino, "Mujeres 'radicales': utópicas, republicanas e internacionalistas en España (1848–1874)," and María Dolores Ramos, "La República de las librepensadoras."
72. Pi y Margall cited in Molas, *Ideario de F. Pi y Margall*, 89.
73. See Odón de Buen, "La mujer española," *Las Dominicales del Libre Pensamiento*, January 20, 1898.
74. María del Pilar Salomón Chéliz, "Resumen de las mujeres en la cultura política republicana," 113.
75. Segismundo Pey Ordeix, "Sicalipsis Monástica," *El Motín*, March 10, 1910.
76. Pey Ordeix, "Sicalipsis Monástica. Abyección Feminina," *El Motín*, March 17, 1910.
77. Pey Ordeix, "Sicalipsis Monástica," *El Motín*, April 28, 1910.
78. Pey Ordeix, "Sicalipsis Monástica. Luna de miel," *El Motín*, March 31, 1910.
79. "Una monja suicida," *El Motín*, April 1, 1893.
80. Alejandro Lerroux, "¡Rebeldes, Rebeldes!" *La Rebeldía*, September 1, 1906, cited in Cowans, ed., *Modern Spain: A Documentary History*, 103.
81. Alvarez Junco, *El Emperador*, 403.
82. *El Noroeste* (Gijón), September 12, 1899, cited in Pamela B. Radcliff, "Política y cultura republicana en el Gijón de fin de siglo," 386. On Belén Sárraga see Maria Dolores Ramos, "Federalismo, laicismo, obrerismo, feminismo: cuatro claves para interpretar la biografía de Belén Sárraga," in *Discursos, realidades, utopías. La construcción del sujeto femenino en los siglos XIX y XX*, 125–164.
83. *El pueblo* (Valencia), April 3, 1910, cited in Cowans, ed., *Modern Spain*, 109.
84. Concepción Arenal, "Estado Actual de la Mujer en España," in *Arenal y Lázaro: la admiración por una mujer de talento (1889–1895)*, 73–108.
85. Demófilo (Fernando Lozano), "A cualquiera mujer del pueblo de C," *Las Dominicales*, July 13, 1906.
86. Concepción Arenal, *El Motín*, January 2, 1897.
87. "Por la mujer," *Las Dominicales*, August 31, 1906 (A similar editorial about Sárraga appeared under the same title in *Las Dominicales*, December 22, 1904).
88. Belén Sárraga de Ferrero, "¡Esas son las madres!" *Las Dominicales*, October 5, 1906.

89. See Stanley Brandes, *Metaphors of Masculinity;* Julian Pitt-Rivers, *The People of the Sierra,* Second edition; and David D. Gilmore, *Aggression and Community: Paradoxes of Andalusian Culture.* See also Celia Valiente, "An Overview of Research on Gender in Spanish Society," *Gender & Society* 16, 6 (December 2002): 767–792.

90. 'Las mujeres poniendose los pantalones que los hombres no sabemos llevar,' *El Motín,* July 16, 1892.

91. *El Motín,* October 5, 1895.

92. *El Pueblo,* April 3, 1910, in Cowans, ed., *Modern Spain,* 109–110.

93. Alvarez Junco, *El Emperador,* 249–254, 264–265; Alvarez Junco, "Racionalismo, Romanticismo, y Moralismo," 373–385.

94. "¡Adelante! ¡Adelante!" *El Motín,* April 8, 1886.

95. "Lenguaje virile," *El Motín,* September 6, 1885. See also "El honor de la patria," *El Globo,* August 19, 1885, and Ingrid Schulze Schneider, "El papel de la prensa madrileña en el conflicto de las Islas Caroliñas," in *La sociedad madrileña durante la restauración,* 2 vols., II: 299–306.

96. José Nakens, *La vuelta de Cristo,* Biblioteca del Apostolado de la Verdad Series, no. 1 (Madrid, 1903?), 20.

97. José Nakens, "¡Pobre mujeres!" *El Motín,* February 9, 1888 (reprinted in *El Motín,* March 27, 1897). See also the excerpts from "An Antiquated Catholic," and the commentary by Nakens in *El Motín,* March 2, 1895.

98. "¡Hasta las mujeres!" *El Motín,* January 15, 1888.

99. Belén Sárraga, *La Conciencia Libre,* 1 (1906), cited in Alvarez Junco, *El Emperador,* 250, n. 69.

100. José Nakens, "Más seriedad," *El Motín,* October 28, 1899.

101. Pierre Conard, "Sexualité et anticlericalisme (Madrid 1910)," *Hispania* XXXI (1971): 103–131.

102. Mitchell, *Betrayal of Innocents.*

103. Alvarez Junco, *El Emperador,* 264–265.

Chapter 6

1. Ullman, *The Tragic Week,* 1, 286, and 326.

2. Julio de la Cueva, "The Stick and the Candle," 260.

3. Ibid.

4. Varela Ortega, *Los amigos politicos,* 337–338.

5. Andrés Gallego, *La política religiosa, 1889–1913,* 511–512.

6. José Andrés Gallego, "Sobre las formas de pensar y de ser: la Iglesia," in *Historia general de España y América,* (Madrid: 1983), vol. XVI-1: 301–302, cited in Callahan, *The Catholic Church in Spain,* 51. See also Manuel Pérez Ledesma, "La sociedad española, la guerra y la derrota," in *Más se perdió en Cuba. España, 1898 y la crisis de fin de siglo,* 134–143.

7. Callahan, *The Catholic Church in Spain,* 68.

8. Alvarez Junco, *Mater dolorosa,* 588.

9. Vicente Gay, *El regionalismo ante el nacionalismo y el imperialismo modernos en la formación de Estados* (Valladolid, 1908), 23–24, cited in Alvarez

Junco, *Mater dolorosa*, 589; 625, n. 107. On post-1898 state "cultural nationalism," see Eric Storm, *La perspectiva del progreso: pensamiento político en la España del cambio de siglo (1809–1914)*, 289–309.

10. Sebastian Balfour, *The End of the Spanish Empire, 1898–1923*, 12–13. See also John Lawrence Tone, *War and Genocide in Cuba, 1895–1898*, 81–96; and Louis A. Pérez, Jr., "Cuba between Empires, 1898–1899," *Pacific Historical Review* 48, 4 (1979); 473–500.

11. Juan Eslava Galán and Diego Rojano Ortega, *La España del 98: El fin de una Era*, 219; Tone, *War and Genocide in Cuba*, 106–112; Balfour, *The End of the Spanish Empire*, 11–12; Carlos Serrano, *Final del Imperio. España, 1895–1898*, 32–41; and Rafael Núñez Florencio, *Militarismo y antimilitarismo en España (1888–1906)*, and his *El ejército español en el Desastre de 1898*.

12. Raymond Carr, *Spain, 1808–1975*, 383–385; Tone, *War and Genocide in Cuba*, 113–121.

13. Tone, *War and Genocide in Cuba*, 153–177. On Weyler see Emilio Diego de García, *Weyler: de la leyenda a la historia* (Madrid, 1998).

14. Alistair Hennessy, "The Origins of the Cuban Revolt," in *The Crisis of 1898: Colonial Redistribution and Nationalist Mobilization*, 89.

15. Tone, *War and Genocide in Cuba*, 209–218. Philip S. Foner, *The Spanish-Cuban-American War and the Birth of American Imperialism*, 2 vols., I: 115, and Juan Pérez de la Riva and Blanca Morejón, "La población de Cuba, la Guerra de Independencia, y la immigración del siglo XX," *Revista de la Biblioteca Nacional de José Martí*, May–August (1971), 17–27, accept 200,000 deaths from the Spanish strategy of reconcentration.

16. Tone, *War and Genocide in Cuba*, 218. See Louis A. Pérez, Jr. "The Meaning of the *Maine*: Causation and the Historiography of the Spanish-American War," *Pacific Historical Review* 58, 3 (1989): 293–322; and John Offner, "United States Politics and the 1898 War over Cuba," in Angel Smith and Emma Dávila-Cox, eds., *The Crisis of 1898*, 24–26.

17. For the assassination, see Tone, *War and Genocide in Cuba*, 225–234; Alvarez Junco, *El Emperador*, 164; and Rafael Núñez Florencio, *El terrorismo anarquista, 1888–1909*, 59–60, 134–137. On Nakens' remembrances of his time with Angiolillo see Nakens, *Trozos de mi vida*, 116–130.

18. On the sinking of the *Maine* see Balfour, *The End of the Spanish Empire*, 24–25; Tone, *War and Genocide in Cuba*, 239–243, and Carr, *Spain, 1808–1975*, 386. For a discussion the meaning of the *Maine*, see Pérez, Jr., "The Meaning of the *Maine*"; Peggy Samuels and Harold Samuels, *Remembering the* Maine; and Hyman G. Rickover, *How the Battleship* Maine *Was Destroyed*.

19. On the Prescott Paradigm and Spanish historiography, see Richard L. Kagan, "Prescott's Paradigm: American Historical Scholarship and the Decline of Spain," *American Historical Review* 101, 2 (April 1996): 423–446.

20. Balfour, *The End of the Spanish Empire*, 39–46.

21. Ibid., 20.

22. In addition to Juan Pan-Montojo, ed., *Más se perdió en Cuba*, Sebastian Balfour, *The End of the Spanish Empire*, Carlos Serrano, *Final del Imperio*.

España, 1895–1898; see also Juan Pablo Fusi and Antonio Niño, eds., *Antes del "desastre": Orígenes y antecedentes de la crisis del 98*; Santos Juliá, ed., *Debates en torno al 98: Estado, Sociedad y Política*; Carlos Serrano, José Luis Comellas, *Del 98 a la semana trágica, 1898–1909: crisis de conciencia y renovación política* (Madrid, 2002); Pedro Laín Entralgo and Carlos Seco Serrano, eds., *España en 1898. Las claves del Desastre*; Octavio Ruiz-Manjón and Alicia Langa, eds., *Los significados del 98: la sociedad española en la genesis del siglo XX*; and Rafael Sánchez Mantero, ed., *En torno al 98: España en el tránsito del siglo XIX y XX: actas del IV Congreso de la Asociación de la Historia Contemporánea*.

23. Juan Pro Ruiz, "La política en tiempos del *Desastre*," in *Más se perdió en Cuba*, 157–173.

24. Among the many treatments on Costa, see Jacque Maurice and Carlos Serrano, J. *Costa: Crisis de la Restauración y populismo (1875–1911)*; Eric Storm, *La perspective del progreso*, 97–144; Rafael Pérez de la Dehesa, *El pensamiento de Costa y su influencia en el 98*; George J. G. Cheyne, *Joaquín Costa: el gran desconocido*; Balfour, *The End of the Spanish Empire*, 71–91; and Carr, *Spain, 1808–1975*, 525–528.

25. Balfour, *The End of the Spanish Empire*, 64–65.

26. Carr, *Spain, 1808–1975*, 546.

27. Ibid; Joseph Harrison, "The Catalan Industrial Élite, 1898–1923," in *Élites and Power in Twentieth-Century Spain. Essays in Honour of Sir Raymond Carr*, ed. Frances Lannon and Paul Preston (Oxford, 1990), 53–55; and Balfour, *The End of the Spanish Empire*, 142–143. On Prat de la Riba's and Francesc Cambó's discursive vision for Catalonia, see Enric Ucelay-Da Cal, *El imperialismo catalán: Prat de la Riba, Cambó, D'Ors y la conquista moral de España*.

28. Alvarez Junco, *El Emperador*, 225–370. See also Romero Maura, *La rosa del fuego*.

29. See Julio Busquets, *Pronunciamientos y golpes de Estado en España*.

30. Juan Pro-Ruiz, "La política en tiempos del *Desastre*," 232–248; Balfour, *The End of the Spanish Empire*, 164–187. See also Stanley G. Payne, *Politics and the Military in Modern Spain* (Stanford, 1967); Manuel Balbé, *Orden público y militarismo en la España constitucional (1812–1983)* (Madrid, 1983); Carolyn P. Boyd, *Praetorian Politics in Liberal Spain*; and Geoffrey Jensen, *Irrational Triumph: Cultural Despair, Military Nationalism, and the Origins of Franco's Spain*.

31. Joaquín Romero Maura, *The Spanish Army and Catalonia. The '¡Cu-cut! Incident' and the Law of Jurisdictions, 1905–1906*, 25; see also Balfour, *The End of the Spanish Empire*, 178–182.

32. Geoffrey Jensen, *Irrational Triumph*, especially 99–114.

33. Sebastian Balfour, *Deadly Embrace: Morocco and the Road to the Spanish Civil War*.

34. Carlos Serrano, *El turno del pueblo: crisis nacional, movimientos populares y populismo en España (1890–1910)*, 48–62; Demetrio Castro Alfín, "Protesta popular y orden público: los motines de consumo," in *España entre dos siglos (1875–1931): continuidad y cambio*, 109–123.

35. Angel Smith, "The People and the Nation: Nationalist Mobilization and the Crisis of 1895–1898 in Spain," 171–176.
36. Carr, *Spain, 1808–1975*, 532.
37. Balfour, *The End of the Spanish Empire*, 151–152. For more on the *Lliga*, see Borja de Riquer i Permanyer and Josep Fontana i Lázaro, *Lliga Regionalista: la burguesía catalana i el nacionalismo (1893–1904)* (Barcelona, 1977).
38. Balfour, *The End of the Spanish Empire*, 49–63.
39. Christopher Schmidt-Nowara, "Imperio y crisis colonial," in *Más se perdió en Cuba*, 36–37.
40. Martin Blinkhorn, "Spain, the Spanish Problem and the Spanish Myth," *Journal of Contemporary History* 15, 1 (January 1980): 5–11.
41. José Alvarez Junco, "La nación en duda," in *Más se perdío en Cuba*, 411.
42. Alvarez Junco, *El Emperador*, 397-ff.
43. María Cruz Seone and María Dolores Sáiz, *Historia del periodismo en España*, Vol II: El Siglo XIX, 285–291; and Henry F. Schulte, *The Spanish Press, 1470–1966: Print, Power, and Politics*, 211–212.
44. Sebastian Balfour, *The End of the Spanish Empire*, 49. See also Sebastian Balfour, " 'The Lion and the Pig': Nationalism and National Identity in Fin-de-Siècle Spain," in *Nationalism and the Nation in the Iberian Peninsula*, 107–117; and Carlos Serrano, *Fin de Imperio*, 89.
45. "Cantares," *La Publicidad*, April 24, 1898, cited in Balfour, *The End of the Spanish Empire*, 100.
46. See for example the Archbishop of Seville's words in *El Imparcial*, September 8, 1898.
47. A detailed account is Miguel Morayta, *Masonería Española. Páginas de su historia*, with elaborations and rebuttals by Maurcio Carlavilla, 361–396.
48. Andrés Gallego, *La política religiosa, 1889–1913*, 156; Stanley G. Payne, *Spanish Catholicism*, 127. On the few women in Spanish Freemasonry see AHN-GCE (Salamanca), Sección Teosofía, Legajo 29, no. 2217; and AHN-GCE (Salamanca), Sección Masonería A, Legajo 355, exp. 2. See also Natividad Ortiz Albear, *Las mujeres en la masonería*; and María José Lacalzada de Mateo, *Mujeres en Masonería : antecedentes históricos entre las luces y las sombras (1868–1938).*
49. Celso Almuñia, "Clericalismo y anticlericalismo a través de la prensa española decimonona," 123–175.
50. Luis Morote, *Los frailes en España*, 63–64.
51. Andrés Gallego, *La política religiosa*, 143. See also José Andrés Gallego, "El separatismo filipino y la opinión española," *Hispania* XXXI (1971): 77–102.
52. See for example, Mosen El Nasaar, "Los Frailes en Filipinas," *Las Dominicales del Libre Pensamiento*, April 7, 1898. See also Viriato Díaz-Pérez, *Los frailes en Filipinas*, which was available at the *El Motín* editorial office.
53. See Ramiro Reig, *Blasquistas y Clericales*, 290–292.
54. Ullman, *The Tragic Week*, 37–38, 326–328.
55. José Alvarez Junco, *The Emergence of Mass Politics in Spain*, 161.
56. José Alabern to the Bishop Morgades, August 10, 1899, cited in Andrés Gallego, *La política religiosa*, 154–155.

57. Beginning in April of 1897, *El Motín* began running a column called "Los crímenes carlistas" (Carlist crimes).
58. Salvador Forner Muñoz, "La crisis del Liberalismo en Europa y en España: Canalejas en la encrucijada de la Restauración," in *La Restauración entre liberalismo y democracia*, 199–200.
59. On Canalejas see Diego Sevilla Andrés, *Canalejas*; and Forner Muñoz's, *Canalejas y el partido Liberal Democrático*.
60. *Diario de las Sesiones de Cortes. Congreso de los Diputados*, December 18–19, 1900, 512–517.
61. Ibid., see also O'Connell, "The Spanish Parliament and the Clerical Question," 112–113.
62. *Diario de las Sesiones de Cortes*, December 19, 1900, 517. It must be noted that within the same speech, Canalejas admonished the republicans and freemasons in the Parliament for being too exuberant with their anticlerical propaganda, and undermining the state's authority to do battle with ultramontane, anarchist, and socialist enemies.
63. O'Connell, "The Spanish Parliament and the Clerical Question," 117–118.
64. Berkowitz, *Pérez Galdós*, 118.
65. Berkowitz, *Pérez Galdós*, 370–379.
66. Ibid., 364; and Timothy Mitchell, *Betrayal of Innocents*, 55–59.
67. "Los teatros," *El Imparcial*, January 31, 1901; Berkowitz, *Pérez Galdós*, 350–353. See also E. Inman Fox, " 'Electra,' de Pérez Galdós (Historia, literatura y la polémica entre Martínez Ruiz y Maeztu)," in *Ideología y política en las letras de fin de Siglo (1898)*, 65–95.
68. "El estreno de *Electra*," *La Epoca*, January 31, 1901.
69. Alvarez Junco, *El Emperador*, 398.
70. "Tumulto en la Plaza de Santa Ana," *El Imparcial*, February 2, 1901. "El Sainete de anoche," *El Siglo Futuro*, February 2, 1901.
71. Fox, *Ideología y política*, 75–77.
72. See for example, Vicente Blasco Ibáñez, "Causas de nuestra incultura," *Electra* 5 (1901): 157; and Carlos del Río, "De dónde nos viene el fanatismo," *Electra* 9 (1901): 266–267.
73. "Mentira religiosa," *El Motín*, April 2, 1904 and May 21, 1904.
74. Pío Quinto, "El jesuita y Jesús," 1 (1901): 32, and José Martínez Ruiz, "Los jesuitas," *Electra* 1 (1901): 97. According to María Pilar Celma Valero, *Literatura y Periodismo en las Revistas del Fin de Siglo. Estudio e Indices (1888–1907)*, 76, Pío Quinto was most probably one of the pen names employed by the anarchist novelist Pío Baroja.
75. José Martínez Ruiz, "La religion," *Electra* 9 (1901): 257–258.
76. O'Connell, "The Spanish Parliament and the Clerical Question," 127–128.
77. Ibid., 127.
78. Forner, *Canalejas*, 110–129; Ullman, *Tragic Week*, 40–42; O'Connell, "The Spanish Parliament and the Clerical Question," 127–128.
79. For commentary on these developments in France see José Ferrandiz, "Francia y la Iglesia," *El Motín*, April 29, 1905; and "Cuestión Gravísima," *Las Dominicales*, December 22, 1905.

80. On the Nozaleda affair see Ramiro Reig, *Blasquistas y clericales. La lucha por la ciudad en la Valencia de 1900* (Valencia, 1986), 290–294.

81. Ullman, *The Tragic Week*, 42. For Maura see María Jesús González, *El universo conservador de Antonio Maura. Biografía y proyecto de Estado.* See also Storm, *La perspectiva del progreso*, 270–287.

82. Ullman, *The Tragic Week*, 326.

83. Ibid., 283–297.

84. Ibid., 322–332.

85. Romero Maura, *La rosa del fuego*, 271.

86. On Lerroux's successes between 1901 and 1905 see Alvarez Junco, *El Emperador*, 225–243.

87. From Lerroux's often cited "¡Rebeldes! ¡Rebeldes!" article in an issue of *El Progreso*, September 1, 1906, cited in Ullman, *The Tragic Week*, 88.

88. Payne, *Spanish Catholicism*, 133.

89. Ullman, *The Tragic Week*, 228.

90. Ibid.

91. Callahan, *The Catholic Church in Spain*, 82.

92. On the Ley del "Candado" and its background, see Andrés Gallego, *La política religiosa*, 370–404; Sevilla Andrés, *Canalejas*, 354–372; Payne, *Spanish Catholicism*, 134–135; and Ullman, *The Tragic Week*, 330–334.

93. Andrés Gallego, *La política religiosa*, 384.

94. Julio de la Cueva Merino "La democracia frailófoba. Democracia liberal y anticlericalismo," in *La Restauración, entre liberalismo y democracia*, 248–249. On remarkable pro-clerical demonstrations in Álava see Onésimo Díaz Hernándcz, " 'La ley del candado' en Álava," *Sancho el Sabio: revista de cultura e investigación vasca* 11 (1999): 143–160.

95. See Julio de la Cueva, "Cultura y movilización en el movimiento católico," 187–188.

96. Pérez Ledesma, "José Nakens," 323.

97. Ibid., 324.

98. Ibid, 324–325.

99. See AHN, Audencia Territorial de Madrid, Criminal Section, leg. 253/1, 174/921.

100. Pérez Ledesma, "José Nakens," 327.

101. Ibid.

102. Alvarez Junco, *El Emperador*, 333.

103. Ibid., 419–431.

104. Holguín, *Creating Spaniards*, 6–7.

Conclusion

1. On reaction to Salisbury's speech on national vigor see "La nación muerta," *Las Dominicales del Libre Pensamiento*, August 21, 1903; Rosario de la Torre del Río, "La prensa madrileña y el discurso de Lord Salisbury sobre 'las naciones moribundas' (Londres, Albert Hall, May 4, 1898)," *Cuadernos*

de Historia Moderna y Contemporánea, 6 (1985): 163–180; and "Cosas de España," *El Motín*, May 4, 1899.

2. Balfour, *The End of the Spanish Empire*, 129.
3. Balfour, *The End of the Spanish Empire*, 131; Ullman, *The Tragic Week*, 282–304.
4. Bruce Lincoln, "Revolutionary Exhumations in Spain, July 1936," 252.
5. Tracy Henderson, "Language and Identity in Galicia: The Current Orthographic Debate," in *Nationalism and the Nation in the Iberian Peninsula*, 237–251.
6. Michael Richards, *A Time of Silence: Civil War and the Culture of Repression in Franco's Spain, 1936–1945* (Cambridge, 1998), 11–12, 26–46; Holguín, *Creating Spaniards*, 195–196.
7. Alvarez Junco, *Mater dolorosa*, 20.
8. Ibid, 607. See also Edurne Uriarte, *España, Patriotrismo y nación*, especially 233-ff.
9. See Víctor M. Pérez-Díaz, *The Return of Civil Society: The Emergence of Democratic Spain*.

Bibliography

(A) Archives

Archivo Histórico Nacional, Madrid (AHN):
  Fondos Contmporáneos–Audencia Territorial de Madrid, Criminal Section (Madrid);
  Fondos Contemporáneos–Ministerio de Interior, General Series;
  Fondos Contemporáneos–Tribunal Supremo.
Archivo Histórico Nacional de la Guerra Civil Española, Salamanca (AHN-GCE):
  P.S. Madrid, Sección Masonería.
Archivo Regional de la Comunidad de Madrid.
Archivo de la Villa de Madrid (AVM), Sección 7, Legajo 97.
Biblioteca Nacional, Madrid (BN).
Hemeroteca Municipal, Madrid (HMM).
Hemeroteca Nacional, Madrid (HNM).
Herbert Southworth Collection, Mandeville Special Collections at Geisel Library, University of California, San Diego, Francisco Ferrer Collection. MSS 0248, Series 1A, 1C, 1D, 2, 3A, 4C, 5A, 5D.

(B) Newspapers and Periodicals

El Ateo (Barcelona).
La Carcajada (Barcelona).
El Cencerro (Madrid).
El Clarín (Madrid).
El Correro Español (Madrid).
La Correspondencia de Madrid (Madrid).
El Debate (Madrid).
Los Desheredados (Sabadell).
Las Dominicales del Libre Pensamiento (Madrid).
Electra (Madrid).
La Epoca (Madrid).
El Escándalo (Barcelona).
La España Moderna (Madrid).
España Nueva (Madrid).

La Flaca (Barcelona).
Germinal (Madrid).
Gil Blas (Madrid).
El Globo (Madrid).
El Imparcial (Madrid).
Jeremías (Madrid).
El Liberal (Madrid).
Madrid Cómico (Madrid).
El Motín (Madrid, weekly).
El País (Madrid, daily).
El Progreso (Barcelona, daily).
La Publicidad (Barcelona).
El Resumen (Madrid).
Revista de las Prisiones (Madrid).
El Siglo Futuro (Madrid).
El Socialista (Madrid).
El Solfeo (Madrid).
La Unión Católica (Madrid).
Vida Nueva (Madrid).

(C) Official Publications

Boletín Eclesiástico del Arzobispado de Toledo (Toledo).
Colección Legislativa de España (BN/AHN).
Diario de las Sesiones de Cortes. Congreso de los Diputados (Madrid).
La Gaceta de Madrid (HNM/HMM).
Ministerio de Gracia y Justicia. *Causa por regicido frustrado, 1906–1909. Atentado de 31 de de mayo de 1906. Causa contra Mateo Morral, Francisco Ferrer, José Nakens, Pedro Mayoral, Aulinio Martínez, Isidro Ibarra, Bernardo Mata, y Concepción Pérez Cuesta.* 5 vols. Madrid: Sucesores de J. A. García, 1911.
Ministerio de la Guerra. *Causa contra Francisco Ferrer Guardia, instruída y fallada por la jurisdicción de Guerra en Barcelona: Año 1909.* Madrid: Sucesores de J. A. García, 1911.
Ministerio de Instrucción Pública y Bellas Artes. *Estadística de la Prensa periódica de España (Referida al 1.o de Abril del año 1913).* Madrid: Dirección General del Instituto Geográfico y Estadístico, 1914.

(D) Primary Works by José Nakens*

Nakens, José (with collaboration from S. Pey Ordeix). *Almanaque de la Inquisición, por "El Motín."* Madrid, n.d. (1911?).

*A date is almost never printed in Nakens' works. However, wherever possible I have attempted to approximate a date in the parenthesis based on tracking advanced publicity for these books in *El Motín* and other newspapers.

Nakens, José. *Anticlericalism al por menos.* Biblioteca Anticlerical de Bolsillo. Madrid, n.d. (1915?).

———. *Asuntos diversos (Colección de artículos).* Madrid, n.d. (1915?).

———. *Calumnias al clero, inventadas por José Nakens. Robos, estafas, captaciones, explotaciones, violaciones, estupros, adulterios, atropellos, crueldades, riñas, asesinatos, infanticidios, homicidios, parricidios, etc., etc.* Madrid, n.d.

———. *Cantares, epigramas y cuentos anticlericales en verso, publicados por "El Motín."* Madrid, n.d.

———. *Cartas y dedicatorias.* Madrid, n.d. (1909?).

———. *La celda número 7 (Impresiones de la cárcel).* Madrid, 1908.

———. *Clericalismo en solfa.* Madrid, n.d.

———. *Cosas que he dicho (Esbozos de ideas).* Madrid, n.d. (1912?).

———. *Cuadros de miseria, copiados del natural por José Nakens.* Madrid, 1907.

———. *De todo un poco (Colección de artículos).* Madrid, n.d. (1909?).

———. *Degradaciones y cobardías.* Madrid, n.d. (1906?).

———. *La dictadura republicana.* Madrid, n.d. (1904?).

———. *En broma y en serio. Artículos anticlericales.* Madrid, n.d. (1909?).

———. *Espejo moral de clérigo.* Madrid, 1883.

———. *Garrotazo limpio: colección de artículos.* Madrid, n.d. (1889?).

———. *Humorismo anticlerical.* Madrid, n.d. (1909?).

———. *Juan Lanas.* Madrid, n.d. (1897?).

———. *Lo que no debe decirse.* Madrid, n.d. (1882?).

———. *Mi paso por la cárcel.* Madrid, n.d. (1908?).

———. *La moral y la Iglesia.* Biblioteca del Apostolado de la Verdad, Third Series. Madrid, n.d. (1911?).

———. *Muestras de mi estilo.* Madrid, 1906.

———. *¡Ojo al Cristo!* Madrid, n.d.

———. *Pequeñeces. Juguete cómico en un acto y en verso.* Madrid, n.d.

———. *La piqueta. Colección de artículos.* Madrid, n.d. (1883?).

———. *Trozos de mi vida.* Madrid, n.d. (1914?).

———. *Verdades al Pueblo (Juan Lanas).* Madrid, n.d. (1908?).

———. *Viaje al infierno.* Biblioteca del Apostolado de la Verdad, Second Series. Madrid, n.d. (1906?).

———. *Virtudes del clero divulgadas por los Sacrosantos Concilios celebradas desde el siglo I de la era cristiana, hasta fin de XII, y comentadas por José Nakens.* Madrid, n.d. (1881?).

———. *La vuelta de Cristo.* Biblioteca del Apostolado de la Verdad, First Series. Madrid, n.d. (1901?)

———. *Yo, hablando de mí (Colección de artículos).* Madrid, 1915.

(E) Other Primary Sources

Anonymous. *La lujuria del Clero según los concilios.* Biblioteca del Apostolado de la Verdad. Madrid, n.d.

Arenal, Concepción. "Estado Actual de la Mujer en España." In *Arenal y Lázaro: La admiración por una mujer de talento (1889–1895)*, ed. Carmen Simón Palmer, 73–108. Madrid, 2002.

Baroja, Pío. *El cura Santa Cruz y su partida*. Madrid, 1918.

Cansinos Asséns, Rafael. *La novela de un literario*. 3 vols. Madrid, 1982.

Costa, Joaquín. *Oligarquía y caciquismo, Colectivismo agrario y otros escritos (Antología)*. Edited by Rafael Pérez de la Dehesa. Third edition. Madrid, 1973.

———. *Oligarquía y caciquismo como la forma actual del gobierno en España*. Madrid, 1902.

Delaunay, Gaétan. *Memoirs sur l'infériorité des civilizations précoces*. Paris, 1885.

Díaz-Pérez, Viriato. *Los frailes en Filipinas*. Madrid, 1904.

Estévanez y Murphy, Nicolás. *Pensamientos revolucionarios*. Barcelona, 1978; originally published in 1906.

Ferrer (y Guardia), Francisco. *La escuela moderna: póstuma explicación y alcance de la enseñanza racional*. Edited and with a Prologue by Lorenzo Portet. Barclona, 1912?; republished in 1976.

Gramsci, Antonio. *Selections from Prison Notebooks*. Edited and translated by Quintan Hoare and Geoffrey Nowell Smith. New York, 1971.

"Hugo, Víctor." *Cristo en el Vaticano*. Madrid, n.d.

Meslier, Jean. *Superstition in all Ages by Jean Meslier, a Roman Catholic Priest, Who, after a Pastoral Service of Thirty Years at Etrepigny and But in Champagne, France, Wholly Abjured Religious Dogma, and Left His Last Will and Testament to His Parishioners, and to the World, to be Published after His Death, the Following Pages Entitled Common Sense*, edited and translated by Paul Henry Thiry and Baron d'Holback. New York, 1920.

———. *El Testimonio de Juan Meslier*. Madrid, n.d. (1887?).

Michelet, Jules. *Le prêtre, la femme et la famille*. Paris, 1912.

Molas, Isidre, ed. *Ideario de F. Pi y Margall*. Madrid, 1966.

Mónita Secreta: Instrucciones reservados de los jesuítas. Translated from the Latin by Anonymous. Biblioteca del Apostolado de la Verdad. Madrid, n.d.

Morayta, Miguel. *La Libertad de Cátedra: Sucesos Universitarios de la Santa Isabel*. Madrid, 1911.

———. *Masonería Española. Páginas de su historia*. With elaborations and rebuttals by Mauricio Caravilla. Madrid, 1956.

Morote, Luis. *Los frailes en España*. Madrid, 1904.

———. *La moral de la derrota*. Introduction by Juan Sinisio Pérez Garzón. Madrid, 1997; originally published in 1900.

Morphy, Michel. *Les mystères de la pornagraphie cléricale; sécrets honteaux de la confession, immoralitiés, et guerre aux prêtre, corrupteurs de la jeunes*. Paris, 1884.

Ortega y Gasset, José. *Reactificación de la República. Artículos y discursos*. Madrid, 1931.

Pardo Bazán, Emilia. *Campoamor. Estudio biográfico*. Madrid, 1893?.

Pérez, Miguel (pseud. *Siffler*). *Don Manuel Ruiz Zorrilla ante la ARM. Noticias sobre la formación y desarrollo de la misma. Historia de la conspiración militar que produjo la sublevación de Badajoz y la de Seo de Urgell y detalles interesantes del ejercito. Escrito por Siffler-725.* Madrid, 1883.

Pérez Galdós, Benito. *La de San Quintín; Electra.* Edited by Luis F. Díaz Larios. Letras hispánicas Series, no. 535. Madrid, 2002.

Pey Ordeix, Segismundo. *Sor Sicalipsis.* Barcelona, 1931.

Potvin, Charles. *La democracia y la iglesia.* Biblioteca del Apostolado de la Verdad. Madrid, n.d.

Proudhon, Pierre-Joseph. *La Pornocratie ou les femmes dans les temps modernes.* Paris, 1875.

Romanones, Count of (a.k.a. Alvaro Figueroa y Torres). *Notas de una vida (1868–1901).* Vol. I. Madrid, 1934.

Rousseau, Jean-Jacques. *The Basic Political Writings.* Edited and translated by Donald A. Cress. Indianapolis, 1987.

Ruiz Zorrilla, Manuel. *Tres negaciones y una afirmación. Cuatro folletos.* Madrid, 1864.

Samaniego, Félix M. *Cuentos y poesías más que picantes.* Barcelona, 1899; originally published in 1799.

Sardá y Salvany, Félix. *El Liberalismo es Pecado. Cuestiones Candentes.* Second edition. Barcelona, 1884.

Urales, Federico. *Mi vida.* Barcelona, 1930.

(F) Books and Articles

Aguado, Ana. "Entre lo público y lo privado: sufragio y divorcio en la Segunda República." In *República y republicanas*, ed. María Dolores Ramos, 105–134. *Ayer* Series, Vol. 60. Madrid, 2005.

Aguilar, A. "Los motivos de Mateo Morral." *Historia y vida*, no. 56, extra (August 1973): 24–29.

Agulhon, Maurice. *Marianne into Battle: Republican Imagery and Symbolism in France, 1789–1880.* Translated by Janet Lloyd. Cambridge, 1981.

Agulhon, Maurice and Pierre Bonte. *Marianne. Les visages de la République.* Paris, 1992.

Almuñia, Celso. "Clericalismo y anticlericalismo a través de la prensa española decimonona." In *La cuestión social en la Iglesia española contemporánea*, ed. Carlos Seco Serrano et al., 123–175. Real Monasterio de El Escorial, 1981.

Alvarez Junco, José. "Los 'Amantes de la Libertad': la cutural republica española a principios del siglo XX." In *El republicanismo en España (1830–1977)*, ed. Nigel Townson, 265–292. Madrid, 1994.

———. "El anticlericalismo en el movimiento obrero español." In *Octubre 1934. Cincuenta años para la reflexión*, ed. Gabriel Jackson et al., 283–300. Madrid, 1985.

———. "La creación de los símbolos nacionalizadores en el siglo XIX español." In *Les nationalismes dans l'Espagne contemporaine: Idéologies, mouvements, symbols*, ed. Jean-Louis Guereña, 53–76. Paris, 2001.

———. *The Emergence of Mass Politics in Spain: Populist Demagoguery and Republican Culture, 1890–1910.* Portland, OR, 2003.

Alvarez Junco, José. *El Emperador del Paralelo: Lerroux y la demogogia populista*. Madrid, 1990.

———. "The Formation of Spanish Identity and Its Adaptation to the Age of Nations." *History & Memory* 14, 1 and 2 (Fall 2002): 13–36.

———. "Hobsbawm sobre nacionalismo." *Historia Social*, 60 (1996): 179–187.

———. *La ideología política del anarquismo español, 1868–1910*. Madrid, 1976.

———. "Los intelectuales: anticlericalismo y republicanismo." In *Los orígenes culturales de la II República*, ed. José Luis García Delgado, 101–126. Madrid, 1993.

———. "La invención de la Guerra de la Independencia," *Studia Historica*, 12 (1994): 75–99.

———. "Magia y ética en la retórica política." In *Populismo, caudillage y discurso demagógico*, ed. José Alvarez Junco, 219–270. Madrid, 1987.

———. *Mater dolorosa: la idea de España en el siglo XIX*. Madrid, 2001.

———. "La nación en duda." In *Más se perdió en Cuba. España, 1898 y la crisis de fin de siglo*, ed. Juan Pan-Montojo, 405–475. Madrid, 1998.

———. "The Nation-Building Process in Nineteenth-Century Spain." In *Nationalism and the Nation in the Iberian Peninsula: Competing and Conflicting Identities*, ed. Clare Mar-Molinero and Angel Smith, 89–106. Oxford, 1996.

———. "El populismo como problema." In *El populismo en España y América*, ed. José Alvarez Junco and Ricardo González Leandri, 11–38. Madrid, 1994.

———. "Racionalismo, romanticismo y moralismo en la cultura política republicana de comienzos del siglo." In *Clases populares, cultura, educación. Siglos XIX y XX*, ed. Jean-Louis Guereña and Alejandro Tiana, 355–376. Madrid, 1989.

Alvarez Villamil, V. and Rodolfo Llopis, eds. *Cartas de conspiradores. La Revolución de Septiembre. De la emigración al poder*. Madrid, 1929.

Amezcua, Manuel. "La vida contradictoria de la beata." *Demófilo: revista de cultura tradición* 7 (1991): 33–43.

Anderson, Benedict. *Imagined Communities: Reflections on the Origins and Spread of Nationalism*. Revised edition. New York, 1991.

Anderson, Margaret Lavinia. "The *Kulturkampf* and the Course of German History." *Journal of Modern History* 63 (1991): 82–115.

Andrés Gallego, José. *La política religiosa en España, 1889–1913*. Madrid, 1975.

———. "El separatismo filipino y la opinión española." *Hispania* XXXI (1971): 77–102.

———. "Sobre las formas de pensar y de ser: la Iglesia," in *Historia general de España y América*, XVI-1: 287–303. Madrid, 1983.

Andrés Gallego, José, ed. *Estudios históricos sobre la iglesia española contemporánea*. El Escorial, 1979.

Angosto, Pedro L. "Carlos Esplá: anticlericalismo y masonería en un republicano español del siglo XX." *Espacio, tiempo y forma. Serie V. Historia contemporánea* 15 (2002): 229–258.

Apte, Mahadev L. *Humor and Laughter: An Anthropological Approach*. Ithaca, NY, 1985.

Arbeloa, Víctor Manuel. *La Semana Trágica de la Iglesia en España (1931)*. Barcelona, 1976.

———. *Socialismo y anticlericalismo*. Madrid, 1973.

Artola, Miguel. *Partidos y programas políticos 1808–1936*. Madrid, 1974.

Aston, Nigel and Matthew Cragoe, eds. *Anticlericalism in Britain, c. 1500–1914*. Gloucestershire, 2001.

Aston, Nigel. *Religion and Revolution in France, 1780–1804*. Washington, DC, 2000.

Azcárate, Pablo de. *La Guerra del 98*. Madrid, 1968.

———. *Gumersindo de Azcárate: Estudio biográfico documental*. Madrid, 1969.

Bahamonde Magro, Angel and Jesús A. Martínez-Martín. "La desamortización y el mercado inmobilario madrileño (1836–1868)." In *Urbanismo e historia urbana en el mundo hispano*, ed. Antonio Bonet Correa, II: 939–956. Madrid, 1985.

Balbé, Manuel. *Orden público y militarismo en la España constitucional, 1812–1983*. Madrid, 1983.

Balcells, Albert. *Historia contemporánea de Cataluña*. Barcelona, 1983.

———. *Historia de Cataluña*. Madrid, 2006.

Balcells, Albert and Geoffrey J. Walker, eds. *Catalan Nationalism: Past and Present*. New York, 1995.

Balfour, Sebastian. *Deadly Embrace: Morocco and the Road to the Spanish Civil War*. Oxford, 2002.

———. *The End of the Spanish Empire, 1898–1923*. Oxford, 1997.

———. " 'The Lion and the Pig': Nationalism and National Identity in *Fin-de-Siècle* Spain." In *Nationalism and the Nation in the Iberian Peninsula: Competing and Conflicting Identities*, ed. Clare Mar-Molinero and Angel Smith, 107–117. Oxford, 1996.

———. "Riot, Regeneration and Reaction: Spain in the Aftermath of the 1898 Disaster." *Historical Journal* 39, 2 (1995): 405–423.

Barrio Alonso, Angeles. "Anarquistas, republicanos y socialistas en Asturias (1890–1917)." In *El anarquismo español y sus tradiciones culturales*, ed. Bert Hofmann, Pere Joan i Tous, and Manfred Tietz, 41–56. Vervuert, 1995.

Barry, Edouard. *España y españoles: paisaje, monumentos, tipos de la corte y de provincias, usos yo costumbres, leyendas y tradiciones*. Paris, 1913.

Bell, David. *The Cult of the Nation in France: Inventing Nationalism, 1680–1800*. Cambridge, MA, 2001.

Bell, Donald H. *Sesto San Giovanni: Workers, Culture, and Politics in an Italian Town, 1880–1922*. New Brunswick, NJ, 1986.

———. "Worker Culture and Worker Politics: The Experience of an Italian Town, 1880–1915." *Social History* 3 (January 1978): 1–21.

Berkowitz, H. Chonon. *Pérez Galdós: Spanish Liberal Crusader*. Madison, WI, 1948.

Bertocci, Philip A. *Jules Simon: Republican Anticlericalism and Cultural Politics in France. 1848–1886*. Columbia, MO, 1978.

Biedermann, Hans. *Dictionary of Symbolism*. Translated by James Hulbert. New York, 1992.

Blackbourn, David. *Class, Religion, and Local Politics in Wilhelmine Germany: The Center Party in Württemberg before 1914*. New Haven, 1980.

Blas Guerrero, Andre de. *Tradición republicana y nacionalism español (1876–1930)*. Madrid, 1991.

Blinkhorn, Martin. "Spain, the Spanish Problem and the Spanish Myth." *Journal of Contemporary History* 15, 1 (January 1980): 5–25.

Blum, Carol. *Rousseau and the Republic of Virtue: The Language of Politics in the French Revolution*. Ithaca, NY, 1986.

Bonet Correa, Antonio, ed. *Urbanismo e historia urbana en el mundo hispano*. Madrid, 1985.

Botti, Alfonso. *Cielo y dinero. El nacionalcatolicismo en España (1881–1975)*. Madrid, 1992.

Boyd, Carolyn P. *Historia Patria: Politics, History and National Identity in Spain, 1875–1975*. Princeton, 1997.

———. *Praetorian Politics in Liberal Spain*. Chapel Hill, NC, 1979.

Bozal Fernández, Valeriano. *La ilustración gráfica del XIX en España*. Madrid, 1979.

Brandes, Stanley. *Metaphors of Masculinity: Sex and Status in Andalusian Folklore*. Philadelphia, 1980.

Bredin, Jean-Denis. *The Affair: The Case of Alfred Dreyfus*. Translated by Jeffrey Mehlman. New York, 1986; originally published in French as *L'Affair* in 1983.

Burleigh, Michael. *Earthly Powers: The Clash of Religion and Politics in Europe from the French Revolution to the Great War*. New York, 2005.

Busquets, Julio. *Pronunciamientos y golpes de Estado en España*. Barcelona, 1982.

Cacho Viu, Vicente. *La Institución Libre de Enseñanza. I. Orígenes y etapa universitaria (1860–1881)*. Madrid, 1962.

Calhoun, Craig, ed. *Habermas and the Public Sphere*. Cambridge, MA: MIT Press, 1992.

———. "Introduction: Habermas and Public Sphere." In *Habermas and the Public Sphere*, ed. Craig Calhoun, 1–48. Cambridge, MA, 1992.

———. *Nationalism*. Concepts in Social Thought Series. Minneapolis, 1997.

Callahan, William James. *The Catholic Church in Spain, 1875–1998*. Washington, DC, 2000.

———. *Church, Politics and Society in Spain, 1750–1874*. Cambridge, MA, 1984.

———. "An Organization and Pastoral Failure: Urbanization, Industrialization, and Religion in Spain, 1850–1930." In *European Religion in the Age of Great Cities, 1830–1930*, ed. Hugh McLeod, 43–60. London, 1995.

———. "The Origins of the Conservative Church in Spain, 1793–1823." *European Studies Review* 10 (1980): 199–223.

———. "The Spanish Parish Clergy, 1874–1930." *Catholic Historical Review* LXXV (1989): 405–422.

———. "Two Spains and Two Churches, 1760–1835." *Historical Reflections* 2 (1975): 158–182.

Calvo Poyato, José. *El Desastre del 98*. Barcelona, 1997.

Camacho Pérez, Salvador. "Violencia anticlerical en Madrid en julio de 1834." *Almatocín. Revista de la E.U. del Profesorado de EGB de Almería* 9 (January–June 1987): 68–101.

Canal, Jordi. "Manuel Ruiz Zorrilla (1833–1895): de hombre de estado a conspirador compulsivo." In *Liberales, agitadores y conspiradores*, ed. Isabel Burdiel and Manuel Pérez Ledesma, 267–299. Madrid, 2000.

Cannadine, David. "The Context, Performance, and Meaning of Ritual: The British Monarchy and the Invention of Tradition, c. 1820–1977." In *The Invention of Tradition*, ed. Eric Hobsbawm and Terrence Ranger, 101–164. Canto edition. Cambridge, 1992.

———. "Splendor Out of Court: Royal Spectacle and Pageantry in Modern Britain, c. 1820–1977." In *Rites of Power*, ed. Sean Wilentz, 206–243. Philadelphia, 1985.

Capel, Rosa. *El sufragio femenino en la Segunda República*. Madrid, 1992.

Cárcel Ortí, Vicente. *Iglesia y revolución en España (1868–1874): estudio histórico-jurídico desde la documentación vaticana inedita*. Pamplona, 1979.

———. *La persecución religiosa en la Segunda República (1931–1939)*. Madrid, 1990.

———. *Política eclesial de los gobiernos españoles, 1830–1840*. Pamplona, 1975.

Caro Baroja, Julio. *Introducción a una historia contemporanea del anticlericalismo español*. Madrid, 1980.

Carr, Raymond. *Spain, 1808–1975*. Second edition. Oxford, 1982.

Carro Celada, Esteban. *Curas guerrilleros en España*. Madrid, 1970.

Carroll, Michael P. *The Cult of the Virgin Mary. Psychological Origins*. Princeton, NJ, 1986.

Castro Alfín, Demetrio. "Cultura, política y cultural política en la violencia anticlerical." In *Movilización y cultura en la España contemporánea*, ed. Rafael Cruz and Manuel Pérez Ledesma, 69–97. Madrid, 1997.

———. "De la clandestinidad republicana a la clandestinidad anarqusta." In *El anarquismo español y sus tradiciones culturales*, ed. Bert Hofmann, Pere Joan i Tous, and Manfred Tietz, 41–56. Vervuert, 1995.

———. "Protesta popular y orden público: los motines de consumo." In *España entre dos siglos (1875–1931): continuidad y cambio*, ed. Michael Alpert and José Luis García Delgado, 109–123. Madrid, 1991.

Celma Valero, María Pilar. *Literatura y periodismo en las Revistas del Fin de Siglo. Estudio e índices (1888–1907)*. Gijón, 1991.

Chadwick, Owen. *The Secularization of the European Mind*. Canto edition. Cambridge, 1991.

Chartier, Roger. *The Cultural Origins of the French Revolution*. Translated by Lydia G. Cochrane. Durham, NC, 1991.

———. "Texts, Printings, Readings." In *The New Cultural History*, ed. Lynn Hunt, 154–175. Berkeley, 1989.

Cheyne, George J. C. *Joaquín Costa: El gran desconocido*. Barcelona, 1972.

Chodorow, Nancy J. *The Reproduction of Motherhood: Psychoanalysis and the Sociology of Gender.* Second edition. Berkeley, 1999.

Christiansen, Eric. *The Origins of Military Power in Spain, 1800–1854.* Oxford, 1967.

Clark, Christopher and Wolfram Kaiser, eds. *Culture Wars: Secular-Catholic Conflicts in Nineteenth-Century Europe.* Cambridge, 2003.

Clark, Lorenne M. G. and Lynda Lange, eds. *The Sexism of Social and Political Theory: Women and Reproduction from Plato to Nietzsche.* Toronto, 1979.

Clark, Martin. *Modern Italy, 1871–1982.* London, 1984.

Clarke, John, Stuart Hall, Tony Jefferson, and Brian Roberts. "Subcultures, Cultures and Class: A Theoretical Overview." In *Resistance Through Rituals: Youth Subcultures in Post-War Britain,* ed. Stuart Hall and Tony Jefferson, 9–74. London, 1976.

Clemente, Josep Carles. *Historia de una disidencia social (1833–1976).* Barcelona, 1990.

Colley, Linda. *Britons: Forging the Nation, 1707–1937.* New Haven, CT, 1994.

Comellas, José Luis. *Del 98 a la semana trágica,1898–1909: crisis de conciencia y renovación política.* Madrid, 2002.

Comín Comín, F. *Hacienda y economía en la España contemporánea (1800–1936).* Madrid

Conard, Pierre. "Sexualité et anticléricalisme (Madrid 1910)." *Hispania* XXXI (1971): 103–131.

Conversi, Daniele. *The Basques, the Catalans, and Spain: Alternative Routes to Nationalist Mobilization.* Reno, NV.

———. "Language or Race? The Choice of Core Values in the Development of Catalan and Basque Nationalisms." *Ethnic and Racial Studies* 12, 1 (1990): 52–70.

Coppa, Frank J. "Anticlericalism." In *Dictionary of Modern Italian History,* ed. Salvatore Saladino, 15–16. Westport, CT, 1985.

Coverdale, John. *The Basque Phase of Spain's First Carlist War.* Princeton, NJ, 1984.

Cowans, Jon, ed. *Modern Spain: A Documentary History.* Philadelphia, 2003.

Cowling, Maurice. *Religion and Public Doctrine in Modern England.* 3 vols. Cambridge, 1980–2001.

Cruz, Rafael. "La cultura regresa al primer plano." In *Cultura y movilización en la España contemporánea,* ed. Rafael Cruz and Manuel Pérez Ledesma, 13–34. Madrid, 1997.

———. "Introducción." In *El Anticlericalismo,* ed. Rafael Cruz, 11–13. Ayer Series no. 27. Madrid, 1997.

Cruz Seoane, María. *Historia del Periodismo en España.* Volume II, El Siglo XIX. Madrid, 1983.

———. *Oratoria y política en la España del siglo XIX.* Madrid, 1977.

Cruz Seoane, María and María Dolores Sáiz. *Historia del Periodismo en España.* Volume III: El Siglo XX: 1898–1936. Madrid, 1996.

Cuadrat, Xavier. "La Setmana Tràgica i el moviment obrer a Catalunya," *L'Avenç* 2 (1977): 44–48.

Cubitt, Geoffrey. *The Jesuit Myth: Conspiracy Theory and Politics in Nineteenth Century France*. Oxford, 1993.

Cuenca Toribio, José Manuel. "El catolicismo español en la Restauración (1875–1931)." In *Historia de la Iglesia en España*, ed. Ricardo García Villoslada, 5 vols., Volume V, 277–336. Madrid, 1979.

Cueva Merino, Julio de la. "El anticlericalismo en la Segunda República y la Guerra Civil." In *El anticlericalismo español contemporáneo*, ed. Emilo LaParra López and Manuel Suárez Cortina, 211–301. Madrid, 1998.

———. "Atrocities against the Clergy during the Spanish Civil War." *Journal of Contemporary History* 33, 3 (July 1998): 359–369.

———. *Clericales y anticlericales. El conflicto entre confesionalidad y secularización en Cantabria. 1875–1923*. Santander, 1994.

———. "Cultura y movilización en movimiento católico de la Restauración (1899–1913)." In *La cultura española de la Restauración*, ed. Manuel Suárez Cortina, 169–192. Santander, 1999.

———. "La democracia frailófoba. Democracia liberal y anticlericalismo." In *La Restauración, entre liberalismo y democracia*, ed. Manuel Suárez Cortina, 229–271. Madrid, 1997.

———. "Movilización política e identidad anticlerical, 1898–1910." In *El Anticlericalismo*, ed. Rafael Cruz, 101–126. Ayer Series, no. 27. Madrid, 1997.

———. "The Stick and the Candle: Clericals and Anticlericals in Northern Spain." *European History Quarterly* 26, 2 (April 1996): 241–256.

Culla i Clarà, Joan. B. *El republicanisme lerrouxista a Catalunya (1901–1923)*. Barcelona, 1986.

Dardé Morales, Carlos. "Biografía política de Nicolás Salmerón (ca. 1860–1890)." In *Republicanismo y repúblicas en España*, ed. José A. Piqueras and Manuel Chust, 135–161. Madrid, 2000.

———. "Los republicanos." In *Historia general de España y América*, ed. José Andrés Gallegos, Vol. XVI-2: 130–156. Madrid, 1981.

Davis, John A. "Italy." In *The War for the Public Mind: Political Censorship in Nineteenth-Century Europe*, ed. Robert Justin Goldstein, 81–124. Westport, CT, 2000.

Delgado Ruiz, Manuel. "Anticlericalismo, espacio y poder. La destrucción de los rituales católicos, 1931–1939." In *El Anticlericalismo*, ed. Rafael Cruz, 149–180. Ayer Series, no. 27. Madrid, 1997.

———. *La ira sagrada. Anticlericalismo, iconoclastia y antirritualismo en la España contemporánea*. Barcelona, 1992.

———. *Las palabras de otro hombre. Misoginia y anticlericalismo*. Barcleona, 1993.

Dendle, Brian J. *The Spanish Novel of Religious Thesis, 1876–1936*. Madrid; and Princeton, NJ, 1968.

Devlin, John. *Spanish Anticlericalism. A Study in Modern Alienation*. New York, 1966.

Díaz Hernández, Onésimo. " 'La ley del candado' en Álava." *Sancho el Sabio: revista de cultura y investigación vasca* 11 (1999): 143–160.

Díaz Mozaz, José María. *Sociología del anticlericalismo. Estructura social, política y religión en España.* Madrid, 1976.

Diego García, Emilio de. *Weyler. De la leyenda a la historia.* Madrid, 1998.

Dijkstra, Bram. *Idols of Perversity: Fantasies of Feminine Evil in Fin-de-Siècle Culture.* New York, 1986.

Dobbelaere, Karel. *Secularization: A Multi-Dimensional Concept.* A special issue of *Current Sociology* 29, 2 (Summer 1981): 1–216.

Dommanget, Maurice. *Francisco Ferrer.* Grandes Educateurs Socialistes Series. Paris, 1952.

Drochon, Paul. "Juan Valera et la liberté religieuse." *Mélanges de la Casa de Velázquez* 8 (1972): 407–444.

Duara, Prasenjit. "Historicizing National Identity, or Who Imagines What and When." In *Becoming National: A Reader*, ed. Geoff Eley and Ronald Grigor Suny, 151–177. Oxford, 1996.

Duarte, Angel. "La esperanza republicana." In *Cultura y movilización en la España contemporánea*, ed. Rafael Cruz and Manuel Pérez Ledesma, 169–200. Madrid, 1997.

Duarte, Angel and Pere Gabriel, eds. *El republicanismo español.* Ayer Series 39. Madrid, 2000.

Dufour, Gérard. *Clero y sexto mandamiento: la confesión en la España del siglo XVIII.* Valladolid, 1996.

Dykema, Peter A. and Heiko A. Oberman. *Anticlericalism in Late Medieval and Early Modern Europe.* Studies in Medieval and Renaissance Thought. Volume 51. Leiden, 1993.

Eastman, Scott. "Constructing the Nation Within a Catholic Tradition: Modernity and National Identities Across the Spanish Monarchy, 1793–1823." Ph.D. diss, University of California, Irvine, 2006.

Eguillor, José R. Manuel Revuelta, and Rafael María de Diego, eds., *Memorias del P. Luis Martín, General de la Compañia de Jesus (1846–1906).* Volume II. Rome, 1988.

Eisenstein, Elizabeth L. "Some Conjectures about the Impact of Printing on Western Society and Thought: A Preliminary Report." *Journal of Modern History* 40 (March 1968): 1–56.

Eley, Geoff and Ronald Grigor Suny. "Introduction." In *Becoming National: A Reader*, ed. Geoff Eley and Ronald Grigor Suny, 3–37. New York, 1996.

Elshtain, Jean Bethke. *Public Man, Private Woman: Woman in Social and Political Thought.* Princeton, NJ, 1981.

Elwitt, Sanford. *The Making of the 3rd Republic: Class and Politics in France, 1868–1884.* Baton Rouge, LA, 1975.

Enciclopedia Universal Illustrada Europea Americana. Vol. XXVII. Madrid, 1987.

Esdaile, Charles J. *Fighting Napoleon: Guerrillas, Bandits and Adventurers in Spain, 1808–1914.* New Haven, CT, 2004.

———. *The Peninsular War.* New York, 2003.

———. *Spain in the Liberal Age: From Constitution to Civil War, 1808–1936.* Oxford, 2000.

Esenwein, George. *Anarchist Ideology and the Working-Class Movement in Spain, 1868–1898.* Berkeley, 1989.

Eslava Galán, Jaun and Diego Rojano Ortega. *La España del 98: El fin de una Era*. Madrid, 1997.

Espigado Tocino, Gloria. "Mujeres 'radicals': utópicas, republicanas e internacionalistas en España (1848–1874)." In *República y republicanas en España*, ed. Maria Dolores Ramos, 15–43. *Ayer* Series 60. Madrid, 2005.

Esteban, José. *Mateo Morral, el anarquista. Causa por un regicidio*. Madrid, 2001.

Evans, Eric J. "The Church in Danger? Anticlericalism in Nineteenth-century England." *European Studies Review* 13 (1983): 201–223.

Farr, Ian. "From Anti-Catholicism to Anticlericalism: Catholic Politics and the Peasantry in Bavaria, 1860–1900." *European Studies Review* 13 (1983): 249–269.

Fauré, Christine. *Democracy without Women: Feminism and the Rise of Liberal Individualism n France*. Translated from French by Claudia Gorbman and John Berks. Bloomington, IN, 1991; orginally published in French in 1985.

Faury, Jean. *Cléricalisme et anticléricalisme dans le Tarn (1848–1900)*. Series A, no. 4. Toulouse, 1980.

Fenn, Richard. *Toward a Theory of Secularization*. Storrs, CT, 1978.

Fermon, Nicole. *Domesticating Passions: Rousseau, Woman and Nation*. Hanover, NH, 1997.

Fernández Almagro, Melchor. *Historia del Reinado de Alfonso XIII*. Second Illustrated edition. Barcelona:, 1934.

———. *Historia política de la España contemporánea. Vol I: 1868–1885*. 3 vols. Madrid, 1968.

Fernández de la Reguera, Ricardo and Susana March. *La boda de Alfonso XIII*. Barcelona, 1966.

———. "¿Fue culpable Ferrer Guardia?" *Historia y vida*, 8 (November 1968): 92–105.

———. "La muerte de Mateo Morral, el regicidia frustrado." *Historia y vida*, 6 (September 1968): 90–103.

Ferrer Sanmartí, Sol. *Le veritable Francisco Ferrer*. Paris, 1948.

———. *La vie et l'oeuvre de Francisco Ferrer: un Martyr au Xxe siècle*. Preface by Charles August Bontemps. Paris, 1962.

Foner, Philip S. *The Spanish-Cuban-American War and the Birth of American Imperialism*. 2 vols. New York, 1972.

Ford, Caroline. *Creating the Nation in Provincial France: Religion and Political Identity in Brittany*. Princeton, NJ, 1993.

———. *Divided Houses: Religion and Gender in Modern France*. Ithaca, NY, 2005.

Forner Muñoz, Salvador. *Canalejas y el Partido Liberal Democrático*. Madrid, 1993.

———. "La crisis del Liberalismo en Europa y en España: Canalejas en la encrucijada de la Restauración." In *La Restauración entre liberalismo y democracia*, ed. Manuel Suárez Cortina, 199–221. Madrid, 1995.

Fox, Inman. *Ideología y política en las letras de fin de Siglo (1898)*. Madrid, 1988.

———. *La invención de España: nacionalismo liberal e identidad nacional*. Madrid: Cátedra, 1997.

Freeze, Gregory L. "A Case of Stunted Anticlericalism: Clergy and Society in Imperial Russia." *European Studies Review* 13 (April 1983): 177–200.

———. *The Parish Clergy in Nineteenth-Century Russia: Crisis, Reform, Counter-Reform.* Princeton, NJ, 1983.

Frías Fernández. "Percepciones, imágenes y explicaciones de la recuperación económica de la iglesia: los anticlericales entre 1876–1899." In *Iglesia, Sociedad y Estado en España, Francia e Italia (s. XVIII al XX)*, ed. Emilio La Parra López and Jesús Pradells Nadal, 173–184. Alicante, 1992.

Fusi, Juan Pablo. "El estado español en el fin de siglo: ¿era normal en relación con Europa?" In *Debates en torno al 98: Estado, Sociedad y Política*, ed. Santos Juliá, 59–70. Madrid, 1998.

Fusi, Juan Pablo and Antonio Niño, eds. *Antes del Desastre. Orígenes y antecedentes de la crisis del 98.* Madrid, 1996.

Gadille, Jacques. "On French: Some Reflections." *European Studies Review* 13 (April 1983): 127–144.

García Rovira, Anna M. *La revolució liberal a Espanya i les clases populars (1832–1835).* Vic, 1989.

Gauchet, Marcel. *The Disenchantment of the Modern World: A Political History of Religion.* Princeton, NJ, 1997.

Geertz, Clifford. "Centers, Kings, and Charisma: Reflections on the Symbolics of Power." In *Culture and Its Creators: Essays in Honor of Edward Shils*, ed. Joseph Ben-David and Terry N. Clark, 150–171. Chicago, 1977.

Gellner, Ernest. *Nations and Nationalism.* Oxford, 1983.

———. *Thought and Change.* London and Chicago, 1964.

Gibson, Ralph. "Hellfire and Damnation in Nineteenth-Century France." *Catholic Historical Review* LXXIV (July 1988): 383–402.

———. *A Social History of French Catholicism, 1789–1914.* London, 1989.

Gilmore, David D. *Aggression and Community: Paradoxes of Andalusian Culture.* New Haven, CT, 1987.

———. "The Anticlericalism of the Andalusian Rural Proletarians." In *La religiosidad popular. Vol I: Antropología e historia*, ed. María Jesús Buxó i Rey, Salvador Rodríguez Becerra, and León Carlos Alvarez y Santaló, 278–298. Barcelona, 1989.

Goldberg, Harriet, ed. *Motif—Index of Medieval Spanish Folk Narratives.* Tempe, AZ, 1998.

Gómez Aparicio, Pedro. *Historia del periodismo español.* 4 vols. Madrid, 1967, 1971, 1974, 1981.

Gómez Chaix, Pedro. *Ruiz Zorrilla. Un ciudadano ejemplar.* Madrid, 1934.

González, María Jesús. *El universo conservador de Antonio Maura. Biografía y proyecto de Estado.* Madrid, 1997.

González Casanova, José Antonio. *Federalismo y autonomía: Cataluña y el estado español, 1868–1938.* Barcelona, 1979.

Goode, Joshua. "Corrupting a Good Mix: Race and Crime in Late Nineteenth- and Early Twentieth-Century Spain." *European History Quarterly* 35 (2005): 241–265.

———. "The Racial Alloy: The Science, Politics, and Culture of Race in Spain, 1875–1923." Ph.D. diss., University of California, Los Angeles, 1999.

Graham, Helen. "Community, Nationalism and State in Republican Spain, 1931–1938." In *Nationalism and the Nation in the Iberian Peninsula: Competing and Conflicting Identities*, ed. Clare Mar-Molinero and Angel Smith, 133–147. Oxford, 1996.

Greenfeld, Liah. *Nationalism: Five Roads to Modernity*. Cambridge, MA, 1992.

Gross, Michael B. *The War Against Catholicism: Liberalism and the Anti-Catholic Imagination in Nineteenth-Century Germany*. Ann Arbor, MI, 2005.

Habermas, Jürgen. *The Structural Transformation of the Public Sphere: An Inquiry into a Category of Bourgeois Society*. Translated by Thomas Burger and Frederick Lawrence. Cambridge, MA, 1989.

Haliczer, Stephen. *Sexuality in the Confessional: A Sacrament Profaned*. Oxford, 1996.

Halperin, S. William. "Italian Anticlericalism, 1871–1914." *Journal of Modern History* 19, 1 (March 1947): 17–34.

Harrison, Joseph. "The Catalan Industrial Élite, 1898–1923," in *Élites and Power in Twentieth-Century Spain. Essays in Honour of Sir Raymond Carr*, ed. Frances Lannon and Paul Preston, 45–70. Oxford, 1990.

Hastings, Adrian. *The Construction of Nationhood: Ethnicity, Religion and Nationalism*. Cambridge, 1997.

Hause, Steven C. and Anne R. Kenney. *Women's Suffrage and Social Politics in the French Third Republic*. Princeton, NJ, 1984.

Hayes, Carlton. *Nationalism: A Religion*. New York, 1960.

Hazareesingh, Sudhir. *Political Traditions in Modern France*. Oxford, 1994.

Henderson, Tracy. "Language and Identity in Galicia: The Current Orthographic Debate." In *Nationalism and the Nation in the Iberian Peninsula: Competing and Conflicting Identities*, ed. Clare Mar-Molinero and Angel Smith, 237–251. Oxford, 1996.

Hennessy, Alister. "The Origins of the Cuban Revolt." In *The Crisis of 1898: Colonial Redistribution and National Mobilization*, ed. by Angel Smith and Emma Dávila-Cox, 65–95. New York, 1999.

Hennessy, C. A. M. *The Federalist Republic in Spain: Pi y Margall and the Federalist Republican Movement, 1868–1874*. Oxford, 1964.

Hernández Girbal, F. "José Nakens ampara a Mateo Morral." *Historia y vida*, 126 (September 1978): 44–59.

Herr, Richard. *An Historical Essay on Modern Spain*. Berkeley, 1971.

Hibbs-Lissourgues, Solange. *Iglesia, prensa y sociedad en España (1868–1904)*. Alicante, 1995.

Hobsbawm, Eric. "Mass-Producing Traditions: Europe, 1870–1914." In *The Invention of Tradition*, ed. Eric Hobsbawm and Terence Ranger, 263–308. Canto edition. Cambridge, 1992.

———. *Nations and Nationalism since 1780: Programme, Myth, Reality*. Canto edition. Cambridge, 1992.

Hobsbawm, Eric and Terrence Ranger, eds. *The Invention of Tradition*. Canto edition. Cambridge, 1992.

Holguín, Sandie. *Creating Spaniards: Culture and National Identity in Republican Spain*. Madison, WI, 2002.

Hoover, Arlie J. *The Gospel of Nationalism: German Patriotic Preaching from Napoleon to Versailles*. Stuttgard, 1986.

Hroch, Miroslav. "From National Movement to the Fully Formed Nation: The Nation-Building Process in Europe." In *Becoming National: A Reader*, ed. Geoff Eley and Ronald Grigor Suny, 60–77. New York, 1996.

Hunt, Lynn. *The Family Romance of the French Revolution*. Berkeley, 1992.

———. *Politics, Culture, and Class in the French Revolution*. Berkeley, 1986.

Jensen, Geoffrey. *Irrational Triumph: Cultural Despair, Military Nationalism, and the Origins of Franco's Spain*. Reno, NV, 2001.

Jover, José María. "1898. Teoría y Práctica de la redistribución colonial." In *Debates en torno al 98: Estado, Sociedad y Política*, ed. Santos Juliá, 13–58. Madrid, 1998.

Juliá, Santos, ed. *Debates en torno al 98: Estado, Sociedad y Política*. Madrid, 1998.

Juliá, Santos, David Ringrose, and Cristina Segura. *Madrid: Historia de una capital*. Madrid, 1994.

Julien, Nadia. *The Mammoth Dictionary of Symbols: Understanding the Hidden Language of Symbols*. New York, 1996.

Kagan, Richard L. "Prescott's Paradigm: American Historical Scholarship and the Decline of Spain." *American Historical Review* 101, 2 (April 1996): 423–446.

Kedourie, Elie. *Nationalism*. Fourth, expanded edition. Oxford, 1993, originally published in 1960.

Keene, Judith. " 'Into the Clear Air of the Plaza': Spanish Women Achieve the Vote in 1931." In *Constructing Spanish Womanhood: Female Identity in Modern Spain*, ed. Victoria Lorée Enders and Pamela Beth Radcliff, 325–348. Albany, NY, 1999.

Kern, Robert W. *Liberals, Reformers and Caciques in Restoration Spain, 1875–1909*. Albuquerque, NM, 1974.

Kertzer, David. *Ritual, Politics, and Power*. New Haven, CT, 1988.

Kley, Dale K. van. *The Religious Origins of the French Revolution: From Calvin to the Civil Constitution, 1560–1791*. New Haven, CT, 1996.

Kohn, Hans. *Nationalism, Its Meaning and History*. Revised edition. New York, 1965.

La Parra López, Emilio. "Los inicios del anticlericalismo español contemporáneo (1750–1833)." In *El anticlericalismo español contemporáneo*, ed. Emilio La Parra López and Manuel Suárez Cortina, 17–68. Madrid, 1998.

La Parra López, Emilio and Jesús Pradells Nadal, eds. *Iglesia, Sociedad y Estado en España, Francia e Italia (ss. XVII al XX)*. Alicante, 1991.

La Parra López, Emilio and Manuel Súarez Cortina, eds. *El anticlericalismo español contemporáno*. Madrid, 1998.

Lacalzada de Mateo, María José. *Mujeres en masonería: antecedentes históricos entre las luces y las sombras (1868–1938)*. Barcelona, 2006.

Laín Entralgo, Pedro and Carlos Seco Serrano, eds. *España en 1898: Las claves del Desastre*. Barcelona, 1998.

Lalouette, Jacqueline. "El anticlericalismo en Francia, 1877–1914." In *El Anticlericalismo*, ed. Rafael Cruz, 15–38. Ayer Series 27. Madrid, 1997.

Landes, Joan. *Women and the Public Sphere in the Age of the French Revolution.* Ithaca, NY, 1988.

Lange, Lynda. "Rousseau: Women and the General Will." In *The Sexism of Social and Political Theory: Women and Reproduction from Plato to Nietzsche,* ed. Lorenne M. G. Clark and Lynda Lange, 41–52. Toronto, 1979.

Lannon, Frances. *Privilege, Persecution, and Prophecy: The Catholic Church in Spain, 1875–1975.* Oxford, 1987.

Lears, T. J. Jackson. "The Concept of Cultural Hegemony: Problems and Possibilities." *American Historical Review* 90 (June 1985): 567–593.

Lebovics, Herman. *True France: The Wars over Cultural Identity, 1900–1945.* Ithaca, NY, 1992.

Lida, Clara. "Literatura anarquista y anarquismo literario." *Nueva Revista de Filología Hispánica* 19 (1970): 360–381.

Lincoln, Bruce. "Revolutionary Exhumations in Spain, July 1936." *Comparative Studies in Society and History* 27 (April 1985): 241–260.

Linz, Juan L. "The Party System of Spain: Past and Future." In *Party Systems and Voter Alignments: Cross-National Perspectives,* ed. Seymour M. Lipset and Stein Rokkan, 198–282. New York, 1967.

Litvak, Lily. *Erotismo fin de siglo.* Barcelona, 1979.

———. *Musa Libertaria: Arte, literatura y vida cultural del anarquismo español (1880–1913).* Barcelona, 1981.

Llorca, Carmen. *Emilio Castelar. Precursor de la democracia cristiana.* Madrid, 1966.

Llorens i Vila, Jordi. *La Unió Catalanista (1891–1904).* Barcelona, 1991.

Longare, Jesús. "El pensamiento de Lamennais criticado por un católico español de la época isabelina." *Hispania Sacra* XXV (1972): 379–390.

López Morrillas, Juan. *Krausist Movement and Ideological Change in Spain.* Cambridge, 1981.

López Ruiz, José María. *La Vida Alegre: Historia de las revistas humorísticas, festivas y satíricas publicadas en la Villa y Corte de Madrid.* Madrid, 1995.

Lovett, Gabriel. *Napoleon and the Birth of Modern Spain.* 2 vols. New York, 1965.

Lyttelton, Adrian. "An Old Church and a New State: Italian Anticlericalism, 1876–1915." *European Studies Review* 13 (1983): 225–248.

Maddox, Richard. "Revolutionary Anticlericalism and Hegemonic Processes in an Andalusian Town, August 1936." *American Ethnologist* 22, 1 (February 1995): 125–143.

Marcos Orteruelo, Alfredo. *El pensamiento de Gumersindo de Azcárate.* León: Institución Fray Bernardino de Sahagún, 1985.

Martí Gilabert, Francisco. *La Iglesia en España durante la revolución francesa.* Pamplona, 1971.

Martin, David A. *A General Theory of Secularization.* Oxford, 1978.

Martín Arranz, Raúl. "El liderazgo carismático en el contexto del estudio del liderazgo." In *Populismo, caudillaje y discurso demagógico,* ed. José Alvarez Junco, 73–99. Madrid, 1987.

Martínez Cuadrado, Miguel. *La burguesía conservadora (1874–1931).* Madrid, 1986.

Martínez Cuadrado, Miguel. *Elecciones y partidos en España (1868–1931)*. Madrid, 1969.

Marx, Anthony W. *Faith in Nation: Exclusionary Origins of Nationalism*. Oxford, 2003.

Mateo Avilés, Elías de. *El anticlericalismo en Málaga (1875–1923)*. Málaga, 1990.

———. *Paternalismo burgués y beneficiencia religiosa en Málaga desde la segunda mitad del siglo XIX*. Málaga, 1985.

Maurice, Jacques and Carlos Serrano. *J. Costa: Crisis de la restauración y populismo (1875–1911)*. Madrid, 1977.

McManners, John. *The French Revolution and the Church*. London, 1969.

McMillan, James F. "Clericals, Anticlericals and the Women's Movement in France under the Third Republic." *Historical Journal* 24 (1981): 361–376.

McPhee, Peter. *A Social History of France, 1780–1880*. London, 1992.

Mercader Riba, Joan. "La feria tradicional de San Narciso y las autoridades napoleónicas," *Anales del Instituto de Estudios Gerundenses* 3 (1984): 222–225.

Mercader Riba, Juan. "Origenes del anticlericalismo español." *Hispania* 33 (1973): 100–123.

Millán, Fernando. *La revolución laica: de la Institución Libre de Enseñanza a la escuela de la República*. Valencia, 1983.

Mitchell, Timothy. *Betrayal of Innocents: Desire, Power, and the Catholic Church in Spain*. Philadelphia, 1998.

Molina Martínez, José Luis. *Anticlericalismo y literatura en el siglo XIX*. Murcia, 1998.

Montero Alonso, José. *Sucedió en Palacio*. Fifth edition. Madrid, 1991.

Montero Moreno, Antonio. *Historia de la persecución religiosa en España, 1936–1939*. Madrid, 1961.

Moody, Joseph N. *The Church as Enemy: Anticlericalism in Nineteenth Century French Literature*. Washington, DC, 1968.

Mosher, John R. "The Birth of Mass Politics in Spain: Lerrouxismo in Barcelona." Ph.D. diss., University of California, San Diego, 1977.

Mosse, George L. "Caesarism, Circuses, and Monuments." *Journal of Contemporary History* 6 (1971): 167–182.

———. *Nationalism and Sexuality: Respectability and Abnormal Sexuality in Modern Europe*. New York, 1985.

———. *The Nationalization of the Masses: Political Symbolism and Mass Movements in Germany from the Napoleonic Wars through the Third Reich*. Ithaca, NY, 1975.

Nash, Mary. *Defying Male Civilization: Women in the Spanish Civil War*. Denver, 1995.

———. "Género y ciudadanía." In *Política en la Segunda República*, ed. Santos Juliá, 105–134. Ayer Series, Vol. 20. Madrid, 1995.

Neuhas, Richard J. *The Naked Public Square: Religion and Democracy in America*. Grand Rapids, MI, 1984.

Niccoli, Ottavia. *I sacerdoti, i guerrieri, i contadini. Storia di un'immagine della società*. Turin, 1979.

Nord, Philip. *The Republican Moment: Struggles for Democracy in Nineteenth Century France.* Cambridge, MA, 1995.

Núñez, Clara Eugenia. *La fuente de la riqueza: educación y desarrollo económico en la España contemporánea.* Madrid, 1992.

Núñez Florencio, Rafael. *El ejército español en el Desastre de 1898.* Madrid, 1997.

————. *Militarismo y antimilitarismo en España (1888–1906).* Madrid, 1990.

————. *El terrorismo anarquista (1888–1909).* Madrid, 1983.

Núñez Seixas, Xosé M. "Historia e actualidade dos nacionalismos na España contemporánea: unha perspectiva de conxunto." *Giral* 128 (1995): 495–510.

O'Connell, Robert. "The Spanish Parliament and the Clerical Question, 1874–1936." Ph.D. diss., Columbia University, 1966.

Offner, John. "United States Politics and the 1898 War over Cuba." In *The Crisis of 1898: Colonial Redistribution and Nationalist Mobilization,* ed. Angel Smith and Emma Dávila-Cox, 18–44. New York, 1999.

Ollero, Andrés. *Universidad y política: tradición y secularización en el siglo XIX español.* Madrid, 1972.

Ortiz, Jr., David. "Opposition Voices in Regency Spain: Liberalism, the Press, and the Public Sphere, 1885–1902." Ph.D. diss., University of California, San Diego, 1995.

————. *Paper Liberals: Press and Politics in Restoration Spain.* Westport, CT, 2000.

Ortiz Albear, Natividad. *Las mujeres en la masonería.* Málaga, 2005.

Oyarzúra, Román. *Historia del Carlismo.* Third edition. Madrid, 1965.

Ozouf, Mona. *Festivals and the French Revolution.* Translated by Alan Sheridan. Cambridge, MA, 1988.

————. "Space and Time in Festivals of the French Revolution." *Comparative Studies in Society and History* 17 (1975): 372–284.

Palomares Ibáñez, José María. "La Iglesia española y la asistencia social en el siglo XIX." In *Estudios históricos sobre la Iglesia española contempóranea,* ed. José Andrés Gallego, et al., 119–149. El Escorial, 1978.

————. "La recuperación económica de la iglesia española (1845–1931)." In *Iglesia, Sociedad y Estado en España, Francia e Italia (s. XVIII al XX),* ed. Emilio La Parra López and Jesús Pradells Nadal, 153–172. Alicante, 1991.

Pan-Montojo, Juan, ed. *Más se perdió en Cuba. España, 1898 y la crisis de fin de siglo.* Madrid, 1998.

Partin, Malcolm O. *Waldeck-Rousseau, Combes, and the Church: The Politics of Anticlericalism, 1899–1905.* Durham, NC, 1969.

Pateman, Carole. *The Sexual Contract.* Stanford, CA, 1988.

Payne, Stanley G. *Basque Nationalism.* Reno, NV, 1975.

————. *Politics and the Military in Modern Spain.* Stanford, CA, 1967.

————. *Spanish Catholicism: An Historical Overview.* Madison, WI, 1984.

Paz, D. G. *Popular Anti-Catholicism in Mid-Victorian England.* Stanford, CA, 1993.

Pérez, Jr., Louis A. "Cuba between Empires, 1898–1899," *Pacific Historical Review* 48, 4 (1979): 473–500.

————. *Cuba and the United States: Ties of Singular Intimacy.* Athens, GA, 1990.

Pérez, Jr., Louis A. *The War of 1898: The United States and Cuba in History and Historiography.* Chapel Hill, NC, 1998.

Pérez de la Dehesa, Rafael. "El acercamiento de la literatura finisecular a la literatura popular." In *Creación y público en la literatura española*, ed. J. F. Botrel and Serge Salaün, 156–161. Madrid, 1974.

———. *El pensamiento de Costa y su influencia en el 98.* Madrid, 1966.

Pérez de la Riva, Juan and Blanca Morejón. "La población de Cuba, la Guerra de Independencia, y la inmigración del siglo XX." *Revista de la Biblioteca Nacional José Martí.* May–August (1971): 17–27.

Pérez-Díaz, Víctor M. *The Return of Civil Society: The Emergence of Democratic Spain.* Cambridge, MA, 1993.

Pérez Garzón, Juan Sinisio. "Curas y liberales en la revolución burguesa." In *El Anticlericalismo*, ed. Rafael Cruz, 67–100. Ayer Series 27. Madrid, 1997.

———. "Los mitos fundacionales y el tiempo de unidad imaginada del nacionalismo español." *Historia Social* 40 (2001): 7–28.

Pérez Gutiérrez, Francisco. *El problema religioso de la generación de 1868: la leyenda de Dios.* Madrid, 1976.

Pérez Ledesma, Manuel. "José Nakens (1841–1926): pasión anticlerical y activismo republicano." In *Liberales, agitadores y conspiradores*, ed. Isabel Burdiel and Manuel Pérez Ledesma, 301–330. Madrid, 2000.

———. "La sociedad española, la guerra y la derrota." In *Más se perdió en Cuba: Espana, 1898 y la crisis de fin de siglo*, ed. Juan Pan-Montojo, 91–150. Madrid, 1998.

———. "Studies on Anticlericalism in Contemporary Spain." *International Review of Social History* 46, 2 (2001): 227–255.

Perrot, Michelle. "El elogio del ama de casa en el siglo XIX." In *Historia y género. Las mujeres en la Europea moderna y contemporánea*, ed. James Amelang and Mary Nash, 224–268. Valencia, 1990.

Philips, Roderick G. "History of the Family." *Encyclopedia of European Social History, from 1350 to 2000*, ed. Peter N. Stearns, Vol 4, 135–144. New York, 2001.

Pick, Daniel. *Faces of Degeneration: A European Disorder, c. 1848–1918.* Cambridge, 1989.

Pilbeam, Pamela M. *Republicanism in Nineteenth-Century France, 1814–1871.* New York, 1995.

Piqueras Arenas, José A. "Detrás de la política: República y federación en el proceso revolucionario español." In *Republicanos y repúblicas en España*, ed. José A. Piqueras Arenas and Manuel Chust, 1–44. Madrid, 2000.

Piqueras Arenas, José A. and Manuel Chust, eds. *Republicanos y repúblicas en España.* Madrid, 2000.

Pitt-Rivers, Julian. *The People of the Sierra.* Second edition. Chicago, 1971.

Pope, Barbara Corrado. "The Influence of Rousseau's Ideology of Domesticity." In *Connecting Spheres: Women in the Western World, 1500 to the Present*, ed. Marilyn J. Boxer and Jean H. Quataert, 136–145. New York, 1987.

Portero Molina, José Antonio. *Púlpito e ideología en la España del siglo XIX.* Zaragoza, 1978.

Prados de la Escosura, Leandro. *De imperio a nación. Crecimiento y atraso ecónomico en España (1780–1930)*. Madrid, 1988.

Pro Ruiz, Juan. "La política en tiempos del *Desastre*." In *Más se perdio en Cuba: España, 1898 y la crisis del fin de siglo*, ed. Juan Pan-Montojo, 151–260. Madrid, 1998.

Pryke, Sam. "Nationalism and Sexuality, What Are the Issues?" *Nations and Nationalism* 4 (1998): 529–549.

Puelles Benítez, Manuel de. *Educación e ideología en la España contemporánea*. Second edition. Barcelona, 1991.

———. "Secularización y enseñanza en España (1874–1917)." In *España entre dos siglos (1875–1931)*, ed. José Luis García Delgado, 191–212. VII Coloquio de Historia Contemporánea de España. Madrid, 1991.

Puerto, Javier and Carlos San Juan. "La epidemia de cólera de 1834 en Madrid." *Estudios de Historia Social* 15 (1980): 9–61.

Radcliff, Pamela Beth. "The Emerging Challenge of Mass Politics." In *Spanish History since 1808*, ed. José Alvarez Junco and Adrian Shubert, 137–154. London, 2000.

———. *From Mobilization to Civil War: The Politics of Polarization in the Spanish City of Gijón, 1900–1937*. Cambridge, 1996.

———. "Política y cultura republicana en el Gijón de fin de siglo." In *El republicanismo español (1830–1977)*, ed. Nigel Townson, 373–394. Madrid, 1994.

———. "La representación de la nación. El conflicto en torno a la identidad nacional y las práctica simbólicas en la Segunda República." In *Cultura y movilización en la España contemporánea*, ed. Rafael Cruz and Manuel Pérez Ledesma, 305–326. Madrid, 1997.

Ramos, María Dolores. "Federalismo, laicismo, obrerismo, feminismo: cuatro claves para interpretar la biografía de Belén Sárraga." In *Discursos, realidades, utopias. La construcción del sujeto femenino en los siglos XIX y XX*, ed. María Dolores Ramos and María Teresa Vera, 125–164. Barcelona, 2002.

———. "La república de las librepensadoras (1890–1914): laicismo, emancipismo, anticlericalismo." In *República y republicanas en España*, ed. María Dolores Ramos, 45–74. *Ayer* Series 60. Madrid, 2005.

Rapport, Michael. *Ninteenth-Century Europe*. New York, 2005.

Read, Jan. *The Catalans*. London, 1978.

Rearick, Charles. "Festivals in Modern France: The Experience of the Third Republic." *Journal of Contemporary History* 12 (1977): 45–460.

Reglá, Juan. *Historia de Cataluña*. Madrid, 1974.

Reig, Ramiro. *Blasquistas y clericales: La lucha por la ciudad en la Valencia de 1900*. Valencia, 1986.

———. "Entre la realidad y la ilusión: el fenómeno blasquistas en Valencia, 1898–1936." In *El republicanismo español (1830–1977)*, ed. Nigel Townson, 395–423. Madrid, 1994.

———. "Vicente Blasco Ibáñez (1867–1928): promotor de rebeldías." In *Liberales, agitadores y conspiradores*, ed. Isabel Burdiel and Manuel Pérez Ledesma, 331–361. Madrid, 2000.

———. "Populismes." *Debats* 12 (June 1985): 6–21.

Rémond, René. "Anticlericalism: Some Reflections by way of Introduction." *European Studies Review* 13, 2 (April 1983): 121–126.

——. *L'anticlericalisme en France de 1815 à nos jours.* New and revised edition. Brussels, 1985.

——. *Religion and Society in Modern Europe.* Oxford, 1999.

Revuelta González, S. J., Manuel. *El anticlericalismo español en sus documentos.* Barcelona, 1999.

——. "Clero viejo y clero nuevo en el siglo XIX." In *Estudios históricos sobre la Iglesia española contemporánea,* ed. José Andrés Gallego, 153–197. El Escorial, 1979.

——. *La exclaustración, 1833–1840.* Madrid, 1976.

——. *Política religiosa de los liberales en el siglo XIX.* Madrid, 1973.

——. "La recuperación eclesiástica y el rechazo anticlerical en el cambio de siglo." In *España entre dos siglos (1875–1931),* ed. José Luis Garcia Delgado, 213–234. VII Coloquio de Historia Contemporánea de España, dirigido por Manuel Tuñón de Lara. Madrid, 1991.

——. "Religión y formas de religiosidad." In *Historia de España, Ramón Menéndez Pidal.* Volume XXXV, 213–327. Madrid, 1989.

——. "La supresión de la Compañía de Jesús en España en 1820." *Razón y Fe* 170–171 (1970): 103–120.

Rhodes, Anthony. *The Power of Rome in the Twentieth Century: The Vatican in the Age of Liberal Democracies, 1870–1922.* London, 1983.

Rich, Norman. *The Age of Nationalism and Reform, 1850–1890.* Second edition. New York, 1977.

Richards, Michael. *A Time of Silence: Civil War and the Culture of Repression in Franco's Spain, 1936–1945.* Cambridge, 1998.

Rickover, Hyman G. *How the Battleship Maine Was Destroyed.* Washington, DC, 1976.

Ringrose, David R. *Spain, Europe, and the "Spanish Miracle," 1700–1900.* Cambridge, 1996.

Riquer i Permanyer, Borja de. "La débil nacionalización española del siglo XIX." *Historia Social* 20 (1994): 97–114.

Riquer i Permanyer, Borja de and Joseph Fontana i Lázaro, *Lliga Regionalista: la burguesía catalana i el nacionalismo (1893–1904).* Barcelona, 1977.

Rodríguez de Coro, Francisco. "Anticlericalismo y sociedad madrileña en el siglo XIX." *Anales del Instituto de Estudios Madrileños* 28 (1990): 355–381.

Romero Maura, Joaquín. *La rosa del fuego; republicanos y anarquistas: la política de los obreros barceloneses entre el desastre colonial y la semana trágica, 1899–1909.* Barcelona, 1975.

——. *The Spanish Army and Catalonia. The '¡Cu-cut! Incident' and the Law of Jurisdictions, 1905–1906.* Beverly Hills, CA, 1976.

——. "Terrorism in Barcelona and Its Impact on Spanish Politics, 1904–1909." *Past and Present* 41 (1968): 130–168.

Roper, Lyndal. *Oedipus and the Devil: Witchcraft, Sexuality, and Religion in Early Modern Europe.* London, 1994.

Ross, Ronald J. *Beleaguered Tower: The Dilemma of Political Catholicism in Wilhelmine Germany.* Notre Dame, IN, 1976.

Rueda Hernanz, Germán, ed. *La desamortización en la península ibérica.* Ayer Series 9. Madrid, 1993.

Ruiz-Manjón, Octavio and Alicia Langa, eds. *Los significados del 98: La sociedad española en la genesis del siglo XX.* Madrid, 1999.

Sábato, Hilda. "Citizenship, Political Participation, and the Formation of the Public Sphere in Buenos Aires, 1850s–1880s." *Past and Present* 136 (1992): 139–163.

Sahlins, Peter. *Boundaries: The Making of France and Spain in the Pyrenees.* Berkeley, 1989.

Salomón Chéliz, María del Pilar. "Beatas sojuzgadas por el clero: la imagen de las mujeres en el discurso anticlerical en la España del primer tercio del siglo XX." *Femenismo/s: revista del Centro de Estudios sobre la Mujer de la Universidad de Alicante* 2 (2003): 41–58.

———. "El discurso anticlerical en la construcción de una identidad nacional española republicana (1898–1936)." *Historia Social* 54, 110 (2002): 485–498.

———. "Resumen de las mujeres en la cultura política republicana: religion y anticlericalismo." *Historia Social* 53 (2005): 103–118.

Samuels, Peggy and Harold Samuels. *Remembering the Maine.* Washington, DC, 1995.

Sanabria, Enrique A. "Anticlerical Politics: Republicanism, Nationalism, and the Public Sphere in Restoration Madrid, 1874–1912." Ph.D. diss., University of California, San Diego, 2001.

Sánchez, José. *Anticlericalism: A Brief History.* Notre Dame, IN, 1972.

Sánchez Agesta, Luis. *Historia del constitucionalismo español.* Second edition. Madrid, 1964.

Sánchez Mantero, Rafael, ed. *En Torno al "98": España en el tránsito del siglo XIX al XX. Actas del IV Congreso de la Asociación de Historia Contemporánea.* 2 vols. Huelva, 2000.

Sanfeliu, Luz. "El blasquismo en Valencia (1898–1911). Un proyecto político y la transformación de las identitades genérica." In *Cultura Republicana. 70 años después*, ed. Nicolás Sánchez Durá, Rafael Maestre Marín, and Pilar Molina Beneyto, 121–135. Valencia, 2002.

———. "Familias republicanas e identidades femeninas en el blasquismo: 1896–1910." In *República y republicanas en España*, ed. María Dolores Ramos, 75–103. Ayer Series, Vol. 60. Madrid, 2005.

Sarti, Roland. *Mazzini: A Life for the Religion of Politics.* Westport, CT, 1997.

Schapiro, J. Salwyn. *Anticlericalism: Conflict between Church and State in France, Italy, and Spain.* Princeton, NJ, 1967.

Schmidt-Nowara, Christopher. "Imperio y crisis colonial." In *Más se perdió en Cuba. España, 1898 y la crisis de fin de siglo*, ed. Juan Pan-Montojo, 31–90. Madrid, 1998.

Schulte, Henry F. *The Spanish Press, 1470–1966: Print, Power, and Politics.* Urbana, IL, 1968.

Schulze Schneider, Ingrid. "El papel de la prensa madrileña en el conflicto de las Islas Caroliñas." In *La sociedad madrileña durante la restauración, 1876–1931*, ed. Angel Bahamonde Magro and Luis Enrique Otero Carvajal, Vol. II, 299–306. Madrid, 1989.

Schumacher, John N. "Integrism: A Study in Nineteenth Century Spanish Politico-Religious Thought." *Catholic Historical Review* 48 (1962): 343–364.

Schwartz, Joel. *The Sexual Politics of Jean-Jacques Rousseau*. Chicago, 1984.

Scribner, R. W. *For the Sake of Simple Folk: Popular Propaganda for the German Reformation*. Cambridge, 1981.

Seco Serrano, Carlos. *Militarismo y civilismo en la España contemporánea*. Madrid, 1984.

Serrano, Carlos. "Conciencia de la crisis: conciencias en crisis." In *Más se perdió en Cuba. España, 1898 y la crisis de fin de siglo*, ed. Juan Pan-Montojo, 335–404. Madrid, 1998.

———. *Final del Imperio. España, 1895–1898*. Madrid, 1984.

———. *El nacimiento de Carmen. Símbolos, mitos y nación*. Madrid, 1999.

———. *El turno del pueblo: crisis nacional, movimientos populares y populismo en España (1890–1910)*. Translated from French y María del Mar Duró. Barcelona, 2000.

Sevilla Andrés, Diego. *Canalejas*. Barcelona, 1956.

Shklar, Judith N. *Men and Citizens: A Study of Rousseau's Social Theory*. Cambridge, 1969.

Shorter, Edward. *The Making of the Modern Family*. New York, 1975.

Shubert, Adrian. *A Social History of Modern Spain*. Second edition. London, 1992.

Simón Segura, Francisco. *La desamortiazción española del siglo XIX*. Madrid, 1973.

Sipe, A. W. Richard. "The Problem of Sexual Trauma and Addiction in the Catholic Church." *Sexual Addiction and Compulsivity: The Journal of Treatment and Prevention* 1 (1994): 130–137.

———. *Sex, Priests, and Power: The Anatomy of a Crisis*. New York, 1995.

Sluga, Glenda. "Identity, Gender, and the History of European Nations and Nationalism." *Nations and Nationalism* 4 (1998): 87–111.

Smith, Angel. *Anarchism, Revolution and Reaction: Catalan Labour and the Crisis of the Spanish State, 1898–1923*. New York, 2007.

———. "The People and the Nation: Nationalist Mobilization and the Crisis of 1895–1898 Spain." In *The Crisis of 1898: Colonial Redistribution and Nationalist Mobilization*, ed. Angel Smith and Emma Dávila-Cox, 152–179. New York, 1999.

Smith, Angel and Clare Mar-Molinero. "The Myths and Realities of Nation-Building in the Iberian Peninsula." In *Nationalism and the Nation in the Iberian Peninsula: Competing and Conflicting Identities*, ed. Clare Mar-Molinero and Angel Smith, 1–30. Oxford, 1997.

Smith, Angel and Emma Dávila-Cox, eds. *The Crisis of 1989: Colonial Redistribution and Nationalist Mobilization*. New York, 1999.

Smith, Anthony D. *The Ethnic Origins of Nations*. Second edition. Oxford, 1998.

———. "The Origins of Nations." In *Becoming National: A Reader*, ed. Geoff Eley and Ronald Grigor Suny, 106–130. Oxford, 1996.

Smith, Helmut Walser. *German Nationalism and Religious Conflict: Culture, Ideology, Politics, 1870–1914*. Princeton, NJ, 1995.

Spadolini, Giovanni. *L'Italia repubblicana: attraverso i simboli, i dipinti, le foto d'epoca, e i documenti revive una straordinaria storia per immagini dell'idea repubblicana*. Rome, 1988.

———. *I repubblicani dopo l'unità*. Florence, 1960.

Spencer, Philip. *The Politics of Belief in Nineteenth-Century France*. London, 1954.

Sperber, Jonathan. "Festivals of National Unity in the German Revolution of 1848–1849." *Past and Present* 136 (1992): 114–138.

———. *Popular Catholicism in Nineteenth-Century Germany*. Princeton, NJ, 1984.

Sternhell, Zeev. *La droite révolutionnaire. Les Origines françaises du fascisme*. Paris, 1978.

———. "The political culture of nationalism." In *Nationhood and Nationalism in France: From Boulangism to the Great War, 1889–1918*, ed. Robert Tombs, 22–37. London, 1991.

Stone, Lawrence. *The Family, Sex and the Marriage in England, 1500–1800*. New York, 1977.

Storm, Eric. *La perspectiva del progreso: pensamiento político en la España del cambio de siglo (1890–1914)*. Madrid, 2001.

Suárez Cortina, Manuel. "Anticlericalismo y republicanismo en la Restauración, 1874–1898." *Bulletin d'Histoire contemporaine de l'Espagne* 23 (June 1996): 59–92.

———. *El Gorro Frigio: Liberalismo, Democracia y Republicanismo en la Restauración*. Madrid, 2000.

———. "La quiebra del republicanismo histórico, 1898–1931." In *El republicanismo en España, 1830–1977*, ed. Nigel Townson, 139–163. Madrid: Alianza, 1994.

Sutton, Michael. *Nationalism, Positivism, and Catholicism: The Politics of Charles Maurras and French Catholics, 1890–1914*. Cambridge, 1982.

Tackett, Timothy. *Religion, Revolution, and Regional Culture in Eighteenth-Century France: The Ecclesiastical Oath of 1791*. Princeton, NJ, 1986.

Tapia, Francisco Xavier. "Las relaciones Iglesia-Estado durante el primer experimento liberal en España (1820–1823)." *Revista de Estudios Políticos* 173 (1970): 69–89.

Thomas, Paul. "Jean-Jacques Rousseau, Sexist?" *Feminist Studies* 17, 2 (1991): 195–217.

Timoteo Alvarez, Jesús. *Restauración y prensa de masas*. Pamplona, 1981.

Tone, John Lawrence. *War and Genocide in Cuba, 1895–1898*. Chapel Hill, NC, 2006.

Torras, Juame. *Liberalismo y rebeldía campesina, 1820–1823*. Barcelona, 1976.

Torre del Río, Rosario de la. "La prensa madrileña y el discurso de Lord Salisbury sobre 'las naciones moribundas' (Londres, Albert Hall, 4 May 1898)." *Cuadernos de Historia Moderna y Contemporánea* 6 (1985): 163–180.

Tortella, Gabriel. *The Development of Modern Spain: An Economic History of the Nineteenth and Twentieth Centuries.* Translated by Valerie Herr. Cambridge, MA, 2000.

Townson, Nigel, ed. *El republicanismo en España (1830–1977).* Madrid, 1994.

Trask, David F. *The War with Spain in 1898.* New York, 1981.

Tuñón de Lara, Manuel, ed. *La crisis del estado español, 1898–1936.* Madrid, 1977.

Turin, Yvonne. *La educación y la escuela en España de 1874 a 1902. Liberalismo y tradición.* Translated from French by Josefa Hernández Alfonso. Madrid, 1967.

Tusell, Javier. *Historia de la democracia cristiana en España.* 2 vols. Cuadernos para el diálogo Series. Madrid, 1974.

———. *Oligarquía y caciquismo en Andalusía, (1890–1923).* Barcelona, 1976.

Ucelay Da Cal, Enric. *El imperialismo catalán: Prat de la Riba, Cambó, D'Ors y la conquista moral de España.* Barcelona, 2003.

Ullman, Joan Connelly. *The Tragic Week: A Study of Anti-Clericalism in Spain, 1875–1912.* Cambridge, MA, 1968.

———. "The Warp and Woof of Parliamentary Politics in Spain, 1808–1939: Anticlericalism versus 'Neo-Catholicism.'" *European Studies Review* 13 (1983): 145–176.

Uriarte, Edurne. *España, Patriotrismo y Nación.* Madrid, 2003.

Valiente, Celia. "An Overview of Research on Gender in Spanish Society." *Gender & History* 16, 6 (December 2002): 77–792.

Valverdú, Francesc. "A Sociolinguistic History of Catalan." *International Journal of the Sociology of Language* 47 (1984): 13–29.

Varela Ortega, José. "Aftermath of Splended Disaster: Spanish Politics before and after the Spanish American War of 1898." *Journal of Contemporary History* 15 (1980): 317–344.

———. "Los amigos políticos: funcionamiento del sistema caciquista." *Revista de Occidente* 127 (1973): 45–74.

———. *Los amigos políticos. Partidos, elecciones y caciquismo en la Restauración (1875–1900).* Madrid, 1977.

Vilar, Pierre. *La Catalonge dans l'Espagne moderne: Recherches sur les fondements économiques des structures nationals.* Paris, 1977.

Vincent, Mary. *Spain 1833–2002: People and State.* Oxford, 2007.

Weber, Eugen. *Peasants into Frenchmen: The Modernization of Rural France, 1870–1914.* Stanford, CA, 1976.

White, Sarah L. "Liberty, Honor, Order: Gender and Political Discourse in Nineteenth-Century Spain." In *Constructing Spanish Womanhood: Female Identity in Modern Spain,* ed. Victoria Lorée Enders and Pamela Beth Radcliff, 233–257. Albany, NY, 1999.

Wiesner-Hanks, Merry E. "Patriarchy." In *Encyclopedia of European Social History, from 1350 to 2000,* ed. Peter N. Stearns, Vol 4, 15–24. New York, 2001.

Willner, Ruth Ann. *The Spellbinders: Charismatic Political Leadership.* Princeton, NJ, 1984.

Wilson, A. N. *God's Funeral: A Biography of Faith and Doubt in Western Civilization.* New York, 2000.

Winks, Robin W. and Joan Neuberger. *Europe and the Making of Modernity, 1815–1914.* Oxford, 2005.

Wolffe, John. *The Protestant Crusade in Britain, 1829–1860.* Oxford, 1992.

Zeldin, Theodore. *Conflicts in French Society: Anticlericalism, Education and Morals in the Nineteenth Century.* London, 1970.

Index